3302387450

| WN 9/10 | HE 11/11 | DI 2/12 | WI 1/13 | AB | BA |

Henley Library
Ravenscroft Road
Henley-on-Thames
Oxon RG9 2DH
Tel: 01491 575278

DIDCOT LIBRARY
THE BROADWAY
DIDCOT
OX11 8ND
TEL 01235 813103

WITNEY LIBRARY
Witney
Oxon OX28 6JH
Tel: 01993 702659

To renew this book, phone 0845 1202811 or visit
our website at www.libcat.oxfordshire.gov.uk
You will need your library PIN number
(available from your library)

OXFORDSHIRE
COUNTY COUNCIL
SOCIAL & COMMUNITY SERVICES
www.oxfordshire.gov.uk

Victim of Success

Victim of Success
Civilization at Risk

Peter J. McManners

Published by Susta Press a division of Susta Limited
www.susta.co.uk

Copyright © Peter J. McManners 2009

All rights reserved. No part of this publication may be reproduced, stored in a retrieval system, or transmitted, in any form or by any means, without the prior permission in writing of the copyright holder.

Copy-editing by Hilary McGlynn
Production management by Stacey Penny
Cover and page design by Stefan Brazzo

Typesetting by Florence Production Ltd
Stoodleigh, Devon

Printed and bound in the UK by
MPG Books Ltd, Bodmin, Cornwall

A CIP catalogue record for this book is available from the British Library

ISBN 978–0–9557369–1–9

The paper used for the text pages of this book is FSC certified. FSC (the Forest Stewardship Council) is an international network to promote responsible management of the world's forests.

OXFORDSHIRE LIBRARY SERVICE	
3302387450	
Askews	17-Aug-2010
304.28	£17.99

For all the people who support real change: our time has come.

Table of Contents

Foreword ix

Preface xiii

Introduction 1

PART 1 OUR SUCCESS 7

Chapter

1 One Earth, One Chance   9

2 Survival   19

3 The Selfishness of Human Nature   23

4 Choices   27

5 Breaking the Stalemate   31

6 Climate Change Hits Home   37

7 The Boom before the Bust   41

8 Scraping the Bottom of the Barrel   45

9 The Collapse of Civilization   49

PART 2 CHANGING DIRECTION 53

10 Altering the Future   55

11 Show Respect for the Earth   59

12	Stop Breeding	73
13	The Three-Way Balancing Act	85
14	Plan to Ban Fossil Fuel	97
15	Melting the Wings of Icarus	117
16	Cities for People	129
17	Harness the Power of Community	147
18	No Compromise over Food	165
19	Rescue Poseidon	183
20	Support Real Change	203
PART 3	**THE FUTURE**	**213**
21	Living Sustainably	215
22	Fight for the Future	223
23	My Generation: Villains or Heroes?	231
Epilogue		237
Notes		239
Index		253

Figure:

| Figure 13.1 | The three-way balancing act of a sustainable society | 87 |

Foreword

Everyone appreciates that societies all over the world are at different stages of economic and social development, leading to contrasting values and perspectives on everyday life. When it comes to our shared environment, it is the common human mindset – our nature of complacency and selfishness – that requires fundamental change. It is crucial for civilization to re-chart its course away from the imminent 'cliff edge of collapse', as Peter McManners graphically portrays in this eye-opening book.

Humans are born with the innate ability to learn from experience but we are also quick to forget, easily deceived and readily swayed into making selfish choices. The wave of success and consumerism sweeping the world has blunted our ability to see the risks. In the West, industrialization has driven our farmed landscape to the brink of destruction and altered our natural heritage beyond recognition. This modern pattern of behaviour could undo thousands of years of progress during which mankind harvested natural resources and altered the landscape to meet the basic human needs of food, shelter and fuel without significant impact. The rapid explosion in population and technological advances over the last century have moved the goal posts and substantially increased our ecological footprint. Some innovative progress has been made to rectify our mistakes, but we do not have the luxury of time on our hands – we only have one planet and cannot afford to continue making mistakes in the name of short-term economic gains.

As a result of our growing success, we have sadly lost sight of our roots and inextricable relationship with the environment, blissfully ignorant of the fact that the integrity of ecosystems hangs in the balance, waiting to crash. We are all guilty of the most fundamental of crimes: we fail to value something until it is lost. Faced now with what many would consider a more urgent issue, the fight for global economic stability, we risk taking our eye off the ball at the most uncertain and critical of times.

Our population is set to hit the nine billion mark by 2050. We therefore urgently need to reconnect people with the natural environment, helping develop knowledge and new skills to minimize and manage their impact on the finite resources upon which the survival of our species depends. Knowledge is a powerful tool, but this time we cannot afford to 'wait and see' – the lesson begins now.

For the last twenty years, I have witnessed at first hand the Earthwatch commitment to working with companies to demonstrate the business case for conservation, and the development of a learning model designed to raise awareness and encourage action through hands-on scientific field research. According to Marcus Gilleard, our Head of Corporate Partnerships, 'a handful of leading companies truly understand and value the critical importance of the ecosystems on which they impact and depend for their economic success. For them, such issues are no longer banished to the back corridors – they now underpin every decision made in the boardroom.' This is just the start, he claims. All companies, small and large, would be foolish not to follow this path, work collectively and be committed to sustainable prosperity.

Victim of Success: Civilization at Risk is a wake-up call to what may lie ahead if we do not act soon and change our behaviour as a global society. All of us need to understand our place in a rapidly changing world. Every business, community and citizen has their part to play on the road to achieving sustainable livelihoods and the preservation of natural habitats and species diversity – both on land and at sea. It is imperative that we act together – in a sustained, respectful and responsible way that improves and enriches people's lives – to make changes on a scale and of a magnitude that, for most, are incomprehensible in current societal terms. It will require effort, we will face challenges, but it can be achieved and we will then reap the rewards. The time for real change is now.

As the pages that follow poignantly state, our future rests on our working with nature, not against it. It was Konrad Lorenz in *The Waning of Humaneness* who spoke of the need to be 'close to nature, for as long as possible, at the earliest possible age' if we want to begin to understand the complexity of the natural world. Such understanding gives confidence to decide on how best to manage – as a contribution to biodiversity – our window box, our garden, the woods and, beyond, the far hills. This is just good environmental manners.

I hope this challenging work by Peter McManners makes your heart beat a little faster, as you join the same journey of thought.

Nigel Winser
Executive Vice President
Earthwatch Institute
Oxford, UK
14th June 2009

Preface

In this book, I write about the pending collapse of human civilization brought on by the pursuit of economic success at any cost. I also write about how to prevent it. This will mean introducing dramatic changes into society, including constraints on our behaviour and adopting measures that may hold back economic growth. The challenge, as an author, is to write about the changes required in such a way that the reader understands the necessity to act. This means tackling the unpleasant truth about the risks to civilization in order to set the context within which to counter them.

The working title leading up to publication was 'A Blueprint for Saving the World'. I was embarrassed by this, but it is the sort of feel-good title that publishers like. People can read it and sleep easily at night. Such a title implies that that there is a blueprint that we can sign off and then all will be well. This is a delusion that we must reach beyond. I ask you, the reader, to take a journey. This is the same journey of thought that we all must make, and make soon. I have to convince you of the need to act. This requires nothing more of you at this stage than to accept that civilization is indeed at risk. Acceptance of this truth is the single greatest contribution you can make to prevent it from happening. You may then be influenced in how you vote and what measures you will support.

The first part of the book is short and concise, and describes the failure of humanity. It is not a happy story. It is neither scaremongering nor crying wolf. It is a cool, logical analysis of the path humanity is on and a deeply disturbing window on the future. I contend that it is beyond dispute that this analysis is correct. Opinion divides over whether humanity will find an alternative path. Some people urge inaction, arguing that we have always got through every crisis, and will do so again. In most circumstances this is good general advice. Worrying about a possible outcome before it strikes wastes time, effort and leads to needless sleepless nights.

This is no normal human crisis. We are setting up our children for a descent so severe and so rapid that there is nothing in history to compare. We were surprised at the speed of the current financial crisis. The collapse of civilization, when it comes, could be just as surprising and almost as fast. I hope in the decades ahead I will be categorized as a scaremonger. The only way for that to happen is to shift the direction of society. I hope we do, and believe we can, but there is no easy blueprint for how.

The necessary actions to change the direction of society are covered in the second and final parts of the book. Difficult issues are covered that we are reluctant to face. The most awkward of these is to find the circumstances to constrain human breeding. Almost as difficult is the need for effective and realistic plans to ban fossil fuel. The biggest hurdle of all is to persuade people to support such vital alterations to a society that seems to be so successful.

Whilst finalizing the manuscript of this book, I attended a lecture at the Royal Geographical Society. The speaker was Lord Nicolas Stern, famous for the *Stern Review on the Economics of Climate Change*, published in 2006. This was a hugely influential report that concluded it would be cheaper to act early to address climate change compared with the long-term economic costs of delay. This was a simple and powerful message, expressed in the language of economics and numbers.

The event, on 1st April 2009, was the launch of Nicolas Stern's book *A Blueprint for a Safer Planet.* In it, he puts forward a persuasive case for a new global deal to address both climate change and world poverty. He makes the assumption that the world can learn to cooperate in an altruistic manner, and he puts his trust in a global carbon market. The Stern blueprint has a feel-good message: we can solve this problem and it will cost just 2% of world GDP to do so. This is attractive – and dangerous. The problem with a series of optimistic assessments is that they feed complacency. They encourage us to believe that all we have to do is sign up to a handful of targets for the decades ahead and we will sail through the crisis.

We like to listen to optimists, and I still am an optimist, but I am also a realist. Any blueprint to save the world will be tough to implement. It is not possible to avoid difficult and painful decisions. This book contains a blueprint, but its title is closer to reality: *Victim of Success: Civilization at Risk.* This is the uncomfortable and worrying reality that we don't like to hear.

I remain optimistic because I know that when people really understand the risks we are taking on behalf of the next generation, they will be willing to enter crisis mode. The current set of proposals, being worked on for the climate summit in Copenhagen in December 2009, is not enough. A deal will be agreed, but it will then stifle the debate for the next decade whilst we invest in more nuclear power, ramp up carbon trading and then miss the ambitious targets that were agreed.

By then, climate change will be hitting many countries hard, the world population will still be expanding and natural habitats will have been destroyed. We will stop, think, and try again to come up with another blueprint for the planet, but by then the problems will be much more intractable.

This book is not *the* blueprint to save the world. It is a call to action, a plea to open our eyes to reality and an indication of the nature of a new direction for society. The time for complacency and reassuring optimism is long past. Civilization is at risk and it is up to this generation of world leaders to take steps to protect it.

Peter McManners
April 2009

Introduction

Life can only be understood backwards; but it must be lived forwards.

Soren Kierkegaard, Danish philosopher (1813–55)

Living is like making our way into a bank of thick fog. We can see our feet and have an idea where our next footstep will land, but that is all. We can creep forward, carefully, feeling for every step, or charge forward in a rush and take what comes. This book provides a fleeting glance at what may lie ahead for civilization. We can use this insight to change direction, or ignore it and draw comfort from allowing the fog of uncertainty to hide the pitfalls in front of us.

Looking backwards, the view is clear. Laid out behind us is the whole of human history. We can see the route we took, meandering around the obstacles that have crossed our path. History has high points, such as the Renaissance in Europe between the 14th and 17th centuries or, more recently, landing a man on the moon in 1969. There have also been low points where the path of history hit soft ground. World War II was one such low point. Preceding this, in 1938, the British Prime Minister, Neville Chamberlain, came back from Munich clutching the paper he had just agreed and signed with Adolf Hitler. He announced to cheering crowds waiting at Heston Aerodrome that he had achieved 'peace for our time'. He could not see into the fog of the future and the quicksand that lay ahead. Looking back, we can see the whole time line of World War II; the participants at the time could not, not knowing if they would survive, nor which side would prevail.

Looking at the landscape of history, there is a bank of fog slowly rolling away from us, revealing events as they happen. The edge of the fog represents now. Behind us, the path we have followed is well trodden and clear to see. In front, we see a number of possible tracks branching left and right, but where they lead is obscured by the uncertainty of the future. Deciding which direction to take will determine the next phase of human civilization. Our experience is deceptive; it suggests that humankind will prosper whatever choices we make. We can see where humans have made unfortunate choices in the past, and could have chosen a better route, but so far we have always managed to pick ourselves up and resume our progress.

By examining history, it would be a reasonable deduction that humans will find a way to survive and prosper. We always have, and hope that we always will. The problem is that history is not a good guide to help us now. There has never been such instability at the global scale. The surface of the world is changing, literally and metaphorically. Dead ahead, on the path we are on, the route of human history is coming to the top of a cliff.

In Part One, I chart this dangerous path for human society based on the assumption that we continue to give economic success our highest priority. It is a cool, logical look at the consequences of our behaviour. People who regard my analysis as scaremongering should be warned: the only uncertainty is the time frame. The current generation, in positions of power and influence, may be able to see out their working careers without taking action, but the generations to follow will suffer.

The pace of human progress has been quickening. Developments in technologies, such as IT and telecommunications, facilitate rapid action. New opportunities can be exploited and new products launched worldwide by global corporations. Open markets and free trade add further impetus. It seems as if there is nothing we cannot achieve. Human society is running fast into the fog of the future. If we stumble, we hope that we will soon recover our footing; but we do not know that there is a cliff edge coming and there is a huge drop beyond. We will only see the danger when we are going at a pace too fast to take corrective action. We will tumble over the edge, grabbing desperately at anything to arrest our fall, but there may be no way to stop the descent until we reach the bottom.

In the opening chapters of this book, I justify this pessimistic view. Human consumption is already greater than our planet can supply in a sustainable manner, and our demand is rising. This cannot continue indefinitely. As this becomes obvious, defensive measures will be required to secure the resources to continue to run society. Food is our most basic need and shortages will have the worst effect on poorer nations as countries outbid each other for supplies. Our unsustainable thirst for energy will also be exposed as a habit we should have broken decades ago. Communities with fuel supplies will retain them for their own needs. Countries reliant on imports will suffer power cuts and blackouts. Interconnected power grids will start to tumble as one collapsing grid pulls down others. Connections will be shut off deliberately to conserve power for key users, such as hospitals. Data centres will shift to back-up power but will struggle to keep them running continuously, using generators designed for short-term use. Isolated communities will no longer receive fuel supplies as desperate people hijack any vehicle travelling without protection.

In this interconnected world, we will all suffer. The collapse of society, when it comes, could be rapid. As cohesion breaks down, and the rule of law is ignored, looters will ransack what they can find, making shortages more extreme. The apparatus of civilization will no longer offer safe support. As more and more countries are destabilized, global anarchy could break out. Each person will have to do their best to survive.

As real hardship bites, more and more sites and buildings will be ransacked in the search for supplies. Schools and universities will be closed down and pupils sent home due to a lack of reliable power and concerns over security. The break in education may extend from months to years as teachers and lecturers aren't paid and have to join everyone else in surviving as best they can. The education process may suffer terminal damage. As power is not restored, data centres will collapse and the contents of libraries burnt for fuel to keep warm. There is a danger that most records of the civilization that went before will be lost.

There will be groups of people who work hard to retain and defend at least a part of humankind's archives. As the last pieces of equipment able to read electronic storage media break down, the data contained will be lost to us. Some paper archives will remain but, with an education system no longer operating, we will lose the ability to understand what they contain. In the current world, leading scientists and engineers spend decades mastering their particular narrow expertise. A complex mesh of experts and high-technology manufacturing plants deliver the capabilities of the modern world. Trying to recreate that ability using the information in paper archives, by people without formal education, would be impossible.

The modern world is more at risk than we realize. Total collapse is possible. This is the potential future we have lined up for our great-grandchildren.

It does not have to be so: it is possible to glimpse into the fog of the future. The picture is not clear, but we know that straight ahead on the path we are following lies the destruction of civilization. We have a range of immediate problems to deal with as we struggle to stave off recession following the financial crisis of 2008–9. We can behave like Neville Chamberlain and do our best to achieve 'peace for our time' through appeasement, or we can realize that the problems the world faces require dramatic and painful measures.

In Part Two, I explain the change of direction required. It is not a list of actions to be tackled sequentially and ticked off when complete. If only it were that simple. All the actions interact and impinge on each other. Population growth, energy choices, community design, agriculture: all has to be addressed. Attempting to tackle each of these issues in isolation will not work. The world needs wholesale change of a complexity that is hard to comprehend. The focus has to be on building a better society that reinforces the integrity of the ecosystem. This should always have been our aim, and we can succeed, but only if we change the direction of human society.

In Part Three, I look to the future as we would want it to be. Now, we have choices over the future. We can influence the path that humankind takes. If we wait until we teeter on the edge of the cliff, there may be no path back. By believing that our exploitation of the Earth is a threat that applies only to the systems of nature, we are living in deluded ignorance. All that we have worked so hard to build, over thousands of years, is at risk from the short-term focus of modern humans on material success. It is not an exaggeration to say that the human species may be the unwitting architect of its own annihilation.

The good news is that there is still time to mend our ways, but not enough time to allow people to continue in blissful ignorance. Many people who currently have comfortable lives will have to suffer disruption in the short term. This will be a small price to pay to create a sustainable society. Such a society, that incorporates respect for the Earth and its systems, will improve and enrich people's lives and put the future of civilization back on the path to success.

Part One
OUR SUCCESS

1 One Earth, One Chance

We should not be crushing the environment under the heavy boots of industrialization. Like the footprints left by bare feet on a sandy shore, our imprint on the world should be subsumed within the Earth's natural systems, without causing long-term damage.

We are the most successful species ever to have occupied planet Earth – and the most destructive. In our drive to succeed it has been forgotten that we have one planet, for us all to share. To our ancestors, 200 years ago, Earth must have seemed like a huge and limitless resource. For a world of less than one billion people, there was plenty for everyone. The human population was much smaller than now and its demands were less. There was little need to worry about Earth's systems. Human activity was just a small part of the greater ecosystem.

At the beginning of the 21st century, the world population passed the six billion mark. It is projected to exceed seven billion by 2013.[1] Not only are we humans increasing our numbers but also our per capita consumption, as the example set by the developed nations migrates across the globe. We are finding that one planet is no longer enough to satisfy our material desires.

We can quantify the situation we face by considering the Earth's capacity alongside the demands we are placing on it. Scientists have calculated that the Earth has 13.6 billion global hectares (gha)[2] of usable ecological capacity (land and shallow coastal regions). Countries and peoples of the world make a differing range of demands on this resource. The average American requires 9.4 gha to support his or her lifestyle. This ecological footprint is considerably more than the 0.6 gha required by the average Bangladeshi.

A typical European lifestyle falls somewhere in the middle: 4.7 gha. Australians consume 7.8 gha, the Chinese 2.1 gha. The total global consumption of humanity is currently about 17.5 billion gha. This is 30% more than the ecological capacity of our planet.[3]

We are overworking the planet, putting it under growing stress. In the immediate short term we should not be too worried. Earth is a wonderfully benign environment for humans. It is also a very resilient system. I believe that we can rely on Mother Nature to do her utmost to keep the planet stable. She is like a hard-working loyal servant trying to do her very best despite a master who does not notice and does not care. As the problems multiply and stress levels increase, a semblance of normal service can continue but unless the pressure is reduced some aspect of Mother Nature's ecosystem will fail. One failure alone can be handled. When the system is under intense pressure in every quarter, one failure could be enough to initiate a domino effect leading to catastrophic collapse.

We cannot predict what aspect of our life support system will fail first. One thing that we can be very sure about is that human society and our relationship with planet Earth is not sustainable. Without change, the ecosystem will eventually collapse. It is only the timing and the first point of failure that we do not know. We should be asking less of our loyal servant. The planet deserves that we notice the stress it is under and it is in our long-term interests to do something about it.

We know we must reduce consumption. The trouble is that we all want our share. If the entire world's population were to aspire to match European levels of consumption, then we would require the equivalent of 2.6 planet Earths.[4] If the United States is the world's role model, then even four planets will not be enough. Clearly this is not feasible. Another perspective comes from reversing the calculation. If we divide the Earth's ecological capacity by the world population we get a figure of 2.1 gha. It can be argued that this is the equitable share that each person deserves. If the world operated as an egalitarian commune this would be the level of consumption allocated to each of us. Whatever methods we adopt, it is a mathematical fact that the world's average ecological footprint must contract.

There are ways that we can reduce our ecological footprint. As individuals, if we want to make the commitment, we can use the car less, refuse to fly when going on holiday, buy food that has been produced locally and turn down the thermostat at home. These are limited measures; we need to do much more to make a real dent in reducing the impact we have on the planet.

One way to stay within the safe carrying capacity of Earth is to reduce the footprint of everyone on the planet to a safe universal global average. This concept has intellectual appeal because it seems fair and equitable. On closer examination, we soon realize that this would require dramatic changes to lifestyle.

To drive consumption down to the safe figure of 2.1 gha per person would require the adoption of a portfolio of deep-rooted changes. For example, we would have to give up the aspiration to own a car and make all local journeys by bicycle or on foot. People who have become used to large houses for their individual use would have to get used to less space in well-insulated buildings, perhaps shared with a number of other residents. To reduce consumption further, families may find it necessary to occupy just one private room, sharing other facilities such as the kitchen with a number of other families. Many people in the developing world are familiar with such ways of living. Persuading them to continue such low-impact lifestyles will be hard. It will be even harder to persuade the developed world to downsize to such an extent.

When it comes to eating, it can be argued that we should all become vegetarians. The nutritional value of a beef steak and a plate of beans are comparable. Each contains the protein our bodies need in the quantities required. There are detailed nutritional challenges to ensure that vegetarians get a full range of nutrients, but these are easily overcome with careful choice of ingredients. The biggest difference between the steak and the plate of beans is not nutritional value but the area of land required for their production. A beef steak can require five times more agricultural land than an equivalent plate of beans. To minimize our ecological footprint, the logical conclusion is to ban the eating of meat. At one fell swoop we could double or triple the feeding capacity of the world. I do not believe that we should all become vegetarians but the logic is hard to dispute.

As we examine the lifestyle changes required to live within our 'equitable share' of the world's ecosystem, the result is unacceptable to most people in the developed world. It is important that we realize this or we will waste time and effort on impossible targets instead of looking for real practical solutions.

Driving down consumption as low as 2.1 gha per person may not be possible in chilly northern Europe, but we have examples of communities with a significantly lower impact on the environment than the rest of us. The remote Findhorn Foundation and Community in Scotland is one example, with a consumption of 2.6 gha per person. The Beddington Zero Energy Development (BedZED) in London is an example of what can be achieved in big cities with 3.2 gha.[5] This compares with the UK average of 5.3 gha per person. If we all followed these examples we could halve the impact that Britons are having on the planet.

At national level, the UK is consuming much more than its ecological capacity. The sum total of our cropland, grazing land, forest and fishing grounds works out at 1.6 gha per person. This is not enough – even if we did all live in communities like BedZED. There is no escaping the fact that the UK is a tiny crowded island reliant on drawing on the ecological capacity of the rest of the world.

Other countries are running a surplus, such as some of the Nordic countries of Europe. These countries have ecological footprints that are well above the world average but they are succeeding at living within their ecological capacity. Sweden's ecological capacity is 10.0 gha per person and the average Swede consumes 5.1 gha, leaving a surplus of 4.9 gha. Finland has 11.7 gha capacity and Finns consume 5.2 gha; a surplus of 6.5 gha.[6]

There are also big countries such as Brazil and Russia which are running significant surpluses.[7] This is helping the world to cope, but the surpluses are not large enough to offset the excessive consumption of the countries with the biggest overall deficits: China, the United States, Japan and India in that order.[8]

The United States was the prime culprit in putting excessive stress on the world's systems until it was overtaken by China, but it also has a large ecological capacity relative to its population. If the United States can be persuaded to halve its consumption from the current level of 9.4 gha per person down to the European average of 4.7 gha, then it will be living within its ecological capacity. For China and India the problem is far more intractable. Average Chinese consumption is 2.1 gha per person and 0.9 gha for India. These are relatively low figures compared with the developed nations. Even so, the Chinese and Indians are already outstripping their ecological capacity, consuming double the resources available within their own borders.[9] This imbalance between population and resources is a fundamental aspect of the world's problems, which I will return to in Chapter 12.

The problem humanity faces is solvable but the challenge is immense. It is feasible for individual people, small communities and some countries to live within the available resources of the Earth. To extend such thinking to world level and reduce the consumption of the entire world human population to be within the safe carrying capacity of the planet is far more complex.

Usually, when humans face a challenge, there is the opportunity to investigate and experiment. If an idea works we move on to refine the concept. Each time we fail, we rethink, redesign and produce another prototype. We might test to destruction a number of prototypes before we hit on the winning solution. This is how human endeavour is allowed to flourish. Our inquisitive nature and drive to innovate underlies the success of our species and the success of modern society.

The Earth is special and different. We cannot afford to allow human ingenuity free rein. We do not have a series of Earths to experiment with. We have just one, and we are totally reliant on it for survival. The only experimentation we should allow must be totally foolproof. We should think carefully in advance about any activity that could conflict with the natural systems. If we believe it to be safe, then we should try it, first at a small scale, and monitor the results. The period of testing should be long enough that any unforeseen consequences have time to appear.

This is not how we are behaving. We are charging on without seriously considering the consequences. We demand that our scientists deliver incontrovertible evidence that our actions are causing long-term damage before we call a halt.

The danger we face is illustrated by the world's response to climate change. We know that it is happening, that the effects will be serious and that we are the cause; yet we still fail to take substantive action. If we cannot deal effectively with this issue, when the danger is so evident and imminent, then there is little hope of addressing the other problems that will arise, such as the slowly rising levels of radiation in the environment from our nuclear industries. We put off worrying about such things by noting, reassuringly, that the levels are 'within safe limits', and then reassessing what we consider to be safe, allowing the limits to creep up instead of accepting the cost of real action.

The other danger that people cannot be persuaded to take seriously is the gradual poisoning of our oceans. About 70% of the Earth is covered in ocean. It contains a huge reservoir of biodiversity. The attitude of humankind is total disregard and neglect. We allow all the chemicals of our industrial society to make their way to the ocean on the assumption that the oceans are self-cleansing. This viewpoint arises from our experience on land. If we stop releasing pollution, our rivers, lakes and streams are cleansed by Mother Nature. Long-life pollutants are washed away down to the sea. The oceans are so vast that they seem to disappear. This convenient illusion is used to justify inaction. There was life in the oceans long before there was life on land. Millions of years ago, some creatures crawled out of this aquatic ecosystem to evolve into animals that live on land. Humans are at the peak of this process of evolution. It is ironic that people are now, ever so slowly but ever so surely, killing the oceans. This is where life began and where life will end.

I have reached the opinion that the damage we are causing to the oceans is one of the most shameful actions of our species. It is an alien world to us and almost impossible to generate any human concern. Fortunately, careful examination of what is required to protect the oceans uncovers a close synergy with actions that are required to improve human society. It is, therefore, possible to focus on changes that humans will value, in the knowledge that the oceans will also be a beneficiary. The key change required is to bring the waste streams of civilization inside a robust and effective framework. I present such a framework in Chapter 19, 'Rescue Poseidon'.

There will be other problems that we do not anticipate and which have yet to surface. I mention genetic engineering. This is not the worst problem we face, or the most pressing, but our attitude to tinkering with the basis of life shows that our lack of respect for Mother Nature is so complete that we are willing to put at risk the fundamental basis of human survival.

Genetic engineering is happening now. We have herbicide-resistant crops and cloned sheep. The full consequences of such genetic engineering are only likely to appear over many generations. For cash crops and animals raised for food this hardly matters. We can stop planting that particular crop strain or stop using that particular breed, allowing the defective gene line to die out. It is hard to predict whether there will be any negative repercussions for humans from genetic engineering in agriculture and therefore hard to generate any real concern. We have no proof of problems, and proof may not come to light for many decades. We focus on the quantifiable benefits in terms of crop yield and efficiency gains.

The benefits of genetically modified (GM) crops are allowed to mask the problems, such as artificial genes interacting with closely related natural species. Open fields connect with the countryside. As the wind blows pollen around, our artificial genes will, over time, cross-breed with wild species. Field trials have been used to test the growing of GM crops and the results monitored. Nothing bad has come to light. This is not surprising: ecosystems do not respond immediately. We may be storing up long-term changes to the ecosystem as we introduce these man-made genes. Without any evidence to justify caution, legislators working with agricultural policy have no reason to stop the march of technical progress. GM crops are allowed because we have no proof that they should be banned.

As we make further advances in genetic engineering within agriculture we will be tempted to do the same with humans. The debate over genetic engineering of humans has already begun.

It is easy to identify specific cases that draw our compassion. Where a family carries a gene that causes disease (such as haemophilia) it is entirely reasonable to screen potential embryos to eliminate it. Such interference in natural processes is limited in scope and clearly leads to improvement in our genetic stock. We will have to decide whether we allow our scientists and doctors to go further and engage in manipulating our genetic code. At first this will be to tackle those diseases that have a genetic component. The aim could not be more worthy and the arguments in favour of such experimentation are easy to make and hard to dispute. If we allow such genetic engineering and it appears to work, there will be pressure to move on to other outcomes, for example, designer babies with genes manipulated to be more intelligent, better looking and stronger.

When we make mistakes with human genetic engineering, which we do not spot at the early embryonic stage, babies will be born with defective genes. In agriculture these animals would be selected for an early exit to the abattoir and not used to breed from. With humans we do have such an easy choice.

I would not be surprised if there are already scientists who have allowed their curiosity to overcome caution and have implanted genetically engineered human embryos to grow to full term. If I am right, there are children alive today with DNA altered by scientists. As modified human DNA is passed from parent to child over the next two or three generations, there may be no apparent harm. The logical deduction we will make is that genetic engineering is safe. In many cases this may be so, but nature is complex and we cannot know the outcome of the interaction of a number of genetic 'improvements'. Genetic engineering may only show long-term systematic problems after 20 or 30 generations. By then modified human DNA will have spread far and wide.

In these circumstances, we can hope that there will be isolated populations that can continue humanity. If not, we will have destroyed our species from within. If we are lucky, the genetic damage will be confined to the narrow segment of the world's population that could afford genetic engineering. It may be that only the rich who could afford designer babies will be affected.

This is a bleak hypothesis I paint, and I cannot prove it. The common human reaction in such circumstances is to satisfy our curiosity by experimenting. I believe that this would be a mistake. Genetic engineering of human DNA is not an experiment we should be running.

We still have time to win the debate over genetic engineering. I am confident that humans are not so stupid that we will risk the future of the DNA that defines who we are as a species. I am also certain that there are scientists and doctors who will experiment despite the rules. It will take courage and resolve to deal with the consequences of their actions. Mutant humans will still be people and will need to be treated with compassion and respect as we ensure that the faulty genes do not propagate into the main population.

I have focused on genetic engineering to illustrate the dangers of the inquisitiveness of human nature. Genetic engineering of human DNA is, at least, an obvious risk that we should be able to avoid. Killing ourselves off through self-inflicted damage to our DNA is not the way that I believe the human species will be wiped out.

Our downfall will be a complex mixture of overlapping and interconnected problems. It is hard to predict the exact sequence of events that will bring about the collapse of civilization. There are many scenarios that could be painted. Of all the possible futures, those that are a continuation of the Western model of continually rising material consumption will lead eventually to failure.

The human species is too wrapped up in its own success to see the dangers. Certain destruction is waiting just a few generations into the future. But I cannot prove it. Humanity is entering a future where we and the Earth have not been before. Our highly industrialized, globalized society is a unique experiment being run for the first time. Hard evidence will come from continuing this grand experiment. When we have the results it will then be too late.

At the heart of the impending death of humanity is our failure to protect the Earth and respect the processes of nature. This puts our very survival at risk.

2 Survival

The instinct of survival is hardwired into us. 'Survival of the fittest' is the mechanism of natural selection which has led to the set of genes that defines the human species. Without this strong will to survive, we humans would not exist. This may also be the flaw in the human condition that ultimately leads to our downfall.

One of the factors that explain human success is that we have expanded our concept of survival from the individual to a focus on the family or tribe. When we work as a team it becomes far easier to survive and thrive. A team of hunters can corner and kill an animal far better than one person alone. Other people, less physically strong but more dexterous, can make tools and weapons. Many communities have built a culture that can override the individual survival instinct – our warriors are willing to die for the common good. But this is not a sacrifice they make for humanity as a whole. They are only prepared to give up their lives for the community into which they were born and to which they have pledged allegiance.

The power of community values extends from the family, to the village, to the nation state, getting progressively weaker. At the world level, the concept of global loyalty to humanity as a whole is practically non-existent.

In learning to survive, we have tested a myriad of ways to behave. We have stuck with successful behaviours and abandoned those that have led to failure (or the ideas have died along with the community in which they were hatched). We have learnt to collaborate with people close by who can help and support us. Conversely, we have also learnt that we must fight to retain control when another tribe threatens the security of the resources that we need to survive.

In the modern developed world, we have moved beyond the need to worry about basic survival. Food can be taken for granted, as can a minimum level of income. We expect society to provide a roof over our head. We no longer need our ancient survival instinct. Even so, it remains with us. If a resource we have is threatened, we will fight to keep it. Now that we do not have to worry about food, we have translated the concept of necessity to other aspects of modern life: a house, a car and an annual foreign holiday. If these come under threat, our hardwired instinct is to defend them. These aspects of our lifestyle are not vital to survival, and we will not kill other people to defend them, but our subconscious is prodding us to protect what we have.

The proposition of giving up driving a car because the emissions threaten the survival of another tribe far away does not strike a chord with our innate psychology. The other tribe is too remote to appear real and too distant from our own set of genes to activate our concern. Modern civilization should be able to transcend our primeval instinct to defend only our own immediate blood relatives but this bias is never far beneath the surface.

Despite this instinct for self-preservation, pre-industrial people were rather good at protecting the environment. This was more than the simple fact that they did not have the capability that we now have for destruction on a global scale. There are primitive human societies which have evolved a deep respect for the natural world. Examples are Australia's Aborigines or Native Americans. Such attitudes have arisen through spirituality, not science. Living in a world that is so perfectly suited to our needs makes it appear as if the world must have been built for us by gods. It was a reasonable assumption that these same gods were continuing to look after the world, watching humankind's every move. Without the benefit of modern science, such spirituality guides us towards behaving well towards the Earth and its natural systems.

Most modern humans now believe that the reason the Earth suits us so very well is that we have evolved as an integral component of the system. The theory of evolution explains much of the complexity of the world and provides a logical basis with which to understand the world and our place within it. How ironic it would be if arrogance derived from our scientific knowledge leads us to fail to protect the Earth, compared with our superstitious early ancestors who had learnt to protect it through fearing retribution from the gods.

We do not need superstition or religious belief in order to appreciate the need to care for the natural world. We now know, through the logic of our science, that the Earth's natural ecosystems are vital to our survival and that their stability is at risk if we meddle too far. It is not the gods we should fear, but humans.

As the population of the world expands beyond the Earth's ecological capacity, our instinct for survival will be needed once more. An example that illustrates where mankind is heading is provided by the Darfur region in northern Somalia. Over the past decade, it has been hit by increasingly severe drought, reducing the capacity of the region to support its population. The whole region has descended into a conflict over survival. There are not enough resources for everyone so people are killing each other to protect a life for their own tribal group. This is not a situation we want to replicate closer to home, in Europe, or anywhere on the globe.

The genocide of Darfur is a dreadful blot on the world. There are individual people we can blame, of course. We can hope that these people will be held to account by international justice. However, this cannot hide the uncomfortable truth that a human population which does not have the resources to survive will turn against other human communities, putting their own survival before that of people from another tribe, clan or ethnic group.

At world level, if we cannot find a way to eliminate the imbalance between the human demand for resources and the capacity of the Earth to provide them, then many more countries and regions will collapse into a spiral of conflict and decline.

3 The Selfishness of Human Nature

Desiring the best for ourselves, our close family and friends is at the heart of modern society and is a stumbling block in our search for a sustainable future for the world.

It is evident that we must save the world, not only for our generation and our children, but also for our grandchildren and their grandchildren. There may be a few deeply troubled people who would rather see the world destroyed, but fortunately such dangerous views are rare. We can all agree that the world must be saved. Our genuine compassion is confined to the community around us. Those special people, who feel that they are world citizens with a moral responsibility to the world community as a whole, are few.

When we consider the lifestyle changes required in order to conserve the integrity of the Earth's ecosystems, we engage in a hugely important debate. The quality of life of all people across the globe, in this generation and all the generations to come, depends on what we do over the coming decades. The stakes could not be higher. But unless the close community around us is directly affected there is a limit to what we are willing to change within our own lives.

Transportation is a fertile area in which to find examples of selfish behaviour and deeply engrained resistance to necessary change.

One example is the widespread ownership and use of Sports Utility Vehicles (SUVs). These are more damaging to the environment than smaller cars. They consume more fuel and take up more space. For each SUV driver there are advantages. The driving position is higher, giving a clear view of the road and the traffic ahead. Being so much heavier and stronger, they should protect the occupants better in an accident. When it snows, the SUV driver can continue to get around when other cars are stranded. Other SUV owners might engage in outdoor leisure pursuits that justify their ownership. An example from an online forum for the US hunting community provides a good insight. These are people committed to nature and the great outdoors. Just the sort of people you would think would want to preserve nature to keep their sport alive. Amongst a number of discussion threads about the hunter's art was one about the merits of SUVs. The universal view was that they are a necessary hunter's tool and the bigger the better.[1]

Another example is the fixation that many people in the developed world have for exotic holidays. Intercontinental travel is no longer a once-in-a-lifetime experience confined to affluent people. Most people in the developed world can afford to jet off on holiday. Suggesting that this choice should become hugely more expensive meets deep resistance. The argument often quoted is that the rich will still be able to afford to fly but the poor will be priced out, and that this is unfair. We have become used to cheap flying and our instinct is to defend our 'rights'. This is a natural human reaction, but flying on holiday is not a fundamental human need. The human need is to relax and spend time with family and friends. There is a myriad of ways that this can be achieved, not least by improving the quality of day-to-day life.

We have come to feel that the stress of living in modern society is such that we must have at least two 'proper' holidays to recharge our psychological batteries. We do not want to risk wasting valuable holiday time by taking a holiday near to home where the weather can be unreliable. In the summer, we fly to where we can be sure of warm sunshine. In the northern hemisphere, we find that we need another break in the cold dark autumn to carry us through to Christmas. This might be a long weekend in one of Europe's capitals in the warm south. The low-cost airlines have driven the prices so low that the natural choice is to fly. Choosing not to take holidays that require air travel is a restriction that many people are unwilling to accept:

> *But I'm not going to be in the situation of saying I'm not going to take holidays abroad or use air-travel. It's just not practical.*[2]
>
> Tony Blair, 2007

Countries, too, are subject to the same self-interest as they set policy. The United States is a prime example, with an economy that has been leading the world for many decades, and setting a standard for other nations to match. Per capita income levels are some of the highest in the world and so are the associated levels of consumption. The United States is sucking in commodities and goods from around the world. The US demand for energy to fuel its economy and support the American lifestyle emits an average of 20 tons of carbon dioxide per person.[3] For the United States to shift to a low-energy economy and adopt policies with a low impact on the environment would require massive change. It is the fear that such change may undermine the US economy that President George Bush cited during his presidency as he consistently opposed accepting binding emission reduction targets.

If US consumption figures were replicated across the world, then the destruction to the world environment would be massive and rapid. For the United States and other developed nations, the intensive development path has been economically successful. It is only when other large populous nations, such as China, start to follow our lead that the huge potential impact on the Earth's systems is brought into stark relief. We then start to appreciate the arguments of our critics, who claim that the ways of the developed world are excessively extravagant and wasteful. We are accused of having a selfish lifestyle designed to benefit us and our communities, which is, of course, true.

The biggest increase in the pressure we are placing on the Earth's systems is coming from India and China. They are large countries experiencing rapid growth as they exploit the opportunities of globalization. This is exacerbating the world's problems. These two huge countries are unwilling to take action which might restrain their economic growth for the sake of the health of the world as a whole. This is hardly surprising when the world's most prosperous countries are doing so little.

At both the individual level and the state level, our innate selfishness makes it hard to make the right choices in our quest for a sustainable world society.

4 Choices

We have a number of choices open to us. The developed world can choose to carry on as before. Whilst a small proportion of humanity lives a resource-intensive lifestyle, the overall load on the Earth's systems is manageable. It is only when other countries follow our lead that the spectre of disaster appears.

I believe that it is unreasonable and untenable for the developed world to seek to hold down consumption in the developing world in order to maintain high consumption at home. The only workable solution is to bounce past our high-impact industrial past to a sustainable way of life. We may not choose to force the transition now, because of the short-term economic pain. In the end, force of circumstance will prevail. As commodities, including fossil fuels, are depleted we will have to find other ways to run society.

From the perspective of politicians, or government officials responsible for the internal affairs of a developed country, it will be easier to choose a slow transition and ignore the excellent advice of experts such as Nicholas Stern.[1] Those countries, such as Sweden, which have started the process of transformation early may be able to maintain a slow and steady pace and enjoy a smooth transition. However, the governments of most developed countries have chosen to delay making real progress in implementing sustainable policies, fearing the short-term impacts. This is a dangerous choice that denies their economies the time they will need to adjust to the new parameters. It is also dangerous for the world, not only because of the delay in changing their societies, but more importantly for the message this has for the rest of the world.

The greatest danger comes from the developing world. The potential increase in consumption is far greater than the reductions that can be made by developed societies. Populous countries such as China and India have relatively low consumption per capita. As these countries grow their economies, consumption is rising. The overall impact on the Earth's systems will be significant. If the aspiration is to match the consumption levels of the West, then the impact will be catastrophic. This means that the developed nations must move very fast to test and prove that a sustainable and prosperous society is feasible in order to parade a different example.

People within the developed world are slow to understand the full implications of the situation we face. Our success has fooled us into believing that our lifestyle is the perfect example. We have been urging on poorer countries – that were based on rural low-impact economies – to join the industrialization bandwagon. The argument put forward is that such economic development is a way to banish poverty and is therefore to be encouraged. When poverty is defined as a level of income, this is true.[2] But uplifting income in a way that also degrades the environment and undermines the sustainability of society is not an improvement in society. Much well-intentioned advice from the World Bank and other advisors, based on the experience of developed economies, is deeply flawed.

The developed world has a huge intellectual challenge in choosing policy that can lead to a sustainable future, *and* be politically acceptable. We must first accept that a high-consumption industrial economy is the wrong model for the whole world to adopt. We then have to realize that rich countries cannot campaign to hold down the consumption of the poor countries until we do the same at home. Finally, it is in the self-interest of the developed nations to assist the developing world to build sustainable societies, even if that means losing some commercial advantage by sharing technology and know-how before we have fully implemented it ourselves.

The developing world faces a different set of options. One choice available is to shun development, in order to continue to have a low impact on the world's systems. This is not a choice that we can reasonably expect. However, we should admire and support countries that make this choice. This is not what we do. We often undermine their efforts to maintain a low-impact rural-based economy by forcing open competition with our industrialized farming base. On examination, such narrow policy to improve market access for our own farmers is not in our wider self-interest.

Developing nations are much more likely to follow in the footsteps of the developed world and copy our evident success. This will be to repeat our mistakes. It does not have to be like this. There is a third option open to the developing world. This consists of leapfrogging forward to a sustainable society. The examples of telecoms and power generation illustrate this choice. Developing countries in Africa are finding, as they build telecoms infrastructure from scratch, that they do not need a fixed-line network. It is possible to sidestep this stage and go straight to using mobile phones served by a network of base stations. Power generation is another area where underdeveloped countries have the potential to bypass the stage of large centralized power generation to systems that maximize the use of renewable supplies from local sources.

Developing nations have other important choices to make. They own some of the world's most important remaining natural habitats, such as the Amazon rainforest. As the demand for biofuels rises, the pressure to clear the rainforest to grow crops for biofuels will become intense. On the one hand, the developed nations will be urging countries such as Brazil to be conscientious world citizens and protect the virgin rainforest. On the other, these same rich nations will be seeking to reduce their carbon emissions through purchasing biofuel from the world market. Brazil will have the choice to prosper economically from increasing biofuel production, or to earn praise and warm handshakes for preserving the rainforest. If Brazil follows the ways of capitalism (that we have championed so hard around the world), then exports of biofuel will be the government's choice and will take priority in setting policy.

There will be other developing nations that do not have a choice. When a country is poor and its population is starving, it has to do whatever it can to satisfy the immediate humanitarian needs. Stopping encroachment onto nature reserves or preventing the chopping down of virgin forest is not feasible when the people are struggling simply to survive.

It is the countries with sound governance, strong economies and innovative engineers and scientists which are best placed to lead the required transformation. The world is relying on the developed nations to show leadership to make the right choices, whilst we still have viable options available to us.

5 Breaking the Stalemate

There is a clear-cut case for action, but our selfish nature has to be overcome. Our politicians can make statements about the seriousness of the problem, and we can agree with them. But in all this discussion we focus on the changes needed in someone else's lifestyle or another country's pattern of consumption. There is always another person or another place that is a worse offender where we believe action should begin.

In the developed world, it is far easier to carry on as before. As an individual, any action we might take will have little effect. In any case, we suspect that whatever we do will be undermined by other people who do nothing. We will wait until our politicians bring in measures that apply to everyone. Meanwhile, the politicians will wait until there is a majority in support before taking real action.

In the emerging economies, too, there will be resistance. There will be little enthusiasm for measures that put a brake on economic expansion whilst their economies lag behind the richer nations. The industrial route forward is the proven route to economic success. Until the West can show another way to make progress, industrialization will be uppermost in their minds and will dominate their plans.

For the underdeveloped world, there is even a perverse incentive to increase levels of industrial activity as the developed world tightens environmental legislation. In rich countries, many manufacturing processes are becoming subject to more stringent rules. The developing world has the opportunity to win the business of those companies affected, using not only the competitive advantage of a low-cost base, but also less demanding regulations and weaker enforcement.

In the developed world, the local environment is being cleaned up and the environmental credentials of companies are being improved on the back of exporting dirty processes. There is nothing illegal going on (or not necessarily). This is a natural consequence of an open global market. There is no requirement to accept any responsibility for the action of companies on the other side of the world. The focus is on the low price of the goods produced without looking too closely at the methods used. The environmental damage caused is presented as their problem, not ours. Governments of the developed world then berate the governments of developing countries for not doing enough to protect the world environment. Developed nations wash their hands of the problem of environmental degradation in poorer countries without acknowledging any complicity in causing it.

There is a stalemate where each person, community and country is considering their own best self-interest. This will lead to continuing degradation of the shared global environment. We can see that this will lead inexorably to a decline in the quality of life for everyone across the globe. Some people will be affected directly and immediately, others may not experience the full impact for many decades. There may not be the evidence to pin down who, exactly, is the guilty party but the victims will be plain to see.

The stalemate will intensify before it is broken, with accusations and counter-accusations traded as countries avoid any action that is not in their direct interests. Disaffected groups across the world will increasingly blame the West, and the United States in particular, as the environmental degradation becomes more obvious. Blaming the West for what has happened in the past – when the consequences were not understood – would be unfair. Blaming the West for not acting now – when the evidence is so clear – would be fully justified.

But the 'blame game' diverts effort and attention from the more important discussion over what to do.

As the negative effects become more visible, and the press coverage of the problems gets more intense, we will finally decide that we must act. This attitude change has begun and is the vital catalyst for initiating action. It is only when we accept in principle the need for real change and draft policy designed to cut to the heart of the problem that the enormity of the challenge becomes apparent. The problems we face are multifaceted, complex and interconnected.

There are some obvious measures to take, such as tightening regulation on emissions and increasing taxes on fossil fuels. These measures are easy to identify and easy to administer. High fossil-fuel taxes reduce consumption, make alternative energy sources economically viable and provide governments with funds to invest in the infrastructure improvements required for a low-carbon society. It can be seen in hindsight that fossil fuel taxes should have been much higher over the last decade, not only because of growing concern about the climate but also to prepare for a world where oil is in short supply. The easy opportunity that was available to start the process of adaptation whilst oil was cheap has been squandered.

In July 2008, oil prices climbed above $147 a barrel. People accepted this because that was the price set by the market. If politicians had forced prices to this level through taxation, they would have risked being thrown out of office. This problem of political difficulty was highlighted during the US presidential election campaign of 2008. As fuel prices at the pump climbed, hitting voter's pockets, presidential candidate John McCain proposed a reduction in taxes on fuel (a 'gas tax holiday'[1]). His aim was to ease the pain for drivers during the summer. He made the proposal in a speech in Pittsburgh on 15 April 2008 – the day that oil reached a new record high of $113 a barrel. This was pure political opportunism. Responding to rising prices in this way would be counterproductive, undermining attempts to drive down the use of fossil fuel and reducing tax receipts that would be needed to fund investment in a low-carbon infrastructure. Even so, there can be political mileage to be made out of backing off from sensible green taxation.

At the same time as the US presidential election campaign, the British government faced the same issue of rising fuel prices. A series of fuel tax rises had previously been announced. These were sensible and appropriate measures. The UK treasury had planned a 2p per litre tax increase for 1 April 2008. As the price of oil climbed through 2008, the chancellor Alistair Darling delayed the increase until 1 October. In July 2008 the decision was taken not to make any increase until 2009.

As we entered the recession of 2009, oil prices dropped back to pre-2008 levels. Politicians then had another chance to increase fuel taxes. I wrote in *Sustainable Business* magazine in February 2009 that this was a golden opportunity for government to deal with the recession in a very green way by raising fuel taxes and investing the receipts in jobs in the green economy:

> *Oil has now returned to easily affordable levels. Politicians can take this opportunity – if they dare. They should push taxation on fuel to match the price levels determined by the market in summer 2008 – and which we now accept as inevitable. The proceeds should be ploughed into spending on the infrastructure projects required to build a zero-carbon society, such as support for renewable power, much better-insulated public buildings and more efficient public transport.*
>
> *This golden opportunity may not arise a third time. The next oil crisis may come because the world's oil reserves are running out and the price goes into a permanent steep ascent.*[2]

In spring 2009, our leaders did not dare to raise fuel taxes in the midst of a recession. Again, political expediency came before sensible green taxation. As we grapple with breaking the stalemate that threatens to trap the world in a spiral of terminal decline, we are discovering that measures that will lead to both real and lasting improvements and are politically acceptable are hard to find.

At world level, an uncompromising push to prevent further climate change would seem sensible. It is clearly in the self-interest of low-lying countries to do all in their power to support such action. For a poor country such as Bangladesh, this is vital to prevent the loss of a significant area of its land as sea levels rise on the back of global warming. Bangladesh should campaign hard for substantive action, but Bangladesh is not a big contributor to emissions and lacks hard power to influence those countries that are. Bangladesh has to use the soft power of shaming the world into action.

The Netherlands is a country that will support the case made by Bangladesh. Not only out of compassion, but because as a low-lying country it too is threatened by rising sea levels. To set an example to the world, the Netherlands could channel all its effort and investment into growing a zero-carbon economy. But the Netherlands must take a realistic view of the world and assess the degree of change that other nations will also accept. The Netherlands must assume that sea levels will continue to rise, and therefore invest in appropriate sea defences. It would be understandable for the Danish government to give a higher priority to ensuring the country is not submerged by the sea than to increasing its efforts to prevent climate change beyond the level of effort of other countries.

Another example of the conflicting priorities we will face is in agriculture. The fundamental challenge will be maintaining food production whilst at the same time ramping up production of crops for biofuels. We will demand ever higher levels of productivity and convert yet more virgin land to industrialized agriculture. The resulting threat to natural ecosystems will be widespread and hard to reverse.

Water will also become an increasingly valuable commodity. Drawing marginal arid land into agricultural will increase the need for water for crop irrigation. Climate change will also alter rainfall patterns. Where it becomes drier, crop yields will suffer unless we find additional water supplies. So far, we have been able to rely on our engineers to drill boreholes out of which we pump water to allow farmers to continue to grow crops. Our subterranean water supplies seem unlimited: we only have to dig (or drill) deep enough and we always find water. We are slow to understand that over the years our aquifers become depleted and no longer deliver the water we require. In nature, they act as a buffer for drier years, keeping the rivers flowing. We can use aquifers in the same way to cover short-term droughts, but continual pumping at a greater rate than they are replenished is not sustainable.

The impasse we face comes about from our selfish attitude and the difficulty in looking beyond dealing with the symptoms to finding and addressing the causes. The resulting stalemate is so strong, and the difficulties of loosening it so extreme, that the pressure to act has to become enormous before the circumstances are right for real effective action.

Predictions from scientists, no matter how well researched or explained, will not be enough to make society act. Real change will only be discussed seriously when there is dramatic coverage on television screens of people experiencing the negative consequences of climate change. It will not be until the impacts come closer to home that the circumstances will be ripe to act. More powerful storms and increased flooding will be one factor. Power cuts as supplies of fossil fuel are interrupted will be another. The final push to reinforce our resolve will be social problems as society struggles to cope with a huge influx of climate refugees.

Instead of being someone else's problem, climate change will have arrived in our own backyard. That is when the stalemate will finally be broken.

6 Climate Change Hits Home

The majority of people now accept that humankind's activities have increased the levels of CO_2 in the atmosphere and that this is the primary cause of climate change. The level of CO_2 in the atmosphere, measured in 2008, was 387 ppm and was predicted to continue to rise.[1] This is far higher than at any time over the last 650,000 years (180–300 ppm). The cause is the imbalance between the sum total of all the fossil fuel burnt by humankind over the last 200 years and the Earth's capacity to reabsorb it. Whatever we do now, we will have to live with these increased CO_2 levels and the warming of the planet that they are causing. When we finally put a hold on emissions we will have a tense waiting game of something like 50 years to observe the series of consequences without any power to stop it.

The first and most visible change (as seen from satellite) is the reduction of floating ice in the Arctic. The ice is disappearing at an alarming rate. The time when the North Pole becomes ice-free each summer is not far off. The reason why this change is so rapid is that whilst there is ice, the white surface reflects the sun's energy back into space. Where the ice has melted, open water is dark and absorbs this energy. The more open water, the more energy is absorbed, the more the Arctic Ocean warms, so the more ice melts, and so on. This positive feedback loop is accelerating the changes. The 120 polar explorers who are in the record books as having walked unaided to the North Pole will become a very exclusive group as it will no longer be possible to repeat their exploits.

Melting floating sea ice has no effect on global sea levels. According to the Archimedes' principle, such ice displaces its own weight in water. The huge ice sheets of Antarctica are different. The Antarctic ice is made from water that has not been in the ocean for many thousands of years. If we pull the whole of Antarctica out of the deep freeze, and thaw all the ancient ice, then the water pouring back into the ocean would raise sea levels by a staggering 60–65 m.[2] This is not merely speculation. The Earth has been ice-free in the past and the geological record shows the sea levels that resulted.

No one is suggesting that we are likely to thaw out the whole of Antarctica any time soon. The most vulnerable area is the West Antarctic Ice Sheet. When the ice it contains ends up in the ocean, the British Antarctic Survey (BAS) estimates that global sea levels will rise by at least 1.5m.[3] We were surprised when part of the ice sheet (the Larsen B ice shelf) broke off in 2002. This was an area of ice over 200 m thick covering 3,250 km^2 – of similar size to Rhode Island in the United States or the English county of Wiltshire. We will also be surprised when the next piece of the ice shelf breaks away. We have no reliable way to predict the timescale. We are changing the parameters way beyond any comparison we can make with our historic scientific records.

Another feasible scenario over a timescale measured in centuries is that we succeed in thawing the whole of Greenland.[4] Opening this tap into the oceans would raise global sea levels by about 7 m.[5] This is dramatic and significant change, but it still seems a long way off. The sobering thought for those tempted to ignore the issue is that some scientists believe that very soon the Earth's systems will have been pushed so far that it becomes inevitable that the Greenland ice sheet melts.[6] It would take hundreds of years to melt the entire Greenland ice sheet, of course, but if these scientists are right then we are close to the point that we will have no way to stop it happening. Unless we act soon, we are committing humanity to lose all land that is currently lower than 7 m above sea level. This will include most of the world's great cities. Governments will have to make long-term plans for relocation. The couple of centuries that it might take to thaw Greenland completely seem like a long time on the timescale of any one of us. For humanity this is just around the corner. Such a rise in sea levels would be a huge challenge for future generations to deal with. Within one or two decades we will know for sure whether this is the future we have caused, and then there will then be no way to prevent it.

The World Glacier Monitoring Service (WGMS) reports that glaciers around the world are continuing the rapid retreat observed over the last few decades.[7] This is shifting yet more ancient water into the oceans, but also reducing the resilience of the hydrological system. Glaciers provide a reserve of water that melts slowly during the summer to keep many of the great rivers of the world flowing. The Rhine, the Rhone and the Po in Europe are fed by glacier meltwater from the Alps. The Ganges, the Indus and the Brahmaputra in India originate from Himalayan glaciers. The regions through which these rivers pass are all under threat. Significant reduction of the glaciers reduces the summer meltwater and could have dramatic negative impacts on agricultural capacity. Many deserts will get larger and new ones will be formed.

As each year goes by, we will observe and experience whether the predictions made by the climate scientists are playing out. The most reliable assessment is provided by the Intergovernmental Panel on Climate Change (IPCC). They publish a consensus view stating only that for which they have sound evidence. Any extreme opinions are filtered out by the process. This means that the advice from the IPCC about greenhouse gas emissions (GHG) is often understated.

The IPCC is not scaremongering. Its careful conservative language has been pored over for days to ensure that sensationalism does not intrude to colour the science. The grey words that describe the key findings of the 2007 report are made all the more riveting when we know they are completely without any journalistic spin.

> *Anthropogenic warming and sea level rise would continue for centuries even if GHG emissions were to be reduced sufficiently for GHG concentrations to stabilize, due to the time scales associated with climate processes and feedbacks.*
>
> *Some systems, sectors and regions are likely to be especially affected by climate change. The regions are the Arctic, Africa, small islands and Asian and African megadeltas. Within other regions, even those with high incomes, some people, areas and activities can be particularly at risk.*

> *Impacts are very likely to increase due to increased frequencies and intensities of some extreme weather events. Recent events have demonstrated the vulnerability of some sectors and regions, including in developed countries, to heat waves, tropical cyclones, floods and drought, providing stronger reasons for concern as compared to the findings of the Third Assessment Report.*
>
> Robust Findings of the Fourth IPPC
Assessment Report 2007[8]

The IPCC has lodged an independent and carefully researched analysis. It is not to be dismissed. I shall paraphrase the findings of the IPCC to include a level of emphasis that the message deserves.

> *Climate change is an execution warrant hanging over the world as we know it now. We do not know the exact time and place of the execution, but living on death row will become increasingly unpleasant for humanity. It is our duty to consider carefully and decide how to respond. This is not a trivial affair to be given cursory attention until another issue dislodges it from the world's attention.*

7 The Boom before the Bust

We are on the leading edge of a huge wave of innovation as we come to accept that the twin threats of diminishing oil reserves and climate change can no longer be ignored. Governments will be behind the push to shift investment into what they believe to be solutions.

Diminishing oil reserves will grab the headlines and be of more immediate concern to our politicians than threats to the environment. National parks with oil reserves (such as those in Alaska) will become a target. Instead of keeping national parks off-limits, we will start to discuss 'safe' exploitation using advanced technology such as directional drilling. This allows boreholes to be drilled that traverse a long distance underground from the entry point. There are examples of offshore rigs anchored above a splayed array of 40 wells reaching out wide under the seabed from a single production platform. Such wells are slow and expensive to drill. On land, it is cheaper to have many more well heads dotted across the land. Out at sea, the economics favour spending on directional drilling to save the huge expense of a number of offshore platforms. To get permission to pump oil out of national parks, oil companies may propose using such expensive offshore technology. A few well-hidden sites may be sufficient to exploit the oil reservoirs beneath. The case made by oil companies will be that the park will not be adversely affected.

As the scramble for oil takes priority, it is ironic that climate change will assist us. The continental shelf under the Arctic Ocean has been off-limits for exploration. It has been too difficult and prohibitively expensive to build and operate oil production facilities amongst the floating ice. Any rig would soon be damaged or knocked off station by the weight of shifting ice. Now that a greater area of the most northern ocean is becoming ice-free for much of the year,[1] it becomes feasible to use the technology used in other deep-water oil fields such as the North Sea. We can be confident of solving the technical challenges; the problems will be political. Canada, the United States, Russia and Denmark all lay claim to the seabed under the ice. There will be much extended negotiation (and perhaps conflict) over who owns this new oil and gas bonanza.

These new reserves of oil and gas will push back the date when the oil runs out, delaying the need to invest for a world beyond fossil fuels. With the immediate threat of oil shortages removed, the world economy will boom, fuelling another round of globalization.

Out of our concern for climate change, politicians will give carbon markets considerable support. This will put a price to carbon and support investment in all manner of low-carbon technologies, making real improvements in many areas. If we find that such investment is still too expensive, we can buy credits from other companies or countries, helping them to reduce their growth in carbon emissions. In the process, there will be considerable opportunities to sell low-carbon technology, at home and abroad.

During the early days of trading carbon, we have discovered problems with establishing the market. The free allocation of carbon credits, for example, has handed windfall profits to the biggest emitters. Those companies that could make reductions easily have profited. Presumably, these are the companies that had done least to reduce their emissions of greenhouse gases before the market commenced. Governments can see this anomaly, so are likely to auction future permits. Even so, there will be considerable commercial business and trading profits from playing the carbon market.

As the carbon market becomes ingrained, we may be fooled into thinking that we have found the solution to arresting climate change. It will be convenient to forget that trading carbon is only useful as a tool if there is a firm cap on allowable emissions. Our politicians must play their part in agreeing, and implementing, binding global targets that match the recommendations of the world's climate scientists. Politicians will find this tough. Emissions will continue at high levels whilst negotiations proceed, with each country pushing for reduction elsewhere in the world economy, but avoiding putting their own economies at risk.

The economic boom that mankind experiences will not be a positive experience for the natural world. The only polar bears surviving will be in zoos as their natural habitat disappears. Despite the best efforts of our dedicated zoo keepers, many of these will be driven mad by the experience of captivity and only able to breed through artificial insemination. This would be a sad end for this once feared and admired hunter that used to roam across the polar ice.

As summers become hotter and droughts more frequent, investment will be required to adapt to the symptoms of climate change. For example, there will be calls for improved air conditioning in buildings. It is ironic that just when it is realized that fossil-fuel consumption must be reduced, the reaction is to install energy-hungry air conditioning to counter one of the symptoms.

As the glaciers in the Alps retreat, there will be water shortages as less meltwater flows from the mountains to keep Europe's rivers flowing during the summer. There will be calls for more boreholes and larger reservoirs. As the season for Alpine ski resorts becomes shorter, there will be a need to use snow cannons more often to keep the lower slopes open.

Our engineers will deliver ever more energy-efficient solutions to the technical challenges we face due to high energy prices. But energy demand will remain high, or even increase overall, as we deal with adaptation to the symptoms of climate change. Investment in more air-conditioning units, snow cannons, water-supply infrastructure and other responses to climate change will drive the economy forward.

All this buzz of activity will take place whilst the world continues to fail to implement real action to address the causes of climate change. The boom will end as the oil finally runs out.

8 Scraping the Bottom of the Barrel

For many years, there have been commentators who have predicted the end of oil. Nevertheless, the oil has continued to flow. This makes us resistant to yet further warnings. This is dangerous because there is an end to oil. This is a geological fact that cannot be changed. The oil locked up in the Earth's crust contains the embodied energy of millions of years of historic sunshine. We are not making any more; when it is gone it will be gone for ever.

The Organization of the Petroleum Exporting Countries (OPEC) controls the world oil market, adjusting output to maintain a stable market. As oil prices have climbed, our politicians have urged OPEC to increase capacity. Not wishing to undermine the world economy, OPEC has responded by pumping more oil. This choice will no longer be available when the barriers to further exploitation are geological rather than political. There will not be enough oil to go around because reserves are exhausted.

Prices could then surge to much higher levels. There will be nothing to slow the escalation in prices until real damage is inflicted, such that many consumers will not be able to afford to pay. Only then will demand reduce to match the tightly constrained supply. An oil price of double, triple or quadruple current prices is feasible.

Rising oil prices will also spur on the oil companies to explore in more difficult and challenging places. The high price will support heavy investment in small and remote fields that were not viable when oil was cheap. When a new field is discovered, examination of the geology and flow rates from test wells are used to estimate the recoverable reserves. These are then added to the oil company's inventory. As the field comes on-stream, oil is drawn from the inventory. There comes a point where production peaks and the field goes into decline. Engineers consider enhanced recovery techniques to extend the life of the field. There is no hiding from the fact the field is in terminal decline.

So far, oil companies have been able to locate new fields and add them to the inventory. The aim is to try to match new discoveries with the depletion rate of existing fields. It is a scientific impossibility for this to continue indefinitely. It may be that the world oil industry taken as a whole has already passed its peak capacity and has entered the period of terminal decline. It is hard to tell, as figures for the remaining reserves in the world's prime oil fields in Saudi Arabia are a closely guarded state secret.

To hope to rely on oil for a decade or two longer will depend on China. China does not have significant oil reserves. It also has a booming economy. To keep the economy motoring along, the Chinese must secure commodity flows, particularly oil. China will demand a rising share of world oil output, driving the price through the roof as they outbid countries with less financial clout. This scramble for dwindling reserves will bring forward the day when we can no longer rely on oil.

This will further strengthen the case for alternative fuels, particularly renewable fuels. This sector of industry will be insulated from the severe downturn in the economy as the era of cheap and accessible fossil fuel ends.

OPEC countries will hope to milk the long tail of the declining market. As supplies dwindle, prices will climb, with the prospect that overall oil income for OPEC countries could hold at current levels. This cannot hold indefinitely. Prices will rise so high that customers are not prepared to pay. This will be the start of the real transition away from fossil fuels. OPEC should be very worried. As decision makers in the major economies see the looming dangers of continued oil dependency, they may deliberately force early adaptation. The controlled pain of an economic downturn may be judged better than the uncertain risks of continued reliance on oil.

For some time, there will be no choice but to continue to seek supplies of fossil fuel, even at outrageous prices. The cleanest of these is gas. For Europe, there are huge reserves on the doorstep, owned by Russia. Russian leaders can expect their economy to be insulated from the economic downturn as they draw income from selling gas to Europe. In a tight market, Russia will increasingly be able to dictate the price. This situation will continue as long as European leaders are prepared to rely on Russia. Distrust of Russia may steer our politicians towards a greater focus on security of supply, even if such a policy has an economic cost attached.

One place Europe can look is to Qatar in the Middle East. This country has massive gas reserves. A regular shuttle of liquefied gas tankers from Qatar would provide an alternative source to Russian gas. Whether this truly improves security of supply for Europe depends on the political situation in the Middle East. Whatever approach is taken, a Europe that continues to rely on fossil fuel will become increasingly vulnerable to the political situation beyond its borders.

Carbon trading will take on greater significance and help to smooth the transition in the early stages of the fossil-fuel crunch. Whether carbon trading serves any useful purpose in arresting climate change is debatable (as discussed in Chapter 14). You have to be hugely optimistic (or naive) to expect that world politicians can agree, and then implement, a completely watertight and binding global cap on carbon emissions. Carbon trading will therefore do little more than provide stability to the market and provide a sound economic basis from which to exploit marginal fossil-fuel deposits as relatively clean fuels such as gas and oil run low.

The world has low-grade fossil fuels in abundance. For example, the oil sands in Canada have reserves second only to Saudi Arabia. The cost of extraction has been a brake on their exploitation. Canada's National Energy Board (NEB) estimates that the cost of production to extract oil from oil sands is between $12 and $34 per barrel, depending on the method used.[1] When oil was $20 a barrel on the world market (1999),[2] oil sands were uneconomic. At the record oil prices set in summer 2008, these costs become negligible. Canada could become a major petroleum-exporting nation as oil prices return to these levels and climb even higher.

In exploiting the huge low-grade reserves such as oil sands, an inconvenient fact is ignored. Extracting the oil uses energy. Conventional oil production uses some energy for activities like pumping and transportation but these are small compared with the huge energy demands of oil sand production. The sand has to be mined, and then heated to extract the bitumen which is then processed into a suitable fuel. Other methods pump steam or hot water underground to flush out the trapped oil. The NEB calculates that emissions per barrel of oil extracted are 0.075 tonnes of CO_2, dropping to 0.073 tonnes per barrel in 2015 as efficiency improvements are made. This compares with 0.43 tonnes of CO_2 released when one barrel of oil is burnt.[3] On these figures, using oil derived from oil sands emits 17% overall more carbon than using conventional oil. This is a conservative estimate. The main source of the processing energy is gas – a clean fuel with low carbon emissions. If oil sand production was self-contained, using its own oil as the energy source, carbon emissions would be yet higher.

As we move on to increase exploitation of lower grade sources of fossil fuel, such as oil shale and coal, we enter a spiral of diminishing returns. We need to burn ever more fuel and emit increasing quantities of CO_2 simply to maintain energy consumption at the same level.

As we struggle to keep our economies energized, the issue of environmental responsibility will continually thwart many of our efforts (and so it should). There will be no easy way to avoid the negative economic impact of turning away from fossil fuels. If we use foresight to anticipate this huge economic hit, and look around for ways to rebuild the economy in a sustainable way, we will find a wealth of opportunities to exploit. If we put our efforts into scraping the bottom of the barrel, we will be risking economic collapse as well as incurring unnecessary environmental degradation. This would be the price of our procrastination. The price could be even higher. Continuing to deny that we must conserve the ecosystem could be the catalyst for the total collapse of civilization.

9 The Collapse of Civilization

Human civilization has developed capabilities to overcome the threats that species in the natural world are subject to. We have eliminated many diseases, confined our predators to zoos and climate is no longer a direct threat as we heat or cool our indoor spaces as required. The only threat we now face is ourselves.

We have the technology to support enjoyable and healthy lives. It is depressing that, despite this, we are charging towards a collapse in civilization. It is as if we are dancing towards a cliff wearing a blindfold and enjoying the music whilst it plays. When we fall off the edge, and in a panic pull off the blindfold, we will see the true nature of the dance. By then it will be too late as we are dashed on the rocks below.

The swelling of human population from one billion in the year 1800 to six billion at the start of the millennium and then onto a projected nine billion by 2050, is not going to abate easily. To have children is a deep yearning inside us all. We feel uncomfortable when discussing restrictions on human breeding. This is a deep personal issue. Rules and regulations to limit population growth provoke intense emotive resistance. In many cases, this comes from people who, with the very best of intentions, are trying to protect fundamental human rights. The idea that we should allow every one of the six billion people on this planet to have as many children as they desire is dangerously misguided (as discussed further in Chapter 12). We may not like China's enforcement of a one-child-per-couple policy but we should admire the fact that China is trying to find a solution. Avoiding this difficult debate is one part of the blindfold we are wearing.

The future we are dancing towards is a fight for survival.

Some countries will work hard to protect their environment. The prime requirement for clean water will be secured by careful management of watersheds. Agricultural land will be used primarily to supply the population with food. Any excess agricultural capacity will be used for biofuels. This will not match the fuel available in the era of cheap fossil fuel, so we will ramp up renewable energy supplies. This will still fall short of our craving for energy, so we will have to face reductions in consumption.

As the Maldive Islands are submerged by rising sea levels, 300,000 refugees will be looking for a new home. The encroachment of the sea will be slow (unless a major storm forces the pace). So there will be time for discussion and extended wrangling. I believe that, in the end, the developed world will be shamed into providing the Maldivians with a new home.

Some coastal cities such as New Orleans and Venice will be so exposed that there will be no choice but to abandon them. For other cities, like the UK's capital, London, it may be decided to invest in massive sea defences rather than relocate the city.

Bangladesh will not have such a choice. It is estimated that between a fifth and a third of this poor and populous country will be submerged by the end of this century if the upper-end predictions made by the IPCC prove correct. Unless the international community step in with massive aid, Bangladesh will suffer badly. In any case, aid may not be enough. Sea defences on such a scale may not be practical. We can protect a city or put defences across a narrow inlet but the protection of a whole low-lying river delta is an almost impossible engineering task. The subsequent refugee problem will involve millions of people and sorely stretch the charitable intent of other countries.

As we try to feed the growing world population, other factors will be working against us. The demand for biofuels will be sucking 'spare' capacity out of agriculture. Countries that used to export food will export less or none at all. In addition, the increasing affluence of the middle class in the developing world will be increasing the demand for a richer diet. There will not be enough food to go around.

Many developed countries will maintain functioning societies. They will have to work hard to protect their supplies and respond to the demands of the resources squeeze. The effort required will leave little capacity or willingness to help other countries. Many of these weaker countries will collapse into failed states. This will also put pressure on their immediate neighbours. Where every country is stretched and vulnerable, this could become a domino effect. There is a risk that whole regions collapse into anarchy and ruin as individuals and groups seek to defend a future for their family and close 'tribal' group.

There will be countries that have adopted sustainable policies at an early stage which can be observers of the chaos that will engulf the world. Sweden may be an example. This country is at the forefront of adopting sustainable policies. It is also fortunate to occupy a remote geographical location, surrounded by stable countries. Sweden is one of the few countries that may be insulated from the knock-on effects of the crisis.

Throughout this turmoil in human society, there will be one problem we will all share: damage to the shared environment. Now, in the early years of the 21st century, we have spare capacity within society to do something about protecting the global ecosystem. As civilization starts to unravel, the focus of us all will be to survive. In such circumstances, the environment will be a secondary issue. It will become impossible to protect the remaining virgin forests and national parks when the communities nearby are destitute and starving. Many of the nuclear plants that were built in the hope of keeping carbon emissions in check will now be located within dysfunctional societies. The same may be true for stockpiles of nuclear weapons. There is a very real risk of nuclear accidents and nuclear war waged by terrorists. Such outcomes will make our concern over climate change seem almost irrelevant.

Life on planet Earth in one form or another will continue. Civilization may not.

Part Two
Changing Direction

10 Altering the Future

We can learn from the past but we cannot alter it. We cannot know the future but we have the power to change it.

Unless there are major changes, civilization will collapse. Extrapolating current trends leads to this conclusion. This is not scaremongering. This is the result of applying cool, hard logic to the consequences of the behaviours we have adopted.

It is not surprising that others see the same possible future.[1,2] The surprise is that most people choose to ignore the dangers. We cannot be persuaded that civilization is about to collapse around us. If we were persuaded, then we would be prepared to do almost anything to prevent it. The problem is that in the developed world those people born after World War II (which is most of us) expect to live our lives without being directly affected by the world's problems. A new and vibrant Europe arose from the destruction of World War II, leading to over 60 years of peace, security and growth.

During this period of stability, there have been natural disasters such as earthquakes, hurricanes, droughts and the tsunami of 2004; but for most of us these have been in someone else's backyard. Closer to home, the financial system has been hit by a series of setbacks with the bursting of the Internet bubble in 2000 and the major financial crisis of 2008. Each time, there have been headlines and crisis meetings, but our governments have found a way forward. It seems impossible that they cannot pull off the same trick again, whatever befalls us. This is a dangerous delusion. The impact of overpopulation and rising consumption, amplified by the effects of climate change and peak oil and food shortages, are all coming to a head according to the same timetable.

My generation is too young to have experienced the collapse of Europe in the turmoil of World War II. My father and many in his generation did go through such an experience. Those veterans who remain are too old to have further influence in society. This is a shame. My father was a kind and considerate man: an academic, a priest and an expert in the 18th-century history of the church in France. I found it hard to reconcile that such a good man living in the ivory towers of Oxford University had also fought in North Africa in World War II and had been wounded twice. It was only after the war that he was ordained into the church and followed a career in academia. He hardly ever spoke about his years in the desert war. The family finally persuaded him to write down his wartime experiences. The book, *Fusilier*, was eventually published in 2002.[3] His generation was full of people whose stories were never told. They knew at first-hand the terror and brutality of war and would do their utmost to prevent it happening again, but found it hard to communicate this in a way the younger generation could understand.

I only truly understood my father after returning from the Falklands War of 1982. I fought with Britain's parachute forces and experienced first-hand what happens when the normal rules of civilized society are suspended to resolve a dispute that politicians could not resolve themselves. I did my duty, but it was not like a John Wayne film or an adventure novel. War is horrific and nasty – even a relatively short 'clean' conflict such as the recapture of the Falklands from Argentina. Like my father, I could not find the words to explain the reality. To those who are not there, war seems exciting. When we returned home, we were regarded as heroes. This was not true, of course. War is not about excitement and heroes. It is about terrifying ordeals and wasted lives. The danger of a long period of relative peace is that we forget how very lucky we are to live in stable civilized societies.

Most populations in the developed world have grown up in peace (if we ignore a whole series of small conflicts from the former Yugoslavia to Lebanon). This means the people in power do not have the gut feel for the true nature of war that my father and his generation had. We should also remember that war is at least subject to some rules and a certain amount of control. The impending collapse in civilization could be a nasty lawless affair that is far more unpleasant than conventional war. This is not a risk to be ignored or taken lightly.

Some people may be able to live their lives in isolation without worrying about the future. Such selfish fatalism may be a self-defence mechanism. We know we will die. It is better not to think too much about it. The advice we often hear is, 'Live for today because tomorrow we may die.' On an individual basis, this is good advice. For the human species this has always been so. We are the sum total of millions of generations of people who have extracted the best out of life and then handed the world on to the next generation.

We are a special generation and need to behave differently. We can see that the future of humanity is at risk. We need to find the courage to face the issue and do something about it.

Until now, humans have been able to take comfort in knowing that there will be a generation to follow. Children are raised, cared for and educated for the first two decades of their lives. The world is then handed onto them. It is fortunate that as one generation becomes old and cynical there are young fresh bodies and minds to take its place.

Now, if only we could overcome our selfish fatalism, we would see that we are passing a poisoned chalice on to the next generation. We should take the time to imagine the suffering they will have to endure. They will have to fight fellow humans for the resources to survive, without the security of a safe society to fall back on. Elevated levels of background radiation will increase the chances of bearing deformed babies. There will be no more natural wilderness, just isolated 'protected' areas in which the natural flora and fauna have died, killed off by changes to the climate. We are denying future generations the opportunity that we have had. This is irresponsible, unfair and should make us deeply concerned.

Those people who are not swayed by such emotions and do not care a damn for future generations will not help the cause I champion. They should not expect any special treatment. There is no need for restraint as we force change upon this group. I am optimistic that the hard core of those who continue to deny the need for action is reducing. I also believe that their influence and power can be sidelined as the majority view takes over.

Our generation has the responsibility to start the process that will rescue humankind. The dangers are now so real and present that we must act. Now is the time to move beyond the rhetoric.

There are difficult issues that we must confront. This is not the time for easy platitudes. The world needs plain speaking that leads to real action. In the following chapters of this book, I offer a blueprint to reprieve the world.

11 Show Respect for the Earth

The fate of the Earth is in our hands. Dramatic change to the ecosystem will not be immediate. A large and complex system like planet Earth contains considerable inertia. It will take a lot of effort, over a long time, to push it on to a new track. This we are doing, slowly but surely. If we push hard enough, we will not only experience gradual change but the whole balance of the system will be upset. Eventually we will reach the tipping point in Earth's systems that will initiate runaway change to the ecosystem. Climate change is the most visible and immediate consequence, but there will be other outcomes. As species die out and others take over, there may be plagues and infestations that afflict nature, agriculture and humans. Submerged land, new deserts, the spread of malaria from the tropics; there is no limit to the potential damage.

The force for change that each of us can exert is miniscule and cannot be measured on a global scale. Whether we drive a car or not, or what model our car is, or how far we drive hardly seems to matter. Whether we are responsible for a few more kilograms of garbage dumped into landfill, when there is already so much, is of no importance. No one of us can destroy our world, but billions of people all behaving in the same way can. Human society is now on a scale where we are a significant driver on the system. We are no longer simply passive residents. Our progress has given us the capability to destroy the system on which we rely to survive.

The whole world is under threat. Slowly but surely the apparatus of civilization will collapse under the weight of food shortages and huge flows of refugees. Desperate, starving people will do whatever is necessary to survive. As the capacity of our world to support the population shrinks, the structure of world society will come under enormous strain. The number of countries with the spare resources to defend and protect the concept of a fair and civilized society will reduce, and the pressures they have to withstand will become ever more extreme. Even countries that are now beacons of tolerance and charitable intent will be forced to close in on themselves to defend their own survival, finding that there is no easy escape from global catastrophe.

The execution warrant we have prepared for future generations has not yet been signed. A condemned person can remain sane by harbouring the thought that there may still be a last-minute intervention or stay of execution granted by a higher authority. Humankind could take the same approach. We can search out the scientists who advise that there is not a problem. This would reassure us that the lives of our children are not really at risk. But as we discover that such scientists are getting harder to find, and that their views are increasingly marginalized, we should pause to think. When the only 'scientists' we can rely on to give us the reassurance we seek are supported by grants from organizations which cannot survive in a sustainable world (such as the major oil companies) or from academic institutions we have not heard of, then we should be very worried.

The whole sequence of cause and effect is impossible to predict. The detail is far from clear, but there is one observation that can be made. Civilization has become so globally interconnected, with each piece so dependent on every other, that it will be impossible to hide from disruption to the world ecosystem. The world has not been here before. Individual civilizations such as the Roman Empire have collapsed and been replaced. But a systematic failure on a global scale could be far worse. These are not risks we should be running. The time has come to show respect for the Earth.

So far, our growing concern has focused on the level of CO_2 in the atmosphere, and the associated changes in climate that directly affect us, such as reduced crop yields and rising sea levels. There are far more serious issues that are not given the attention they deserve. These range from slowly rising levels of background radiation from our nuclear activities, and the gradual poisoning of the oceans, to the loss of biodiversity and destruction of natural habitats.

Between 1970 and 2005, land-based species fell in number by 25%, marine species by 28% and freshwater species by 29%.[1] These are shocking figures. There is something badly wrong with the way we have run the world since 1970. This period coincides with the careers of my generation, who were at school in 1970 and are now of an age to hold senior positions with power and influence. This generation shoulders a heavy responsibility to reverse direction and choose a different future for the Earth – and for humankind.

It will be a slow process to reverse the changes we have initiated. For CO_2, there are natural mechanisms that could bring the Earth back into equilibrium, provided we stop liberating yet more fossil carbon. For radiation levels and man-made chemicals that nature cannot break down, it is hard to see that there is any realistic way back; except to stop making more, and to do so quickly.

The Amazon rainforest is a spectacular example of the abundance and variety of nature. It is doubtful that we could ever replace the biodiversity of the rainforest once we have destroyed it, as we slowly and surely will without major change to world society.

We will have to change our behaviour. But changing our lives individually will have an insignificant effect, and in any case takes decades to show a discernible improvement. This will make it very hard to persuade people of the need to act. Assuming that initial enthusiasm for action can be generated, it will have to endure for decades. This means that a series of high-profile events, such as pop concerts, conferences or jamborees, is not the answer. These events can be very effective in raising awareness of the problem but people will soon become jaded. It will become increasingly difficult to think of innovative ideas to capture the imagination of the world's population. We need fundamental changes in attitudes that will endure into the long future.

A wholesale attitude shift will be far harder to achieve than winning support for individual policies. Understanding this – that a policy-by-policy approach will not be sufficient – is vital to selecting the most effective early actions. We must not squander the world's concern on initiating short-term temporary measures that will achieve little in the long run. It is better to use the momentum for change to initiate the deep fundamental changes required in society.

These changes reach across all countries and all societies and will impact on all areas of our lives. Anything less will be just a stay of execution, not a reprieve. Those of us who see the future in such a stark way are few. I accept that, currently, most people disagree with this assessment. I understand this; it took me some time to comprehend the implications of my analysis. It is an incredible (and horrendous) insight. The enormity of it is enough to lead to many sleepless nights. There may even be people who share this insight and have been driven insane by it, and are now locked up in our mental asylums. I meet people who believe that my views must have come from such a place. They are surprised when they find that I am as sane and level-headed a person as any you are likely to find in this imperfect world.

The attitude change required is of a similar magnitude to the transition from believing that the Earth is flat to accepting that it is round. If we look towards the horizon the world appears flat. It required a huge leap of understanding to accept that we live on a globe floating in space. Earlier mariners were worried that if they strayed too far offshore they might sail off the edge of the world. It took expeditions by navigators such as Christopher Columbus and Ferdinand Magellan to prove finally that such worries were unfounded. Ferdinand Magellan led the first expedition to complete a full circumnavigation in 1522. Magellan did not survive, being killed in a battle with the indigenous people of the Philippines en route.[2] Of the original 237 men that set sail, only 18 survived to complete the voyage. This small group were amazed to find that they had lost track of one day, even though they had kept a meticulous ship's log. Without accurate clocks, they were not aware of the slight lengthening of each day as they travelled west over the three years of their journey. They arrived exactly a day later than the date shown in the ship's log. This was a consequence of the fact that the Earth is round. No one had thought about this before. This was an amazing finding at the time, but is now simply a fact that we understand from a young age.

The fact that our society must be sustainable is as obvious as the fact that the Earth is round; it is just that it is a belief that has not yet taken hold in modern society. As I campaign for a truly sustainable world, it is clear to me that this is what we must achieve.

But I also see that the change of thinking is so profound that people will not be easily persuaded.

We now know without a second thought that the world is round. As children, this is taught to us from an early age whilst our minds are open and receptive. It is a fact that is easily digested. An adult who already believed in a flat world would be harder to persuade. I have been slow to come to the realization that we must manage our world in a sustainable manner, and that this will be radically different to the way we manage it now. It will be exceedingly hard to make that same attitude shift across all the members of my own generation. But I have confidence that if I, and people who share my views, can succeed, then the momentum of society will be in our favour. For future generations, sustainable living will become a concept that is learnt in nursery and primary schools and accepted as fact.

As our generation reaches retirement age, we will pass on the baton of power to the new generation. Our future leaders are now young people with fresh open minds who are observing our response to this planetary emergency. It would be good if they afforded us a safe and secure old age. On the record of our actions so far, that is not what we deserve. I fear that we will be pilloried as selfish old duffers. The next generation will object, of course, to the legacy of high CO_2 concentrations in the atmosphere, but they will also face stockpiles of radioactive waste, a long list of extinct species and glaciers that exist only in the photographic record. Not only will they be working to contain further damage but also struggling to repair and undo the damage that we have caused.

It is possible, as we enter the second decade of the 21st century, to start a transition to repair the world. If we do, the future generation may look kindly on our efforts. If we fail to act, now that we know we must, we will deserve the condemnation and contempt that the younger generation will heap on us in our old age.

As the evidence of humankind's negative effect on the Earth becomes ever more persuasive, more and more people will be converted to accepting the need for change. However, few people will consider taking unilateral action, and it is hard to argue that they should. A few people changing their behaviour, when everyone else carries on as before, will be both unfair on them and achieve little.

The World at a Tipping Point

There will come a point when the majority of people are persuaded of the need to shift to a sustainable way of living. Then politicians will have the mandate to take action that applies to us all. The measures required for a sustainable world include, of course, constraints and restrictions. These grab our attention and attract resistance. As attitudes shift, we will look beyond the negatives and notice that many of the changes required are in fact improvements in the quality of our lives.

Those people who continue to deny the need for change will be a contracting minority. They will be increasingly marginalized as our collective action penalizes unsustainable practices and behaviours. Politicians will start with the easy wins, for example banning traditional light bulbs that are not much different to the light bulb designed by Thomas Edison and first demonstrated in public in 1879. A ground-breaking invention at the time, such light bulbs should be museum exhibits today. They are inefficient and we have had better technology for many years. Resistance will be short-lived as the old designs are outlawed. Raising taxes on cars with high emissions is also proving to be politically acceptable. We will become amenable to more fundamental lifestyle changes once we can be sure that our wasteful neighbours will also be forced to conform.

Leading up to the tipping point, the resistance to change will be multi-faceted and hard to overcome. When the tipping point is reached, and core attitudes switch in favour of sustainability, change can be dramatic and rapid. Whilst we wait for support for sustainability to grow, the Earth will be displaying the symptoms of increasing damage. By the time we have won over the majority to accept real change, the urgency to act will be greater than it is now. This will give even greater impetus to the wholesale changes that must be made.

Each individual can await the tipping point before taking action. The vital action now, at the individual level, is a mindset change. Each of us must accept the necessity and inevitability of shifting to a sustainable future. We should join the majority call for action – even if for now we do nothing to make changes in our own lives. This means voting for the politicians who promise to act, and supporting measures that apply to us all. We should also persuade our friends, colleagues and associates to vote the same way. This will be far more effective than the individual action we can take to change our own lifestyle. Putting our effort and enthusiasm into changing society will deliver results amplified across whole populations.

For those people not yet persuaded, I offer a sobering thought. It is not just society that has tipping points; the Earth has them too. This has not been brought to our attention because we have not experienced one before. The people alive today have not lived through the changes of the Earth flipping into a different climate. The written historic record does not give any better insight. We have to reach back into the geological record for such evidence. It does not have the impact of television video footage or a well-written eye-witness account to bring it alive, but the facts are there for geologists to see.

Geologists have been able to piece together the evidence that 56 million years ago the Earth warmed by around six degrees.[3] The fossil record shows that many life forms on land and in the sea became extinct. There was a huge turnover of mammalian life leading to the general order of mammals that we have today. A number of theories for the cause have been put forward, ranging from volcanic activity to release of methane stored in deposits of methane hydride under the seabed. Methane is a far more potent greenhouse gas than CO_2 and would have caused the Earth to warm. It is known that the current warming that the Earth is experiencing is warming the tundra in northern regions such as Siberia and releasing methane which had been locked away in the permafrost. As the Earth warms, yet more frozen methane will be released. This could be starting a positive feedback loop that flips the world's climate into a different state. By our actions, humankind may be pushing against a similar tipping point to the one the Earth experienced 56 million years ago.

The big worry is that if we find and pass such a tipping point for our planet, then there will be no way to prevent the runaway climate change that would follow. It is therefore vital that we find, and find quickly, the tipping point in society that initiates the Sustainable Revolution. We will not be safe from an apocalyptic future until we have stopped forcing change on the Earth's systems.

If this warning has still not converted you to the need for rapid action, then take note of this. The changes that we need to make in society, urban infrastructure and community design are so fundamental that our decisions, once we make them, will take decades to enact. The full positive impact of the decisions we take over the coming years may take another 30 years to deliver. Do we have 30 years before the Earth suffers irreversible damage? Opinions differ. Some experts think we still have such a time period. Others think we are already close to the point of no return. The truth is that no one knows for sure.

My opinion is that we should not accept a slow transition. We should take bold, dramatic and painful measures to shorten the transition period. This would be politically and economically difficult. It would also be hugely more costly than working to a plan that replaced infrastructure only when it was due for replacement.

It is likely that our politicians will take a more politically acceptable route and choose a long transition period on our behalf. There will then follow a tense few decades of listening to reports from our scientists, hoping that we have avoided catastrophe. This risky strategy may be the only realistic option in the face of political opposition and an indifferent public. Even this slow option requires that we start now, moving from talk to action.

Talking will continue, of course, but if we use discussion as a substitute for action the problem will become far worse. Failure to initiate action now would be a far bigger disaster than we realize. Further delay and the pressure from human society to tip the world into a new and different climate will remain with us for a very long time. I can envisage the problems of climate change being manageable over the next decade or two. I also believe that there is enough oil to fuel our economies for the next 20 years. That means that my generation can avoid taking action over the rest of our working lives. Such selfish inaction would put back the start of the delivery of change by a further 20 years. Add this to the 30 years we need to make the deep-rooted changes needed and we have accepted 50 years of delay. Only an eternal optimist (or a deluded fool) could believe that the Earth can survive another half century of sustained industrialization without suffering long-lasting damage.

The situation we face is unprecedented in recorded history. The opinions of our scientists differ. We do not know the outcome. In half a century from now we will have the answer at first hand. If I survive, I will be an old man of 100 years old and no longer capable of making a positive contribution to the world. I fear that in 2059 I might observe a debate amongst our scientists in which they say that it would have been possible to do something back in 2009 but that now the options are limited. The discussion – which I don't want to hear – will continue logically, noting that we cannot change history, and agreeing to salvage as much as possible of the remaining natural heritage of the Earth. In 2009, we are in the fortunate position of predicting that conversation whilst there is still the opportunity to do something about it. It would be sheer folly to continue running the risks that modern society is taking with our planet. I hope that scientists and historians will look back on 2009 as the year the Sustainable Revolution[4] took hold.

The Sustainable Revolution

Massive, universal and long-term change is required. This needs to be of a scale and magnitude to match the industrial revolution which brought us to the position we face. There is such a wide divergence between the way we currently run society and the pressing need to move to a sustainable world that only a revolution will do.

I want to ferment such a revolution for the selfish reason that I want to continue to enjoy hiking in the wilderness, snorkelling over corals reefs and living side-by-side with nature. I want to be able to show my children the breathtaking beauty of the natural world. I also want them to prosper.

My views are green, but with a very hard edge. I campaign for pre-emptive action to initiate the revolution and make preparations to exploit the outcomes. I believe that the insiders who join with me to shape a future sustainable society deserve to profit from their commitment. The losers will be those who deny the need for change, oppose the actions I propose, and are then pushed aside by the demands of the Sustainable Revolution. We should have compassion, of course, for the people who are at risk from starvation or death from the collapse of ecosystems or the complete collapse of societies. However, businesses that fold as their production methods are outlawed or people who go bankrupt when their extravagant lifestyles are exposed will be paying the price of opposing the new order.

Whilst we continue to run an unsustainable world, our gas-guzzling cars, large energy-hungry houses and sprawling suburbs in which the car is king all have value. Our mortgages and loans are secured against these assets. All it needs is a change of attitude to burst the bubble of unsustainable society. Those people who buy into the concept of sustainability early, and reconfigure their ownerships to survive the downturn, will profit from the Sustainable Revolution.

Wait too long and it will be too late to escape. The property crash of 2008 and the world recession of 2009 have already hit society and the economy hard. As fuel prices resume their inevitable ascent, property prices in the outer suburbs will never recover their former value. There will be a choice: either to fight the government to retract sustainable policies or to join the Sustainable Revolution. As more people do the latter, the downward spiral in which those in denial are trapped will get tighter and steeper.

The Sustainable Revolution is not to be ignored. Some of us are looking forward to it in the hope that it will secure the future for our world. Others should be very worried that the lifestyles they have worked so hard to build and defend will be destroyed by revolutionary forces they cannot control.

Exploiting the Opportunities

I encourage everyone to exploit the situation we face. Tapping into the selfish desire to improve our circumstances relative to others is a very powerful mechanism to force change upon the world.

We must start by anticipating the future. The future I put forward is a sustainable future. The actions I outline build on my assumption that this will be so. There are other views of the future and therefore other strategies that can be followed. For example, if you believe that the scenario of a collapse of civilization is inevitable, then the logical reaction would be to build an underground bunker hidden away in a remote location and stocked with long-life food. This might allow you to escape the worst of the disorder and chaos for as long as possible.

The future that we believe to be the most likely outcome brings with it an element of self-fulfilment. If we accept the world as it is (as portrayed in Part 1) and plan for failure then we will fail. On the other hand, the more people who bet on a sustainable society, the more likely it becomes that we will succeed. It is hard to foresee that humankind will not choose eventually a sustainable future. My views might be radical within the world of 2009 but I believe I am on the right side of history. Humankind must, and will, shift towards a sustainable society; it is only the timing that can be in doubt.

Choosing when to act will be a tough choice. Whilst waiting for the revolution, people can still profit from our unsustainable world. It is worth structuring your life, and – if you are a business person – your business, to be able to exploit the surge of interest in sustainable policies. Sell on to someone else and lease back assets that you will not need within a sustainable society. If you want to drive an SUV, then take out a lease. You will then be able to hand the vehicle back as the Sustainable Revolution takes hold, leaving the leasing company with the problem of finding someone willing to buy it. If you want to live in a large house in a remote part of suburbia then rent it from a landlord. When you move out, the landlord will have the challenge of what do with the property. For property you own, ensure it is energy-efficient, located near to good mass transport access (such as a train station) and within a high-quality densely populated community. If this is not your ideal lifestyle choice, rent the property out for now; you can be sure that its value will increase. You will then be set to see how the Sustainable Revolution proceeds.

When we are positioned, ready for a sustainable future, we should then campaign hard to bring it about. In other areas of commerce or society, when people or organizations campaign for change that is manifestly to their advantage it is often resisted. When the calls for change are to tighten environmental regulations and force the adoption of sustainable methods and processes, then such resistance will be seen as negative griping. It will be easy for governments to ignore the complaints and agree to regulations that hand the leading companies virtual monopolies whilst their competitors struggle to meet the new requirements.

An example is the truly green car. This would need to be highly efficient, running on a renewable fuel and with every component being fully reusable, recyclable or biodegradable. The development of such a car will require a complete break with the past and huge investment in research and development of car design and manufacturing processes. The demand for such a car, now, is low. Of those people who would like such a car, few will be willing to pay a large premium to have one. As a commercial opportunity, the figures do not add up. Consider that a company designed such a car and lodged a comprehensive suite of patents. The company would still not have a market to sell into. However, it could then indulge in market manipulation by pushing hard for stringent regulations in its home market. It might decide to also draw profits from licensing aspects of the technology to other national competitors allowing them the prospect of surviving tighter regulations. The government may then be persuaded that such a lead in the international market is good for the country and bring in the tougher regulations that make the new design viable. The outcome would be a step further towards a sustainable future, delivered by business with an unabashed profit motive.

Through the following chapters a range of issues are explained and appropriate actions discussed. The Sustainable Revolution will disrupt society and lead to discontinuities that will result in new connections as we counter the problems and challenges. The future is full of uncertainty. Some outcomes flow from direct logical deduction. These we can be sure of. Others may be affected by irrational psychological responses or may require technical solutions that our engineers have yet to devise. Anticipating the non-obvious aspects of a sustainable world is where the most advantage is to be gained. These are selfish words, but tapping into humankind's selfish streak is not a bad way to make progress when the outcome is so evidently desirable.

Saving the world from slow destruction being exerted unwittingly by humankind is becoming increasingly urgent. Rapid action is required to reverse our destructive tendencies before we run out of time to save much of our natural heritage. Forward-looking people and businesses that plan to profit from the disruption can speed our progress. Driving forward the Sustainable Revolution in full knowledge of reaping the benefits is the most powerful mechanism we have to save the world.

We should make an explicit decision whether the natural systems of planet Earth matter to us or not. When we pause and make such a deliberate choice, there is only one realistic option. We must therefore make preparations for a sustainable future. Once our individual preparations are well in hand, we should push for change and vote for the politicians who will bring in the collective regulations that are needed across society. We will then be poised to ride the Sustainable Revolution.

As we consider where the future will lead, the most difficult, intractable and sensitive issue of all is population growth. An open discussion of how to limit the world population soon enters into conflict with fundamental human rights. Rather than risk causing offence, or generating an emotional backlash, we tend to avoid the issue. We can no longer afford such niceties.

12 Stop Breeding

The world population in the year AD 1 is estimated to have been approximately 200 million. By the year 1800 this had risen fivefold to one billion. Commentators at the time questioned whether the Earth could sustain a population larger than this.[1] They were proved wrong. In 2009 the world population is fast approaching seven billion, and is still rising. It is natural that all these people would like to see their bloodline continue and pass their genes on to the next generation. The UN estimates that the world population will increase to eight billion by 2030 and nine billion by 2050.[2] These may be conservative figures if we all get what we desire.

Population growth is an emotive subject that reaches deep into our inner psychology. When writing about it, it is usual to choose words carefully. This allows us to navigate around the issues without causing offence. Such niceties of language have a cost attached. The issues become obscured to such an extent that we can miss the main point, which is contained in the equation:

Population + Consumption = Load on the Earth's systems

The current population is consuming at a rate that is 30% more than the planet can sustain. Each year that we allow this excessive load to continue, the Earth is suffering. It will take time before people in the developed world experience the results first-hand. As the demand for agricultural products and other commodities increases, prices rise, and we complain, but we can afford it. Suffering is confined to the poorer countries and the less well-off elements of society. As we continue to overspend on the resources account, we will strip the Earth bare. There is no denying the truth of the mathematics. We must bring this equation back into balance.

The two terms on the left of the equation have to become smaller numbers. Population and/or consumption have to reduce.

Focusing on consumption is the less sensitive issue. There is a multitude of ways we can change our lifestyles to consume less of the Earth's resources. For example, living in small compact communities is a much less resource-intensive model of living. We could also eat less meat, use public transport to replace private car use, live in well-insulated houses, manufacture fully recyclable products and the list goes on.

Making substantive reductions in consumption in the developed world will cut deep into the lifestyles to which we have become accustomed. Many of these are necessary adjustments but on their own will not be enough.

Looking at the equation as a whole, we notice that a narrow focus on consumption is not going to help us much. The world population is continuing to rise, so consumption has to be driven yet lower to compensate. No matter how low we can drive percapita consumption, a continually growing population will exceed the Earth's capacity. That is the unbiased logic of the maths. There is no avoiding the issue of population growth.

When discussing the populations of other animals, it is possible to decide what a sustainable population would be and then set a culling policy. This may include issuing a specific number of licences to hunters. In this way we can ensure that the animal population and ecosystem remain in balance. Some people object on principle but most people accept this as sound policy. To counter the legitimate concerns of animal rights campaigners, legislation is brought in with regard to the methods used with the aim of avoiding unnecessary cruelty.

With humans, culling is not an option, unless, that is, you believe that the policies adopted by Hitler, Pol Pot and Radovan Karadzic are acceptable. It worries me that if we do not find acceptable and humane policies to limit population growth, then we will witness the circumstances in which a new generation of despots come to power with genocide in mind. Such evil men may even start to look acceptable in the eyes of many of the general population. When a country's resources can no longer cope and starvation beckons, a cull of another tribe or another ethnic group may seem like a reasonable solution.

There is a pressing need to find realistic and humane ways to keep the human population within sustainable limits. This can be done, as I argue later. First, I want to examine the effect of succeeding in bringing population growth under control. This gives an insight into the new world order we can create.

Assuming that that we find and implement a workable mechanism of population control, then let us return to the fundamental equation and see what the maths tells us.

Population + Consumption = Load on the Earth's systems

In a particular region or locality, we can assess its carrying capacity and control numbers to suit. We can also consider the option of increasing consumption, if this is what we desire. In this case we must link the increase with a corresponding population reduction. It becomes entirely feasible to grow consumption in tandem with policies for a declining population.

The policy of deliberately designing measures to lead to a smaller population is not familiar to us. It does not fit with our experience of mainstream economics. A larger population leads to more consumption and greater Gross Domestic product (GDP). More workers generate greater tax receipts. On the other hand, a contracting population throws up a number of challenges. When we slow the rate at which we breed we reduce the size of the next generation. At first this reduces expenditure on schools, education and childcare. Two decades later there is a smaller generation entering the work force. Society has to cope with a higher proportion of retired people supported by a smaller work-age generation. Governments will have to think differently about balancing the finances in a society that is contracting.

The overall reduction in pressure on resources from a smaller population will make it easier to live within the ecological carrying capacity of the locality. There will be transition effects, but these can be overcome, if we plan accordingly. Over time, the bulge of older people will work through the system leading to a smaller sustainable population – even though individual consumption rates may remain high. If we learn how to control population, then many more consumption patterns and choices of lifestyle become viable and sustainable over the long-term.

Back to Basics – Breeding Mechanisms

It is distasteful to talk about humans in the same way that a farmer might discuss livestock. Despite this, I have chosen clarity before sensitivity to draw out the logic.

In the natural world, a population expands when resources are plentiful. It contracts again when resources are tight and the population is under stress. When the shift in resource availability is rapid, then the blunt culling mechanism of starvation eliminates a proportion of the population, starting with the weaker members. The term used by Darwin, 'survival of the fittest',[3] describes accurately the process and is at the heart of the process of evolution.

Nature can be harsh but she also has more subtle mechanisms. For example, an animal that is stressed will not breed (as zoo keepers know). The natural world interprets stress as an indicator that it is not safe to raise offspring. Humans still have this instinct. The urge to procreate is subdued in people who are under great stress (as sex therapists know). There is therefore a natural explanation for the loss of libido in such medical cases.

Fertility is also affected by the level of nutrients in the diet. Natural selection has favoured the behaviour of only breeding when there are spare resources to feed on. This is, of course, entirely sensible and natural. Our genes continue to respond in the same way. The female reproductive system shuts down when nutrients are in short supply and the body is under stress, as some supermodels and top-class marathon runners find out. The advice given to them is to reduce stress and eat greater quantities of nutritious food. Their bodies then respond, as nature intended, by restoring fertility.

In modern society, we have turned off nature's mechanisms. We do not generally experience periods of near-starvation. Quite the reverse: in the developed world overeating is a more common affliction. It is ironic that one problem some couples face in trying to start a family is being too fat to conceive.[4] In general, across most of the world, humans are no longer constrained by the mechanisms of natural fertility control.

We can breed, or not breed, as we decide. Artificial fertility control allows us to make the choice. The technology of birth control, such as pills, condoms and other devices is highly effective, but not self-regulating in the way that nature achieves.

We have an innate desire to have children. The decision is a complex interaction of psychological and economic factors. We do not make the choice on the basis of the ecological capacity of our locality. Somehow we must reintroduce such a linkage. We need to find regulating mechanisms that we can activate within society to complement the technical success of birth control.

China has implemented the policy of one child per couple. In many people's eyes, this is draconian action and a step too far. When Chinese couples selectively abort girls to ensure their one child is a son, the problems start to show through. It is estimated that in 2000 there were 120 male for every 100 female births.[5] This bulge in the population of Chinese males will lead to many men living lonely lives without finding a mate. Another problem is the illegal practice of buying fertility pills on the black market to circumvent the ban by multiple births from a single pregnancy. This is a dangerous practice for mothers and babies. I believe that China should be admired for confronting this tough issue whilst recognizing that it is not a policy we like. China's action conflicts with what we see as fundamental human rights.

Charter of Human Rights

The UN Universal Declaration of Human Rights was adopted in 1948 and has become a cornerstone of international law. The right to marry and found a family is contained in Article 16:

> *Men and women of full age, without any limitation due to race, nationality or religion, have the right to marry and to found a family.*

In 1966, the protection afforded by the Universal Declaration of Human Rights was extended to include the right of everyone to an adequate standard of living for himself and his family. Article 11 of the International Covenant on Economic, Social and Cultural Rights states:

> *The States party to the present Covenant recognize the right of everyone to an adequate standard of living for himself and his family, including adequate food, clothing and housing, and to the continuous improvement of living conditions.*

The two fundamental human rights to 'found a family' and to have an 'adequate standard of living' are difficult to deliver when population is running out of control. We are brought back to the fundamental equation:

Population + Consumption = Load on the Earth's systems

Unfortunately, when discussing population growth and considering measures to limit it, the Universal Declaration of Human Rights is often used to stop further debate. The charter is taken to mean that we should not interfere in decisions over having children. This is unhelpful and, I believe, misinterprets the charter.

We are entering an era when we cannot support complete freedom to have a family without constraint. Unless we tackle this, we will fail in our commitment to 'an adequate standard of living' and 'continuous improvement in living conditions'. The charter has been carefully drafted. It provides a right to have a family but it does not give the explicit right to as many children as desired. Those people drafting the charter had the foresight to see that such a right cannot be ingrained in world society.

We would like to leave people free to have as many children as they desire, but this is more than the world can afford. The ecologist, Garrett Hardin, made this point back in 1968 in the conclusion to his ground-breaking paper 'The Tragedy of the Commons'.[6] Hardin's proposed solution was through 'relinquishing the freedom to breed'. His opinion is even more relevant today.

It should be debated, not thrown out on principle by those who find the subject difficult to face.

At a personal level, we have the same dual responsibilities as states. We have a right to a family and a linked responsibility to provide adequately for our children. The right to breed brings with it the responsibility to bring into this world only the number of children for whom we have the resources to provide healthy and fulfilling lives.

The Population Explosion in the Developing World

The developing world has a rapidly growing population. China is the world's most populous country with a population of 1.3 billion. India is not far behind with 1.1 billion. These populations are also young compared with the developed world. The average age in India is approximately 25 years,[7] whereas in the UK it is 39 years.[8] The young population of India is expected to overtake China as the world's most populous country by reaching 1.7 billion by 2050.[9]

In the developed world, birth rates have stabilized at 2.0 live births per woman in the United States, down to 1.8 in the UK, and as low as 1.3 in Germany.[10] These low birth rates are below replacement level, leading to a contracting population (leaving aside the issue of inward immigration). There are a number of reasons. Having children costs time and money. Childbirth can interrupt career and the responsibility of children can curtail freedom. Some people choose not to breed and enjoy a single lifestyle (with or without a partner). Those people who choose to breed tend to invest in a small brood. The costs of food, housing, education and time are better concentrated to ensure success, rather than spread across more children.

The underdeveloped world has a different set of parameters. When infant mortality is high, more babies are required to ensure that some survive to become adults. Where income in old age relies on children, then a large family brings security. In such circumstances, decisions taken by families that are in their best self-interest conflict with society's concern not to overload the resources of the region.

Bringing the technology of birth control into the underdeveloped world is helpful, of course. But, as in the developed world, it needs to be complemented by other policies if it is to become self-regulating.

One strategy, often championed by NGOs, is to focus on increasing the pace of development in poorer countries. The logic is attractive. In the developed world, we have a high GDP and low birth rate. It would be reasonable to assume that if the poorer countries caught up with our GDP then their birth rates would also fall. If the assumption is wrong and increasing GDP is not enough to slow the birth rate, then we will have an even more severe problem. Rising GDP and rising birth rate would lead to a rampant increase in consumption and potentially cataclysmic environmental consequences.

The logic of taking measures that increase consumption, to find a way out of the population challenge, is dangerous. With the experience we have of the wider impacts that accompany economic development, we can no longer afford to rely on such broad assumptions. The changes needed are improvements in society, not increases in GDP.

In defining actions that will work, we need to reach deep into human psychology. This is where decisions are made about babies and where our action must have an effect.

First, the connection between 'children' and 'security in old age' must be removed. People should be able to observe a stable long-term commitment by society to care for the old. Such care should be appropriate to the society and may not match what Western eyes see as sufficient. That should not prevent action. Long-term commitment to care for the elderly may not be the headline issue that attracts NGOs or aid money, but it is the single most important action and should be given the highest priority.

Second, infant mortality needs to be improved to give parents confidence that their babies will grow into adults. Saving the life of any baby is unmistakably a good thing, but uncoordinated and short-term measures focused on improving the infant mortality statistics simply exacerbate the problem of a growing population. What is needed is highly visible, consistent, reliable and long-term commitment to infant welfare. This is how to eliminate the fear that contributes to large family size.

Third, raising children should have a cost so that there is a clear advantage in raising fewer children. This goes against many well-intended aid packages that offer free support for child health, education and nutrition. It is important that there is a charge for such services. This should be affordable and appropriate to the circumstances of the community. To the donor, such a charge may be insignificant, and aid organizations may feel guilty about charging for delivering aid, but it is important that they do. Local economics will then play their part in influencing choices over family size.

Underlying these three measures is the assumption that birth control is freely and widely available. This is the tool we need, but it is not a policy. Birth control on its own will achieve nothing. However, without it, our efforts may be undermined by the power of sexual desire.

Once a self-regulating population control policy is framed in this way, it becomes clear that it is feasible for even the poorest societies to adopt it. A rich society with spare resources should find it easier, but it is not wealth that is the primary requirement. The requirement is for appropriate social support systems.

In order to initiate an effective response to the world's ballooning population, we must start by acknowledging the problem. Unchecked population growth undermines efforts to achieve sustainable development. When the environment is stressed beyond its carrying capacity, the economy suffers and social structures break down in a fight over diminishing resources.

We should lose our sensitivity to debating how to hold population within sustainable limits. Some potential solutions should be off-limits of course, such as mass exterminations or selective culling. Other real solutions should be considered even if they go beyond choice to use enforcement and include elements of inequity. These will be negative factors, as there are in any real-world analysis. This should be no reason to stifle debate.

The problem of population running out of control is so great that we must give it a high priority. Once a child is born, it is too late to go into reverse. He or she has rights to a fulfilling life and in due course the right to breed. We have to tackle the problem at the root, at the point of decision by adults over whether to have a family, and its size.

For the developed world, we have to accept that a stable or contracting population is required to start to balance demand with resource availability. Ageing populations will be an inevitable consequence. We need to plan our fiscal policy to cope with this, rather than follow the advice of many economists who would argue for policy to push up the birth rate and/or increase immigration.

The biggest problem is in the developing world, where population expansion has been rapid and where there is a huge bulge of young people who will go on to have families of their own. It is in the interests of us all to direct effort and aid to the three policy areas that hit right at the heart of the issue:

- security in old age
- consistent and long-term improvement in infant mortality
- putting a cost to raising children.

There are also other important considerations that go beyond population maths, for example, the status of women. In most of the developed world, women have the same education and career prospects as men. In poorer countries this is often not the case. Educating and raising the status of women is a vital part of bringing population under control. At a simple level, well-educated women know how to limit their fertility. More importantly, women with a full role in society have choices available other than living their lives primarily to have babies and raise children.

The instinct to breed is deeply ingrained in our humanity. Unchecked, it will also be the source of our downfall. We need policies that persuade us not to breed and constrain our capacity to do so. If we fail, there will be no alternative but to turn to enforcement. If we fail to act, then over time we will face a crisis so severe that genocide will be widespread as populations struggle to secure a prosperous future for their own group.

If we do not take population control seriously in the coming decades then, in the long-term, human society cannot survive in a form that we would recognize. Civilization as we know it would collapse. Despite this gloomy warning, I am an optimist. I assume that we will find the resolution to act. We will then need policies that address the other problems we face in building a sustainable future.

13 The Three-Way Balancing Act

At the heart of sustainability is the three-way balancing act between people, profit and planet. It is a tough act to learn but, as with top-class circus acrobats, once the skills have become ingrained, the complex balancing act becomes automatic.

Whilst the population was small, human impact on the ecosystems of planet Earth was limited. If humans made a mess of one place they simply packed up and moved to another. The waste from primitive society was by its nature biodegradable; the same place could be returned to within a generation no matter how badly the tribe behaved. The ecosystem could handle whatever our low-tech ancestors handed out. Becoming too greedy, destroying the capacity of the local ecosystem and starvation, leading to a cull of the weaker members of the tribe, would bring the situation back into balance.

This cycle of expanding population followed by periods of hardship, when only the strong could survive, boosted the process of natural selection. This has been part of the story behind the successful set of genes that defines the human species. It was a hard, harsh life for the individual but also a sustainable way of life.

Civilization has brought numerous benefits and improvements that give structure to society. Complex societies can achieve far more as people work together. Our knowledge expands as each generation of scientists adds further insights and discoveries. These are stored in libraries and databases for us to use and to share. Life for the individual, even the old and infirm, has become generally safe and comfortable. It would be ironic if all the evident improvements that civilization has brought to the individual may put the survival of the human species at risk.

Modern high-tech humankind now has the power to threaten the stability of the whole Earth ecosystem. This brings with it additional responsibilities that humankind has not had before. We are the architects of our economic system and know that when cracks appear we must fix them. We are also architects of society, how people live and are treated; this we accept. We have also become architects of our environment but this we generally do not understand.

A new breed of engineer, termed a geo-engineer, is starting to take seriously humankind's role as environmental designers. They are investigating deliberately engineering the ecosystems of the Earth to suit our ends. Responsible geo-engineers have no intention of taking over from nature. Some of their potential developments are encouraging, looking for ways to reverse the damage human society is causing. For example, I would support geo-engineers if they managed to implement the concept of massive solar-powered machines circling the world's oceans to extract CO_2 from the atmosphere and convert it into pellets that can drop safely to the ocean floor. Such concepts are inspiring, but we should not expect geo-engineers to have godlike powers. Other ideas meddle too far, such as spreading dust in the stratosphere to reflect away an amount of solar energy equivalent to the amount of heat trapped by increased greenhouse gases from human activities.[1] In general, learning to live in harmony with nature is far more likely to succeed than geo-engineering.

There may be no choice but to deploy the technologies of geo-engineers in the centuries ahead if the Earth is to remain habitable for human society. To avoid taking action now, on the assumption that our geo-engineers can fix the problems in the future, would be a dangerous delusion. I have enormous respect for the ability of our engineers. However, I do not expect them to be able to re-engineer the biodiversity of the Amazon rainforest once it is gone.

Living with the hope that a way can be found in the future to fix the damage we are causing is in defiance of logic, astonishingly selfish and deeply troubling. This false hope has to be purged and replaced with real efforts to implement the concepts of sustainability.

Sustainability

The standard definition of a sustainable society is that it meets the needs of the present without compromising the ability of future generations to meet their own needs.[2] Striking the balance is hard. The difficulty becomes clear if we imagine world society as a balancing act using two three-legged stools standing one on top of the other (Figure 13.1).

The upper three-legged stool represents sustainable society, balancing economic, social and environmental issues. Most models of sustainability go no further than this. I have added the lower three-legged stool to represent 'land use'. This is the fundamental basis of our survival. This more complex model gives a clearer insight into the difficulty of the balancing act we must achieve.

'Land use' consists of three components: urban, agricultural and nature. Urban land is the area we choose to use to build our communities, towns and cities. A larger area is used for agriculture, primarily to provide food and materials such as timber, cotton and flax, but increasingly to provide feedstock for the production of biofuels. The land that we leave for nature is enough, we hope, to safeguard the natural ecosystem. We must find a balance between urban, agricultural and natural land use. The total capacity of this

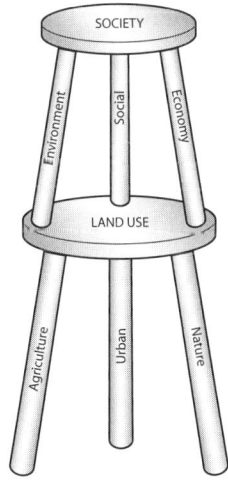

Figure 13.1 The three-way balancing act of a sustainable society

trio is capped by the area of all the continents of the world. If we increase one element we have to find a corresponding reduction in another.

The model is good but not complete. The largest natural habitat is the ocean. Fortunately, building a sustainable human society on land is the single most important action required to protect the ocean. There is, therefore, no need to add further complexity at this stage. The ocean is treated as a special case in Chapter 19. The actions we should take to bring the world system back into balance must start on land, where we live and where we have a direct influence.

When both stools are in balance, we have a robust and stable system. When some legs are longer and stronger than others we risk tipping over. When we have problems with both the sustainability of society and a growing imbalance in land use we could have a dramatic collapse. For example, as we approach the end of the era of cheap oil, two legs of society are coming under pressure. We face economic hardship together with the environmental problems of climate change. Concurrently with these problems within society, land use is coming under pressure to change. To help solve our problems we are pushing to use biofuels to reduce our reliance on oil. This conflicts with the requirement for food. We want to allocate more land to agriculture to be able to continue to feed a growing population. The knock-on effect is a rapid increase in the rate of deforestation and the destruction of natural habitats. The 'nature' leg of the bottom stool is being dramatically weakened.

Society is crumbling as the foundations that underpin it are being undermined. The bottom stool must be stabilized as a matter of priority in order to have a basis from which to rescue society.

Stabilizing Land Use

Stabilizing land use is the foundation of a sustainable society. The most important use for land is that required to ensure the stability of the ecosystem. Take too much away from nature, and the support system on which we rely for survival is undermined. Do this, and other considerations will become irrelevant. The proportion of land that must be left in its natural state is open for discussion. Ideally, this would be so large that our cities and farmland were just patches cut out of the natural world, allowing nature to continue much as before. Humankind has reached a size and a scale that makes this impossible.

One 'solution' is a network of national parks. This could be used to preserve examples of all the world's ecosystems fenced off as living museums. If this is all we do, then all the surrounding areas will, over time, be urbanized or brought into use for intensive agriculture. We may decide that such a land-use profile is an acceptable price to support the continuation of civilization. Even so, national parks cannot survive alone.

Climate change is now inescapable. The excess CO_2 in the atmosphere from the era of fossil fuels will continue to force change even if we manage a dramatic reduction in fossil-fuel burning from this point forward. This means that species of flora and fauna will have to migrate from one area to another to find conditions that suit. The golden toad of Costa Rica is the first species known to have been wiped out in this way.[3] The golden toad lived high in the mountains. As the climate warmed it had moved up to higher altitude looking for cooler conditions. But mountains only go so high. The toad had nowhere left to go and is now extinct. Mountains provide discontinuous habitats. A patchwork of isolated national parks is also discontinuous. Species will have great difficulty jumping from one to another.

A true solution to the challenge of protecting the Earth's ecosystem must go beyond national parks to include the retention of natural land as an integral component of the area occupied by man. This will help protect biodiversity by providing the corridors that species can use to migrate between our nature reserves.

The rainforest is particularly vulnerable. The complexities of the rainforest include its own microclimate. Take away the surrounding forest, and the vegetation may shrivel up and die. Where we hope to have preserved a designated block of rainforest, it may not be viable. Even what appears to be a huge area may not be enough to retain the associated microclimate. It is not known what area of rainforest is required to remain stable into the long future. We hope that the clearance of the Amazon which has already taken place is not enough to destabilize the system. How much more clearance is possible we do not know. Finding out by continued clearance is clearly irresponsible. If we get it wrong, we cannot reinstate such a complex system. Once it is gone, it will be gone forever.

I argue that the clearance of natural land has gone far enough, but the largest remaining areas of natural land are in the underdeveloped regions of the world. I speak as a resident of Europe, a region that cleared most of its natural forest cover many generations back. We cannot be held responsible for the actions of our ancestors, but we are hypocrites if we urge the poorer nations not to follow Europe's example, unless we offer them our support.

Conserving natural habitats is vital, but conventional economics discourages us from trying. Land allocated to nature generates no income. Converting it to agriculture allows crops to be grown that generate cash. Developing land for urban use brings an even greater uplift in value. One of the arguments we use when persuading poor countries to retain their natural heritage is to expand tourism. This is a valid mechanism to earn income, but tourists are fickle and the income stream far from certain.

It is vital that we recognize that the protection of the last great wildernesses matters to us all. We must give our political leaders the mandate to negotiate and agree robust arrangements for their protection.

It seems almost impossible to protect natural assets when there is such intense competition for global resources. The most promising method is alternative forms of ownership. In many places, land is either within a national park, and therefore protected, or privately owned, and subject to exploitation. Land trusts are an alternative model of ownership. The trust owns the land and the trustees are responsible for overseeing it. The aim could be complete protection, as with a conservation trust. Alternatively, a community land trust may aim to blend human needs with those of the ecosystem. Such ownership structures can remove the incentive and means to destroy land for financial gain.

There are also commercial benefits that come from the protection of virgin forests. The concept is based on the assumption that society will find a way to put an economic value to the ecosystem services that they provide. Selling credits into the emerging carbon market is one attempt. In due course, there will be other, better mechanisms. The country or corporation owning the wilderness can profit, but only through careful protection and stewardship.

Another way to value natural assets is to include natural resources in a country's national accounts. Quite how this would lead to improvement is unclear, but it would bring the issue to policy makers' attention. It would show trends from one year to the next. A steady decline in natural resources would have a quantified basis and be hard to ignore.

Protection of the remaining natural wilderness, particularly the rainforest, should take priority. We are in the critical early stage of finding the determination to use our power and influence to protect the natural wilderness. We must also be prepared to pay the price.

Robust long-term protection for the land that nature requires puts a cap on the land available for agriculture. For the finite amount of agricultural land, the balance that has to be struck is between food and biofuels.

In January 2008, the European Commission proposed a 10% binding minimum target for biofuels in transport by 2020. The United States had already brought in similar targets in its Renewable Fuel Standard aimed at achieving 7.5 billion gallons of biofuel blended into gasoline by 2012. These targets were met with a storm of protest from NGOs worried about the effect on world food supplies. Also, whether biofuels – using current methods – are effective in terms of replacing fossil-fuel consumption is doubtful.[4] During 2008, food prices climbed steeply, indicating that the NGOs were right to be concerned. Consider which is more important, food or fuel. There is a moral dilemma. It is hard to justify rich nations converting food crops to biofuel whilst there are poor people who cannot afford to eat.

It is reasonable and sensible for a country to live within its capabilities. When a country is self-sufficient in food, using spare capacity for biofuel can be justified. Outside our own borders, buying food crops on the world market for conversion into biofuels is less acceptable. Outbidding poorer countries who have populations that are hungry is indefensible.

It soon becomes clear that pulling good agricultural land out of food production in order to be able to fill our cars with biofuel is not the solution. There is an important role for biofuels, but only when they can be extracted from waste, or are produced on land not otherwise suitable for agriculture. Ethanol and biodiesel from food crops, such as corn and rape seed, will come to be seen as unacceptable. There will then be a retreat from the policy. The unfairness of it will become evident as world food prices increase steeply.

Bringing the world's land use into balance, with robust protection for the areas required by nature and the retention of agricultural land for food production, will provide a sound foundation for building a sustainable society.

Building a Sustainable Society

Every decision we take must balance the economic benefits with the social and environmental impacts.

Many people have come to accept this statement, which is gaining acceptance for the concept of sustainability. Most decision makers in government would claim that it describes the way they now work. Many responsible business leaders are also thinking this way, being careful to defend the reputation of the corporation and deflect any adverse publicity. This is progress indeed, but it is not enough.

Examining the order of words in the statement above gives an insight into the continuing problem. 'Economic benefits' comes first. In considering our decisions, we give the economic argument priority. The social consequences are simply an impact to consider. The environment is often given even less weight. The environment may be completely ignored in the early stages of planning. Later in the decision process, an environmental impact assessment is produced. This may lead to changes, but such post-design assessments are far short of true sustainable thinking.

Sustainable thinking requires that, from the outset, social outcomes are considered in tandem with economic parameters, whilst at the same time reinforcing the integrity of the environment.

In thinking sustainably, it must be remembered that wealth does not necessarily bring happiness. Studies have shown that as very poor countries become wealthier they also become happier. The obvious conclusion is that pulling people out of poverty makes them happy. However, increasing average annual income beyond $10,000 brings little further improvement.[5] This is counter-intuitive. We presume that rich people are happier – they certainly have the resources to be happy. There is something deeper in the human soul than the desire for material wealth.

The false assumption that wealth is good for us is well established. We measure progress using GDP. Higher GDP should lead to a happier society. It is puzzling that this is not so.

An example from the underdeveloped world illustrates the mental bind that the world finds itself in. With good intentions, attempts are made to improve a poor society. Aid money is used to encourage a multinational company to build a factory. The building and operation of the factory draws people from the poor rural community into work. The income of the region and the country is increased. The GDP divided by the population comes out higher than the UN definition of poverty. To the statisticians, this means that the region has been lifted out of poverty. Economic development has been brought in and the economic outcome delivered.

Look a little closer and a different picture may be seen. Before the factory arrived there may have been little formal economic activity, and very little money flowing in the community. That does not mean that it was a dead and dysfunctional community. Social systems and behaviours had developed over hundreds of years to suit the local environment and circumstances. The economy may have been informal, but we should be very careful in the way we tinker with this complex balance.

Building the factory will have brought monetary wealth to some. The factory owner may have done well, as will the officials who needed to be 'persuaded' (read bribed) to authorize it. The workers will have been paid a competitive local wage, but traditional communities may be suffering as young adults are drawn to live in the slums around the factory. This story is being played out across the underdeveloped world as GDP is used as the measuring stick of progress.

I do not argue that we soften our focus on economics. Economic tools are quantifiable and measurable and the outcome of increased wealth is a tangible improvement. The problem is that a narrow focus on economics does not lead to sustainable outcomes. We need to bring the same level of rigour to the way we deal with social outcomes and protection of the environment.

In improving social provision, and bringing robust protection to the environment, a brake on economic performance should be expected. It should be no surprise if GDP drops. Neither should it cause much concern. The main issue will be whether other metrics such as happiness, health, security and stability show improvement.

When we become familiar with running our lives and society according to the principles of sustainability we may see a return to rising GDP. There are many aspects of a sustainable society that require more effort and more economic activity, but the nature of it is different. Living with much reduced virgin commodity flows requires increased efficiency. Cradle-to-cradle production requires better design. True recycling requires more complexity in how we dispose of obsolete products.

When the concept of sustainability has been embedded into human society, progress can continue to focus on improvement in the quality of life. Material wealth will be seen for what it is, a distraction. Those people who are slow to sense the changing attitude may find their extravagance an embarrassment before they decide to reorder their affairs. Conspicuous consumption will go out of fashion. Other ways will arise to differentiate ourselves.

Keeping in Balance

The balancing act of living in a sustainable society on the finite land we possess will be difficult. We have developed a lifestyle that relies on cheap fossil fuel. As the point of peak oil production is passed, this crutch is about to be pulled. There has been considerable scrabbling around to find a policy for what to do now. Our initial response has been a policy shift in favour of biofuel. This hasty decision threatened to unbalance the whole world system.

Whilst writing this book, I have observed the world's decision-making process. In the search for a quick and easy solution, biofuels were put forward with some fanfare. It was not hard to identify the pitfalls. The world still has to eat, so removing agricultural land from food production leads to hunger and consequent pressure to put yet more natural land under the plough. It was not until politicians tried the policy that the true situation was exposed. Our try-it-and-see approach wastes valuable time. It is possible to generate good policy much more quickly by thinking in terms of balance when we draft policy. The sustainable balance between social provision, the environment and the economy is hard enough; we must also find a balance between the ecosystem, food and energy.

In setting the balance, preventing further climate change requires us to act. We must wean ourselves off fossil fuel. It may be a convenient coincidence that peak oil production and climate change are big issues coming to a head at the same time. The oil runs out just when it is realized that we should not be burning it. Coincidence or not, in the end we will ban fossil fuel and accept the consequences.

14 Plan to Ban Fossil Fuel

In Chapter 8, 'Scraping the Bottom of the Barrel', I outlined how our fatal addiction to fossil fuel is one aspect of the impending collapse of civilization. We are behaving like heroin junkies who put the satisfaction of an immediate fix before long-term health and survival. Of course it will be hard to come off fossil fuel dependency. That difficulty does not hide the necessity that we do so.

In any case, fossil fuel reserves are finite and will run out. There will come a time when society will have to live without fossil fuel. For oil, that time is not far off. It seems odd that some of our biggest corporations employ some of our most able engineers to work on extracting the last hard-to-reach deposits. This investment in time and effort could be applied to ramping up the development of technology to exploit renewable energy.

There are numerous sources of renewable energy. These range from solar and wind to hydro and energy from biowaste. It would require the rest of this book to lay out all the options and analyse them fully. For my argument there is no need. I contend that widespread development of renewable power is stymied by short-term economics. Until it is accepted that the era of cheap fossil fuel is over, we will not make serious inroads into developing the alternatives on the scale needed.

The other barrier to solving fossil-fuel dependency is that renewable energy solutions will not deliver the quantity of energy that we currently draw from fossil fuel. We are resistant to the idea that we do not need such huge amounts of energy. However, not only can we use technology to make reductions through efficiency and better design, but we can make even greater savings when we realize that the whole structure of society is needlessly energy hungry. The important changes, with the biggest impact, are to infrastructure, city design and ultimately our behaviour and lifestyle.

It is possible to envisage a society that does not use fossil fuel. This is not through a reversion to a medieval lifestyle but through being much cleverer with the ways we organize ourselves. In many cases this means shifting the priority away from machines, such as the car, to putting people first. This is how it should always have been. It is not surprising that putting in this extra effort leads to improvement in our lives.

Once it is understood that living without fossil fuel is feasible, a different energy paradigm can be adopted. Now, we regard our energy 'needs' as a demand to be met. When the demand on the electricity grid increases, we build more power stations. The underlying assumption is that the fuel for the power station will be available. Throughout our industrial development we have not had to question this assumption, and so it has become deeply ingrained. The alternative approach is to live within the renewable energy available to us: organizing society to suit the energy budget and designing the infrastructure to match.

Redesigning the infrastructure is not a trivial task. Changes to urban planning and transport systems do not happen overnight. We must plan the infrastructure we will need so that we can migrate to it over the next couple of decades.

Enforcement

In considering how to enforce a ban on fossil fuels, there is a successful example to follow. In 1985 scientists working in Antarctica discovered a hole in the ozone layer. This is the layer of the upper atmosphere that protects us from ultraviolet radiation. Without it, skin cancer would be rife and people without special protection would go blind. This was a clear and present danger to the health of humanity. Governments acted quickly to stop emissions of the most damaging compounds: chlorofluorocarbons (CFCs). The Montreal Protocol on Substances that Deplete the Ozone Layer came into force less than four years later on 1 January 1989.[1] Implementation of the protocol has had a dramatic effect in reducing the production of ozone-depleting chemicals. Scientists predict that the ozone layer will be fully restored by 2050.[2]

The problem of CO_2 emissions is harder to define and tougher to tackle than the ozone hole. The carbon cycle underpins life itself and some of our renewable fuels, such as biofuels, emit CO_2. Carbon is not the problem: the problem is the release of fossil carbon leading to abnormally high levels of CO_2.

Let us consider the factors that made the Montreal Protocol so successful to see if we can learn how to close down fossil carbon release with similar speed. The Montreal Protocol succeeded because:

- the manufacturing process requires large and expensive facilities so that governments have the power to implement controls;
- there are viable alternative substances and technologies;
- the world agreed a united approach, ensuring that no one country or corporation could gain a competitive advantage through continued use of CFCs.

With regard to the first success factor of being able to implement controls, fossil fuels are very different to the specialist compounds in the CFC family of chemicals. Fossil fuels are to be found extensively in the Earth's crust. It seems impossible that production could ever be closed down; delving deeper into the issues shows that we could. The early exploitation of fossil fuel was easy, using available simple technology, but the extraction of many remaining reserves requires high technology. Most of the new oil fields are in deep water far offshore. For existing fields, the first 20–30% of reserves may be easily exploited, but advanced recovery techniques are required to get at what remains. Coal would be harder to control. The world's reserves are massive and it is easy to mine, particularly where seams are found close to the surface. Small-scale mining would be hard to prevent but large-scale exploitation such as strip mining is only possible with government approval. In general, exploiting the remaining fossil fuel requires high technology or government permission. This means that governments have the power to control exploitation – if they want to.

Second, 'there are viable alternative substances and technologies'. This clearly does apply to fossil fuels. There are numerous alternatives. The method for implementing these alternatives is simply to ban fossil fuels. The alternatives then become economically viable. The downside is that energy prices will increase to much higher levels. Currently, a common challenge thrown at potential renewable energy projects is whether they can be cheaper than coal. This is an impossibly high hurdle because coal is so cheap. Remove the coal option, and the figures for renewable energy investment start to look much more attractive. It is time that the world accepts that energy in the post-fossil-fuel era will cost more and adjusts consumption patterns to fit.

It is only the third Montreal Protocol success factor that is difficult to replicate for carbon dioxide emissions. The world must 'agree a united approach'. So far the only agreement that a good chunk of the world community has agreed to is the Kyoto Protocol. This is limited in its aim, limited in the spread of nations included and limited in timescale: it expires in 2012. At the time of writing, replacing the Kyoto Protocol with a much stronger agreement seems unlikely. Discussions are about marginal reductions, holding emissions steady or reducing the rate of increase in emissions. No one is talking seriously about banning fossil fuels.

Repeating the success of the Montreal Protocol requires that we take climate change seriously. If it is decided that the danger from fossil carbon release is a threat to humanity, and we agree to ban such fuels, then enforcement is not a difficulty. Banning the lower grade fossil fuels such as coal should be the priority but it is even possible to ban the fuel to which we have the strongest addiction: oil. The oil terminals of the Middle East only continue to pump because we choose to purchase the oil. If we decided upon a ban (which OPEC would oppose vigorously), Saudi Arabia and other oil nations would not be able to sell oil.

This seems preposterous, but only in terms of our willingness to stop using oil. If we choose a future that does not rely on fossil fuel, a ban is feasible and enforceable.

The Curse of Cheap Fossil Fuel

The Industrial Revolution of the 19th century was built on the ingenuity of our engineers and the drive of our industrialists.

Without cheap and plentiful power, the rate of progress would have been much slower. Fossil fuel was an amazing stroke of luck. It could not be foreseen at the time that fossil fuel would become a curse two centuries later, leading us down a blind alley and preventing us from moving on to better technologies.

In the 19th-century UK, the prime power source was coal. This had been used since Roman times in northern England, where seams of high quality coal break the surface. Small quantities of coal could be gathered by hand and with a bit of digging it was not difficult to get more. As the Industrial Revolution gathered pace, the demand for coal increased exponentially. The capability to mine the deeper seams was developed. Steam engines, using coal for fuel, powered the lifting gear and water pumps that made deep mining possible. As the demand for coal increased, the colliery towns of the 19th century sprouted out of virgin countryside with rows of back-to-back houses clustered around each pit head.

The oil industry was born in Texas. Like the UK coal seams, oil was to be found at the surface, seeping out of the ground to form bitumen ponds. By digging a little deeper with simple hand-powered rigs, the oil came gushing out. Production costs were close to zero. This incredible resource provided the fuel for the internal combustion engine. The vast distances of America could now be conquered with ease. Material, goods and people could move from one place to another cheaply and quickly.

Supplies of fossil fuel were so large that they appeared to be limitless. It became accepted fact within the boardrooms of the big oil companies that investment in exploration could locate enough reserves to balance consumption. Within the timescale of the careers of the business executives making the decisions this was a good strategy. The message coming out of the oil industry has been not to worry, we can keep the oil flowing. This is not surprising: oil companies and oil-rich nations want to continue to draw profits from fossil fuel for as long as possible. An early end to the fossil fuel empire does not suit their interests.

Whilst supplies of fossil fuel have continued to flow, our reliance has become total. The whole transport system is reliant upon cheap fuel supplies. Without such cheap fuel, the infrastructure would have evolved differently, into a more efficient system in which people lived within compact communities and goods were produced closer to the point of consumption. Buildings would also have been very different. In the era of cheap fossil fuel, buildings have been constructed in the sure knowledge that equipment can be fitted to heat or cool them as required. It has not been necessary to spend the time and effort to make our buildings energy neutral.

A farm in southern Scotland where I often spent my summers as a teenager had a large Victorian farmhouse known as the 'new house'. This had been built a century ago in the same era as when the local town became a coal town. It was situated a little away from the main farm complex with beautiful views out across the countryside. It needed a lot of heating to remain comfortable and was built with open coal fires in every room.

Contrast this with the 'old house', as it was called by the farm workers. This had been built as an integral part of the working farm buildings. When the farmer moved to the new house it became a store and workshop. The only power or services in the old house was a single cable for power tools and a work light. The old house was always cool in summer when I visited, and, I was told, held a pleasantly warm temperature in the winter. This was even though the only sources of heat were the people working there and their activities. The old house was built before the era of coal. It was well insulated because that was the only way to stay warm. The thick walls and small windows had a purpose.

Fossil-fuel addiction has led us into building an infrastructure that is inefficient and wasteful. It will take considerable effort to backtrack on this expensive mistake. Ironically, our architects are looking back into history to relearn the old design parameters. This will not be a return to the past. The old designs can be reworked to incorporate the best of two hundred years of technical developments. In this way, we can reach the stage of development where we would have been had we not been hijacked by the curse of fossil fuel.

Fossil fuels also powered the agricultural revolution of the 20th century. Prior to this, up to 25% of the arable land of a farm was required to feed the working livestock. Horses pulled the plough, gathered in the harvest and carried the farmer about his daily business. Replacing horses with tractors (powered by fossil fuel) meant the whole acreage of a farm could be used to grow cash crops. The capacity of the world's agriculture was given a huge boost.

Further increases in yield have come through the use of fertilizer. Once again, cheap fossil fuel is the basis of the production process. Nitrogen from the atmosphere is combined with hydrogen from natural gas under heat and pressure to form ammonia, which is then converted to a fertilizer such as ammonium nitrate.

Farming has become highly industrialized and apparently efficient. The whole process can be run with very few people and the yields are impressive. However, take away fossil fuel and the model of industrialized agriculture collapses.

First, the fuel for tractors would have to come from another source such as biofuel. Using current methods, crops such as rapeseed can be processed into biodiesel or corn into ethanol. Making a few assumptions, it is possible to estimate how much of the farm area is needed to power the farm machinery. A rough calculation comes up with the figure of 10% of the area of a farm.[3] This is a large chunk taken back from the increased yields that the industrialization of farming has brought. If it was known that this would be the outcome, the development of farming would have followed a different course.

Some forward-thinking farmers are considering how to farm using much less fossil fuel. This is what is needed to make agriculture fit for the 21st century, and the methods include: replacing chemical fertilizer with crop rotations and animal manure; processing of waste into bioenergy; and no-till crops that avoid the need for ploughing. There are also cattle farmers returning to ranching instead of the feedlots that dominate the US beef industry. These are the advanced forms of agriculture that we could have retained and refined if farmers had not been seduced by fossil fuels. The progressive farmers using such low-energy methods are currently few and regarded by some as hippies. They are finding a niche premium market for their produce because, although it is more expensive, these methods often produce a higher-quality product.

When the fossil-fuel crunch hits, they will also be carrying the lowest cost base. These 'hippies' will profit from their foresight as the agricultural revolution of the 20th century makes way for the green revolution of the 21st century.

We need to give our engineers, urban planners, farmers and other experts the brief to take us into a sustainable future. First, we have to lift the curse of fossil fuel. Until we do, we will remain blinkered by short-term economics.

Blinkered by Short-Term Economics

The world suffered an oil shock in the 1970s. OPEC implemented steep price rises and an embargo on those countries that had supported Israel in the Yom Kippur war, notably the United States and the Netherlands. Supplies of oil to the UK were not affected as the UK had placed an embargo on arms and supplies to both the Israelis and Arabs so did not draw retaliation from OPEC. However, the UK was hit hard by the combination of higher oil prices and a strike by UK coal miners through the winter of 1973–4. As supply was choked off, there was much talk of how to reduce reliance on oil. Interest increased in sources of renewable power, such as solar and wind. The case for nuclear power was strengthened. In South America, the Brazilian government responded with a major push to promote ethanol made from sugar cane as an alternative fuel to oil. Brazil has continued with this policy and is now the world's largest exporter of ethanol and the second largest producer behind the United States. Unwisely, many other countries backed off from investing in alternatives when the crisis came to an end.

The 1970s oil crisis was soon resolved, with the embargo lifted after five months. Relatively high prices remained, but OPEC members took a more conciliatory approach and avoided further abrupt price increases. I suspect one issue that influenced OPEC was the response of the West to the oil crisis. OPEC may have seen evidence that if they push too hard then the West could choose to break its reliance on oil. OPEC has behaved responsibly over the three decades since the 1970s, ensuring that oil remains affordable, and often increasing production in response to higher prices. The West became less concerned about oil supplies and less interested in investing in alternatives.

At the time of the 1970s oil crisis there was the choice to backtrack on fossil-fuel dependency. Replacing buildings and changing transport infrastructure takes decades. The three decades from then until now is the sort of timescale needed. It is a shame that the opportunity was squandered, but it is not surprising. The situation we faced in the 1970s was different. It was not understood that burning fossil fuel was also damaging the climate.

Now that we understand the negative effects of our addiction to fossil fuel, it is no longer justifiable to allow our decisions to be dictated by short-term economic considerations.

It seemed that our economies were at risk when the price of oil more than doubled as a result of the 1973–4 oil crisis.[4] In 1979–80, as problems erupted in Iran, the second oil crisis hit with the oil price breaking $37 a barrel ($97 at 2007 prices).[5] During the 1980s and 1990s the price eased back, lulling the world into a false sense of security. In 1986 the price dropped to under $15 ($38). In May 2008 steep price rises returned with the price for a barrel of oil exceeding $147 for the first time. Again, despite the protestations, the world economy took these rises in its stride (the financial problems that came later in 2008 were not blamed on the price of oil). We are finding that our economies can live with high oil prices. We are scared to take the next step and discover if our economies can survive without oil.

Coming off oil dependency by free choice is a leap too far for many policy makers. I argue that we can do so, and that our economies will adjust to fit. If we look past short-term economics, as Nicolas Stern did in his report on climate change,[6] we can see that the long-term economic argument supports acting sooner rather than later.

The short-term vested interests of the oil companies and oil-rich nations will have to be overcome. These are very powerful lobbies. Whilst we remain focused on short-term economics, our leaders will listen to them. The financial crash of 2008–9 provided another focus for world concern. It will take courage and foresight for world leaders to look beyond these immediate issues and other distractions, such as carbon trading.

The Distraction of Carbon Trading

Carbon trading is a useful mechanism to help society to adapt but it is not the solution.

Within a tightly controlled market, trading carbon is very good at ensuring the most cost-effective reductions in carbon dioxide emissions are taken first. The market sets a price for carbon and provides a choice between either continuing to emit CO_2 or to invest in CO_2 emission reduction. Those industries and activities that are easy to de-carbonize make the investment to reduce emissions, whilst those where reduction is more expensive buy credits. The overall effect is to reduce CO_2 emissions for the least cost.

The vital component of any carbon market is the cap that applies to overall emissions. This needs to be set in line with the recommendations of scientists. This cap is then screwed down until CO_2 emissions have reduced to a level that the scientists regard as safe. In my opinion, the cap should be screwed down firmly and fast, but let us leave that to the experts. At this stage we need commit only to following the scientists' advice and ensuring that they have the resources to monitor the situation.

The EU Emissions Trading Scheme (ETS) is the largest carbon market that has been set up so far. There have been teething problems. For example, the initial free allocation of carbon permits was too generous. This pushed the price of carbon far too low to have a real impact. It has also become clear that free allocations of carbon credits, based on historic emissions, is unfair and less effective than an auction. Once these problems are ironed out, the ETS could help Europe to move beyond the old technologies of fossil fuel. It could also help to underpin Europe as a world leader in the new energy technologies.

In theory, the carbon market can operate at world level too. CO_2 emitted anywhere in the world joins our shared global atmosphere. Similarly, any reduction, made anywhere, helps to alleviate the problem. When considering the investment required, a global carbon market can direct cash to where it will have the most effect. In Europe and other developed areas, many industrial processes are relatively efficient compared with many poorer countries. The cost of further improvements can be expensive. Rather than make this investment, companies can pay for other companies with very inefficient facilities in the developing world to make improvements in their operations. Such improvements will save more CO_2 than expensive improvements closer to home. This argument can be extended to include the building of new industrial facilities in developing countries. Even though such facilities are adding to global CO_2 emissions, it is argued that more efficient technology will be installed than would otherwise be the case. The global carbon market can have further complexity, such as allowing the planting of new forests to earn carbon credits which can then be sold in the market. All these mechanisms, and more, are being considered as politicians discuss carbon trading as the mechanism to reduce world emissions.

Before jumping to the conclusion that a global carbon market is the solution, there are two closely related issues that must be understood. These must be overcome if carbon markets are to fulfil their potential. The first is fundamental. There has to be a commitment to drive down fossil carbon emissions to safe levels. Unless this underpins policy, the carbon market will facilitate even greater fossil carbon release over the long term (as I explain below). The second is that the market must have tight and effective controls. The two issues relate, in that if we are not serious about making real reductions then a loosely controlled carbon market can be used as an excuse for inaction or delay.

The world community has not agreed a binding cap on carbon emissions, despite over a decade of negotiation and discussion. The result, the Kyoto Protocol, misses out huge parts of the world economy, has no enforceable penalties and expires in 2012. It is expected that world leaders will agree a new agreement at the United Nations Climate Change Conference in Copenhagen, 7–18 Dec. 2009. President Barack Obama has indicated that the US is likely to sign up and the indications are that the deal will have more ambitious targets than the Kyoto Protocol. But we should not hold out hope that the deal will include binding and enforceable penalties. This compares very badly with the world's reaction to CFCs. World leaders took the dangers of CFCs seriously. They moved from the identification of the problem to a binding solution within four years. So far, the world is not serious about making the required reductions in CO_2 emissions. This makes it impossible to set up an effective global carbon market with strong controls and binding penalties.

Despite the failure to progress discussions over a global carbon agreement, we are attracted by the evident benefits of supporting development projects in poor countries that make use of low carbon technology. This is good charitable work, but as a mechanism to reduce global carbon emissions it will have little effect. There are companies that use such projects to offset their carbon emissions and then make claims that their operations are carbon neutral. This is hypocrisy and little better than 'greenwash' whilst we do not have a tightly controlled global carbon market capped to a total emissions figure set by independent scientists.

Let us assume that a global market for carbon is established, despite the lack of commitment to a binding global cap, as this is useful in driving home the point that such a market is fundamentally flawed. In a global carbon market, every fossil-fuel consumer will have a carbon price on which to base investment decisions. This will not only be the current spot price but the carbon futures market will also set the price to support long-term investment decisions. Each decision will be a balance between buying carbon and investing in reduction measures. The fossil-fuel industry too will have a sound basis on which to invest in new capacity.

The global carbon market will favour less carbon-intensive fuels, making them relatively more affordable. Gas is the best, followed by oil. The market will penalize the lower-grade deposits, including oil sands, oil shale and coal. These generate less net energy for every ton of CO_2 emitted. For example, coal combustion emits almost twice as much carbon dioxide per unit of energy as does the combustion of natural gas.[7] In the short term, a global carbon market reduces carbon emissions by ensuring that the cleanest fossil fuels are burnt first.

As the price of fossil fuels increase, driven by an excess of demand over supply, then harder-to-reach and lower-grade deposits of fossil fuel become commercially viable. For example, Canada has huge oil reserves in its Alberta oil sands, second only to Saudi Arabia. It costs around $18 dollars a barrel to extract the oil. When oil was selling at $20 a barrel, these cost were prohibitive. As the price of oil surged past $100 a barrel the financial cost of extraction became insignificant. This is not so for the environmental impact. The normal method is to clear the forest and then strip-mine the oil sand beneath, leaving a moonscape of devastation.

The carbon market should add further costs to low-grade sources such as oil sands. This may delay exploitation in the short term but it provides a firm basis on which to time investment in additional capacity.

In a global carbon market, there will be a mechanism to manage a smooth transition from high-grade to low-grade sources. There will be a sound basis on which to plan investment in oil sands, oil shale and, of course, coal. The Earth has abundant reserves of these low-grade fossil fuels. As the quality of fuel we burn decreases, the carbon emissions increase for the same amount of energy output. This means entering a spiral of diminishing returns, emitting ever more carbon dioxide for ever less energy output.

In 2009, talking about a global cap for carbon emissions leads us towards making reductions through choosing cleaner fuels, such as gas. The carbon market is therefore beneficial in the short term by reducing the carbon output of the energy we generate. Over the longer term, as gas reserves run low and we move on to lower-grade fuels, we will face a situation where we need to reduce our energy consumption significantly just to hold carbon emissions steady. Now we are finding that agreeing a global carbon cap is politically difficult. In the future it will become completely beyond reach if we have become reliant on the carbon market.

The global carbon market delays the point when we are forced to take real action. The short-term benefits are hiding the long-term risks and distracting us from the real task.

Taxing the Carbon Economy

Taxing carbon emissions is a more effective way to make progress, but if government finances become reliant on such taxes then a perverse incentive arises to continue emissions. It is therefore vital that carbon taxes are a transition measure – even if the transition period lasts for one or two decades. After this period, when we have achieved a zero-fossil-carbon society, carbon tax receipts will also drop to zero.

Recognition of the transitional nature of carbon tax receipts makes their application doubly effective. Not only is there a price disincentive attached to fossil fuels but also the funds coming in are not to be used for core government finances. Carbon tax provides the cash flow to support the required adaptation. In political terms, this cash can be used to buy off opposition. Some people, such as the poor and the old, will be deserving cases who need support as fuel prices climb steeply. This needs to be done by reducing energy use with measures such as better insulation. Funds will also be needed for infrastructure, such as improved public transport. There will also be powerful lobby groups that may not deserve special assistance but they too will need to be placated.

Tax on fossil fuels is the most direct carbon tax. The UK decided to commit to escalating transport fuel tax in 1993. By 2000, fuel prices had climbed to become the highest in Europe. This action was quoted as an example of best practice in efforts to reduce greenhouse gas emissions.[8] However, the government faced a rebellion from UK haulage companies (see opposite). The government lost the fight and the fuel tax escalator was abandoned.

Governments should learn from the humiliation of being forced to backtrack and plan to win future battles. First, the tax receipts should be unambiguously and transparently applied to support adaptation to a zero-carbon economy. This will avoid accusations of back-door tax increases. The government should then be sensitive to the needs of those who will lose out. With regard to the example above, I believe that the UK government should have dealt robustly with the haulier's concerns. The fuel tax policy was putting them at a disadvantage compared with their competitors from mainland Europe. The government should have applied taxes, tariffs or road

FUEL TAX REBELLION

In 1993, when transport fuel in the UK was the third cheapest in Europe, the British government brought in a fuel tax escalator. This was set at a 3% increase in real terms, rising to 5% in 1995. By 2000, the UK had the highest fuel taxes in Europe (dramatically higher than the United States and Australia).

In autumn 2000, the price of crude oil rose to over $30 a barrel (at that time, the price was seen as expensive) sparking protest – directed at the fuel tax escalator – led by the haulage companies. They complained that, with the open European market, they were being put at a considerable disadvantage by the policy. The protesters placed blockades on UK oil refineries. The fuel shortages that resulted caused considerable disruption. After a stand-off, the blockades were lifted, but the protesters set a 60-day deadline for their demands for lower fuel taxes to be met. One week before the end of the deadline, the British Chancellor, Gordon Brown, announced in his pre-budget report that fuel duty would be frozen for two years. This signalled the end of the fuel tax escalator.

---

access charges on foreign trucks passing into the UK. Where this broke EU rules, the government should have been willing to push through the measure even if it risked incurring a substantial fine from the EU Commission.

In moving forward, politicians should not be afraid to do the right thing. Consider if the UK had picked a fight with the EU to defend a sensible fuel tax. Gordon Brown (the Chancellor of the Exchequer at the time) would now be hailed as a leader of the climate change movement, rather than remembered as losing the battle with the road hauliers.

I believe that huge rises in the tax on fossil fuels is necessary. I also believe that it is politically possible as our concern over climate change grows. The key to success is a massive commitment of the tax receipts to supporting adaptation.

Security of Supply

Maintaining security of supply is of prime concern, particularly as reliance grows on supplies from remote and unstable regions. For the UK, gas and oil reserves in the North Sea are declining. The UK and Europe are becoming more dependent on oil from the Middle East and gas from Russia. We must decide if such reliance is wise.

One policy option is to revert to coal. This fuelled the Industrial Revolution and there are still massive reserves. From the narrow perspective of energy security, this is a tempting option. The discussions taking place about new technology to burn coal cleanly is an interesting dialogue. We should remain open-minded but also be highly sceptical. Coal is a dirty fuel. There can be little doubt that leaving it underground is the sensible policy option. I believe that a return to reliance on coal would be retrograde and irresponsible.

Another policy option is conventional nuclear power. A nuclear power station emits no carbon. I can understand the predicament of policy makers faced with the task of delivering commitments made under the Kyoto Protocol. Giving a green light to the policy of building new nuclear power stations will deliver carbon reductions. Within stable societies with high-quality management and top-class engineers this seems a reasonably safe option to tide us over the medium-term energy shortages. The long-term radiation legacy is ignored. That is left to future generations to worry about. They will have the problem of our nuclear waste long after we have had the benefits of the energy. This does not seem a fair trade.

Widespread use of nuclear power leads to other problems. We cannot trust some countries to hold to the same rigorous safety standards that we demand. Deciding that some countries are to be trusted and others are not is a recipe for divisive argument. This goes deeper than the safe operation of nuclear power stations. Nuclear power inevitably leads to access to technology that can be diverted to the development of nuclear weapons. These do not have to be high-tech missiles. A dirty radiation bomb is an easy task – if radioactive material is easily available.

The conventional nuclear option will lead to slowly rising levels of background radiation as the sum total of the small unavoidable discharges adds up. There will also be a combustible political mix as a wide range of states acquire nuclear power and, potentially, access to nuclear weapons. Nuclear accidents, or deliberate acts of radioactive terrorism, will be rare but some will be inevitable. Everyone can hope that they will not be a direct victim. However, everyone will be subject to the ratcheted rise in global background radiation that would result. The effects will include higher rates of cancer and more deformities amongst the offspring of all species, but there will be nothing immediate and dramatic. If we are lucky, it will be a slow and insidious poisoning of the global environment.

If we are unlucky, we may suffer a tit-for-tat nuclear exchange initiated by a rogue regime or an extreme terrorist group. The main nuclear powers have more sense than to unleash nuclear Armageddon. There are a number of other organizations and states that are much less predictable. Even the limited use of nuclear weapons would have catastrophic and long-lasting consequences. This would make the problems of climate change – even the flooding of one third of Bangladesh – seem almost irrelevant in comparison.

Nuclear power should be discussed in open debate, but it is wrong that policy makers are pushed down this route. Nuclear power can support a delay in implementing a ban on fossil fuel. That is all. The long-term legacy is unacceptable.

Act Now whilst Oil and Gas Are Still Cheap

Oil and gas prices have been volatile, reaching record highs in the summer of 2008 and dropping back in 2009 as the recession took hold. It is hard to persuade people that oil and gas prices are cheap. Even the record prices set in 2008 are far lower than the high prices we will have to accept as the gap between supply and demand increases when the world economy picks up. We should use this opportunity of cheap fuel to increase tax to fund adaptation.

Europe has already made a start. In the UK, tax accounts for 40% of the price of transport fuel and this is expected to rise. The United States has a far greater challenge. Fuel taxes have been kept very low (about 15% in 2008). This means that the United States is a long way behind Europe in gaining acceptance for high gasoline prices. President George W. Bush consistently opposed higher taxes on fuel. This has left the United States ill-prepared.

It has been found that the world economies can handle an oil price of $100 a barrel. We will find $200 a barrel is also affordable. There will be loud complaints, of course, but in a world of high demand and constricted supplies there will be no choice. The world is so deeply addicted to oil that we will pay almost any price to fund the habit. We should make use of this by increasing the tax take now. Rather than passing so much cash to the oil-producing nations, more of it should be kept at home to fund the shift away from oil.

The UK tax escalator was a good model. This gave a forward commitment to drive prices higher. Such a policy gives business, car drivers and all of us clear and unambiguous information in order to adapt our affairs. However, this will not silence the critics. One way that might is to enshrine such a fuel tax escalator in law. When the measures are first brought in, the impact is low and political acceptance achievable. Later governments then are simply complying with their legal duty. This gives business firm figures to work with and protesters little hope that they can force a U-turn.

None of us should be in any doubt that fuel will become much more expensive. There will be plenty of opposition. The complaints from SUV drivers living in affluent city areas such as Chelsea, London, or Manhattan, New York, will not attract any sympathy. Where people really suffer we will have to take note and act. An example would be pensioners living in remote communities that have no shop or post office. We need to bring in a whole set of policies appropriate to a zero-fossil-fuel society. For example, we need policy that supports small local shops (and/or penalizes big out-of-town stores).

An Opportunity – Liquid Sunshine

This chapter has focused on the need to ban fossil fuel. Until this is accepted as inevitable, we are blind to the future that would follow. This new world will put a much higher price to energy.

The world has ample energy; the problem is capturing it. The world's deserts in particular receive enough solar radiation to replace all our consumption of oil. The difficulty is capturing the energy using technology that is economically viable. When energy prices double, or triple, from current levels many more options open up. There will then be a real commercial incentive to try to harness this sunshine. When this shift takes place, our current solar energy technology will soon look outdated.

My favourite idea is the concept of a liquid biofuel produced from the desert. We have many options that would work, ranging from algae grown within bioreactors to complex chemical processes that mimic photosynthesis. None of these are viable at current oil prices. The challenge for our engineers and scientists will be finding the least-cost method. This will then have an energy price at which it becomes commercially viable. As soon as world energy prices hit this figure, the production of 'liquid sunshine' will boom.

Australia could be at the forefront. It has a huge empty desert interior and – without its own oil fields – should be an enthusiastic supporter. The Middle East also has huge deserts but with oil terminals that can pump conventional oil for almost zero cost it will be harder for Arab leaders to understand the opportunity.

It is important to move fast to show that the intention to ban fossil fuel is genuine in order to start the process of change and give a huge boost to the technical innovation required. Buildings can be designed and communities planned that live within the renewable energy budget available. Where this is not sufficient, local energy supplies can be supplemented from the emerging global market in liquid sunshine.

One sector that will be particularly hard hit, as it becomes clear that fossil fuel will be made obsolete, is aviation. So far, our love of flying has taken precedence over the need to take action to reduce the environmental impact. This will no longer be possible.

15 Melting the Wings of Icarus

One wonderful evening in March 2008 I was sitting relaxing with an international group of skiers gazing out over the frozen wilderness of northern Finland. We were in the bar of a luxury hotel at the top of the ski slopes of the Finnish ski resort, Syötekeskus. Through the wide panoramic window there was nothing to see but stars in a black sky, forest, snow, and the moving lights of an aircraft high above. The hotel was surrounded by ski lifts reaching down off all sides of the mountain. These were out of our direct line of sight and below the field of view. It was as if a small plush capsule had been plonked into the wilderness and we were gazing out of it.

This was a relaxing interlude in what was otherwise a gruelling skiing route across Finland from east to west. We did not fit the normal profile of hotel guests at this downhill skiing resort. Our lightweight ski boots and backpacks were evidence of a different type of skiing. Our cross-country skiing route had started from the Russian border and would end at the border with Sweden. The total route over seven days was 440 km.

The route had begun in deep forest on high ground beside the Russian border. Cold-War watch towers were still in evidence. With an air temperature of −24°C, we were keen to get moving. The initial descent was straight down through the trees and an exciting ride through the forest. The air cut like a knife through our layers of ski clothes. It was not until the terrain flattened out and we had to work to keep the skis moving that the cold seemed less intense.

Whilst skiing, my mind had wandered to thoughts about the airline passengers flying somewhere high above with an outside air temperature considerably colder than down at ground level. This would not bother them, inside the warm cocoon of the aeroplane. They would be in the comfort of man's world. As this thought passed through my mind, a moose ambled across just a few metres in front of me. Until you see a moose, close up, you do not appreciate how big they really are. They make horses look small in comparison. In that remote piece of forest I was in his world, not he in mine, and I felt very small indeed. Fortunately I also remembered the advice I had been given that moose are generally docile creatures. He continued on his way, and I on mine.

Back in the human world, that evening we arrived at the bottom of the mountain of Syötekeskus. It was odd to come out of the wilderness and join a queue of downhill skiers and snowboarders waiting to be dragged up the mountain on the T-bar. We received some odd looks, with our narrow skis and a look of exhaustion on our faces, as we were ushered to the front of the queue. That was the easiest hill that day, sitting back against the T-bar instead of pushing back on the kick wax as we had been doing over the last 55 km. Reaching the top of the mountain, the views out over the Syöte National Park were breathtaking.

After a sauna and a huge meal we listened to a talk about the Syöte National Park through which we would ski the next day. Saara Airaksinen, a senior advisor working on protecting and preserving the wilderness, spoke with passion. She told us about nature and its seasons far from the direct influence of man, in a talk illustrated by beautiful photographs. Special permission had been obtained for us to cross the park and we were required to respect the park, leaving nothing but tracks that would be covered by the next fall of snow. The presentation was part of Saara's job, but as she talked about the wilderness her words came from the heart.

After the lecture, a group of us continued to chat with the speaker. There were a few North Americans amongst this group, one of whom worked for Yellowstone National Park. During the conversation he invited Saara to come to the United States to visit Yellowstone to see how the United States manage their national parks. Her reply made us all stop to think. She said, 'No', in that direct Finnish way that can appear rude. There was a pause in the conversation, then she explained. 'This wilderness and other wilderness areas are at risk from climate change and flying is one of the causes. I don't fly.'

I had to admire her stand. She was not seeking to make a general point or to criticize any of us, she was just explaining her personal decision. If many more of us made the same personal commitment then the impact of flying would, of course, be much reduced. This is what some people argue for; I do not.

Voluntary restrictions on flying will only work with unselfish people like Saara. It would be most unfair that she and people like her be asked to shoulder the burden of everyone else. I can see very good reason for Saara to travel to Yellowstone to share her expertise. I compare this with holidaymakers flying to Ibiza, the Spanish island, intending to spend their time drinking in nightclubs until dawn and snoozing by the pool during the day. This is their choice. It is not for me or others to say they should not. The point is that to tackle the environmental damage of flying, action is needed right across the industry, and such action should apply to everyone.

Aviation Soaring to New Heights

Not long back, flying was too expensive for more than an occasional holiday or a vital business trip. The low-cost airlines have changed all that. New routes have been opened and the capacity on existing routes has been increased. It is now affordable to fly further and more often. Cheap flying has become an expectation. High-capacity national and global flight networks have become a fundamental part of the world's infrastructure. Aviation is firmly entrenched as part of everyday life.

We can afford to fly whenever we have holiday time at our disposal: a summer holiday to the sun and a winter skiing holiday, supplemented by weekend city breaks whenever our batteries need recharging. We no longer have to tolerate the uncertain weather and the lack of exotic appeal of a holiday closer to home.

New commuter profiles are opening up. There are business executives who work in the City of London and live in France. This is not confined to the super rich. One of my colleagues working for a business school (not renowned for high salaries) flies weekly from his home in southern France to England. The flights are convenient and affordable. I also came across a fireman who was weekly commuting from his job in the UK to his family living in Finland. These are lifestyle options that were not feasible until the low-cost airlines came on the aviation scene.

The more globalized our world, the more necessary flying has become. High-value and perishable goods need to be transported. The rose growers in Africa or the asparagus farmers in Peru would not be able to get their produce to market in Europe without the world's high-capacity, integrated and affordable air freight network. We do not pause to wonder if it makes sense for these farmers to be supplying such distant markets with perishable produce.

One area of our lives that no longer requires flying is communicating. Broadband Internet places friends, colleagues, suppliers and customers just a click away, regardless of their physical location. Video conferencing and virtual-reality technologies are improving all the time. Even so, these methods are not as good as face-to-face interaction. If we shake someone's hand, drink a beer with them in a bar or share a sauna, it builds trust and cements relationships in a way that technology struggles to imitate. In a world of cheap flights we do not have to tolerate such limitations. Business meetings and conferences proliferate on every possible theme – including, ironically, the dangers of climate change.

In the developing world, for large countries such as India with a creaking rail system, flying is the fastest way to speed up transportation within the country. Building airports is quicker and easier than upgrading a whole rail network. India and China are now some of the biggest purchasers of passenger jets and have the fastest expanding airlines. Improving the rail network would be a much more sustainable solution, but why bother when there is such an easy way to travel quickly at an affordable price?

We like flying and the industry is booming. It will not be easy to dislodge aviation from the privileged and protected position it has in the world system.

Teflon Aviation

The economic argument in favour of aviation seems robust. This applies not just to tourism: in a globalized world, improving our interconnectivity with the rest of the world is a prerequisite for driving economic success. Within countries (particularly those of large scale), a high-capacity flight network maximizes the economic potential between regions. Our politicians are very wary of testing whether these assumptions are correct. One reason is that their hands are tied by the Chicago Convention. This long-standing international agreement exempts aviation fuel from customs duty.

The Chicago Convention[1] is the agreement that underpins international civil aviation and is administered by the International Civil Aviation Organization (ICAO). Article 24 states:

> ***Fuel****, lubricating oils, spare parts, regular equipment and aircraft stores on board an aircraft of a contracting State, on arrival in the territory of another contracting State and retained on board on leaving the territory of that State,* ***shall be exempt from customs duty****, inspection fees or similar national or local duties and charges.*[2]

This article has ensured that, over the last 65 years, aviation has grown on the back of fuel that is exempt of tax. If one country were to take a national decision to tax aviation fuel, airlines would be within their rights to fly into that country with full tanks and avoid purchasing any fuel. Such action would hit hardest those airlines with operating hubs in the country imposing the tax. Unilateral action would be an economic own goal. No country with its own airline would be so stupid. The fuel tax exemption for aviation fuel in the UK is estimated to be a 3 billion Euro indirect subsidy to airlines, compared with other transport choices.[3]

In 1944, those drafting the Chicago Convention were seeking to: 'create and preserve friendship and understanding among the nations and peoples of the world'. Specifically, the convention aimed to ensure: 'that international civil aviation may be developed in a safe and orderly manner and that international air transport services may be established on the basis of equality of opportunity and operated soundly and economically.' In 1944, no one guessed that Article 24 would act as a barrier to making aviation pay the true price of the environmental impact.

Within the EU, it is acknowledged that the exemption for aviation is an unfair anomaly. Measures are being discussed, such as including aviation within the European Union Greenhouse Gas Emission Trading Scheme (EU ETS). Such action is limited in what it can achieve. Going to the heart of the problem and amending the Chicago Convention would be a more effective course of action. The convention has been ratified by almost all of the countries of the world. If it is to be amended, each country will want its say. This will not be easy. Fortunately there is a way to make early progress. All that is needed is for a group of the largest nations to agree a universal floor to tax charges on aviation fuel.

In the United States, under the Bush presidency, such an agreement would have been impossible. In 2009 and beyond, as world leaders continue to meet to discuss climate change, with little to show for all the talk, aviation will come under the spotlight. The exemption for aviation will become an increasingly powerful image of the world's unwillingness to take real action. It will become increasingly difficult to defend the aviation industry. Its Teflon coating will start to look increasingly scratched and tarnished.

Aviation accounts for 2% of global CO_2 emissions. This figure is often used to justify continuing exemption. The argument is that it would be easier to make carbon reductions in other parts of the world economy. Those making the argument are people who fly. This is most of the people in decision-making positions throughout the world. In the developed world, there is also a large proportion of the electorate who have become accustomed to flying on a regular basis. Even so, it is universally true that flying is not for the poorest elements of world society. It is blatantly unfair that aviation fuel is exempt from the tax treatment that applies to fuel for other transport choices. The argument can be taken further. Given that a tax on aviation fuel will not hit the poor and vulnerable, there is good reason to set the tax disproportionally higher. If this argument gains acceptance, then the coming downturn in the aviation industry could be rapid and steep.

Aviation Crashes to Earth

Aviation is caught in the trap of its own success. The regulatory environment is keeping fuel prices artificially low, which is driving passenger numbers to unsustainably high levels. Whilst this continues, plane manufacturers and airlines do not have the commercial case to transform their industry to fit the needs of the 21st century. I discuss below the vision of 21st-century aviation to which we should aspire. The transition cannot commence until we break the stalemate. It is hard to envisage a smooth transition. It is far more likely that the current airline industry will be brought crashing down to earth.

The meetings of the International Civil Aviation Organization are unlikely to make the changes required – if that means presiding over a bloodbath in the industry. Many people who fly now only do so because it is cheap. As prices rise, they will choose other options: travel less often; holiday closer to home; stop commuting by air; live closer to family and friends. There will still be senior politicians and business leaders who need to travel, but administrators will take a hard look at who needs to fly and why. Raising prices to match the cost of the environmental impact will lead to a major contraction in passenger numbers and a reduction in the demand for air-freight capacity.

The source of substantive action will arise from outside the aviation industry. The venue at which such action will be initiated may be one of the future world summits on climate change. It may not happen this year, next year or the year after, as we still believe we can broker a global agreement to combat climate change that allows aviation to carry on much as before. When all the talk has still not delivered a robust agreement over halting climate change, then world leaders will come under intense pressure to act. An alliance of the smaller nations that are most directly affected by climate change will force the pace. Scientists will also have increased their understanding of the effects of aircraft emissions on the upper atmosphere. There is suspicion that the damage is greater than the CO_2 emitted. If hard evidence backs this up, exemption for aviation will no longer be tenable.

The agreement required is simple and the enforcement straightforward. If world leaders decide to act, they can. All that is needed is a global floor tax on aviation fuel to be applied by all nations. An argument that may undermine the chances of such an agreement is that tax receipts should be held centrally by an agency such as the UN. This would be a mistake. The main purpose of the tax will be to reform aviation; tax receipts should be left with the relevant government. This should make agreement easier to achieve, as governments see this as a way to increase taxation under the collective cloak of international action to combat climate change. The sanction that can be used for enforcement is to suspend flights with non-compliant countries (or impose heavy landing taxes on their planes). A sub-set of countries that choose to remain outside the agreement could emerge, but only flying between one another.

The Phoenix Flies – 21st-Century Aviation

A major contraction in aviation will lead to a lot of disgruntled people who would like to fly but can no longer afford to do so. This demand will drive forward the development of a sustainable aviation industry.

The small group of people who continue to fly will be the rich and the powerbrokers of world society. These people need to get around and are willing and able to pay the high prices. Newer planes with relatively good fuel-economy figures will continue to fly, especially smaller planes such as the Boeing 777 Dreamliner. The Airbus A380 may also do well on a few premium routes, as its fuel-per-passenger-mile figures are better than other current generation planes. Older models will be scrapped, and the companies that own them will go out of business, even though they have many flying hours left in their airframes.

There will be a small and profitable premium market for small efficient conventional jet aircraft, despite the cost. The passengers will pay a substantial premium for the privilege. The taxes levied on aviation fuel can be invested to counter complaints from all those who can no longer afford to fly. Investment in increasing the capacity, speed and efficiency of the rail network is one example.

As the commercial dynamics of aviation change, our engineers will be given a different brief. The task will be to design a plane with zero environmental impact that can fly people at an affordable price. If care is taken not to add further restrictions, and our engineers are given a free hand, it will be interesting to see what they devise. It is possible to guess how such a 'plane' might look.

First, it is likely to be slow and will, therefore, not meet the needs of our busy leaders, but that is not the segment being targeted. Second, the design may use an element of lighter-than-air lift – not necessarily a latter-day airship, but borrowing some of those design parameters. Third, solar power is likely to be an attractive power source. This will mean a huge wing area to gather the energy required. It will need assistance on take-off from another power source. This could be conventional engines or a land-based launch system. Such a system could consist of a long cable attached to a powerful winch on the ground beyond the far end of the runway. On take-off, the winch would pull the plane forward with the cable dropping away as the plane reached a certain altitude. Once cruising above the cloud cover, such a plane would have continuous reliable sunshine. The flight schedule would have to follow the sun with a morning take-off and evening landing.

Such a large, slow plane is a different passenger proposition. In a large aircraft there should be space to move around and be entertained. It could be the 21st-century cruise ship of the skies. This will be important, as holidaymakers will use a day of their holiday in transit. People will then be able to travel from northern Europe to the Mediterranean beaches and from New York to Florida under tax-free renewable power and be able to start to relax for their holiday whilst in flight.

The defence of aviation is so deeply entrenched that we may have to wait some years yet before we start to build an aviation industry fit for the 21st century. Ironically, carbon trading is the biggest barrier. As long as we continue to believe that carbon trading will solve the problem of climate change, the focus will be on forcing airlines to buy carbon credits to offset their emissions. This will be a tough battle. Airlines do not want the additional overhead. When the battle is finally won, we will find that we have expended our resources on the wrong fight.

The shortcomings of carbon trading were covered in Chapter 14. Direct taxation of aviation fuel is what aviation needs to provide the commercial incentive to build a sustainable industry. When setting the rate of tax, governments should also bear in mind that such taxes will hit those who can afford to pay. There are grounds to set a disproportionately high tax rate. To make the taxation more palatable, the income can be earmarked for investment in sustainable ground transport infrastructure, as well as the ground facilities needed by the new 21st-century flying machines.

Governments will need to be tough in protecting their country's self-interest. The current 'policy' of avoiding raising tax to prevent losing competiveness with other nations will need to be reversed. Governments will have to be resolute in pushing through the tax increases and forcing the amendment of international agreements that penalize such actions.

For the rest of us, we should understand that cheap flying will be phased out before there is time to build the 21st-century flying infrastructure. In theory, politicians could broker a deal with escalating tax rates over a number of years to try to force a smooth transition. If they signed such a deal now, it might work. I hope they do, but I suspect they won't. Such a deal will be hard to agree until the crisis is real and imminent. The time for a slow transition will not then be available.

Those people who commute weekly by air would be wise to look for a different job or a different home, and act in good time whilst there are still options available. If you hanker after seeing remote parts of the globe, do it now whilst flights are affordable. I understand that this advice is diametrically opposed to those admirable people who avoid flying and urge others to do the same. I understand and respect their view, and do not want to oppose it. I argue that we should shift our effort to making the changes that will have a real impact.

The key action is for all of us to accept that cheap flying in the current generation of conventional planes should be obsolete, and support politicians in making it so. Then restrictions will apply not just to environmentalists like Saara, but to us all. That would be fair and effective in reducing the impact of aviation on the environment.

There will then follow a delay whilst the aviation industry catches up with the demand for environmentally friendly flying. The wait may not be too long. Some designs have already been drafted, but, at the moment, the business case does not exist to develop them. Universal high taxes on aviation fuel will change the commercial dynamics. Venture capitalists will then pour money into such projects.

The action required is simple: tax aviation fuel. Business will then have the basis for building a 21st-century aviation business. There will be casualties, with many airlines folding, but the forward-thinking operators will be able to profit from the disruption. On a personal note, I would like to see the airlines that oppose the coming changes wiped out as we join together to give our politicians the mandate to act. I may not make many friends in the current industry but the prediction has been in the public domain for some time.[4] An airline failing to prepare is not serving its shareholders well.

Back in 2008, my opinions on making airlines and their passengers pay for the environmental impact was out of step with the views of most people. There was a minority who agreed with me, but almost without exception these same people said that it cannot be done. They thought that it would be impossible to force through the changes required. I disagreed. On 5th August 2008, I was listening to a discussion programme on BBC Radio 4. The theme was the impact on UK business of the credit crunch. One person who phoned the studio ran a narrowboat hire company in England. He explained that his business was doing very well. In previous years, his customers had been primarily from overseas including Americans, Canadians, Australians and New Zealanders. In summer 2008, there were far fewer long-haul customers. However, there had been a huge increase in boat hiring from British people holidaying at home. Overall, his business had benefited. This shows that we should not fear a contracting aviation industry, but watch how the travel industry adjusts to a different set of parameters.

The curiosity we have to see foreign places will remain with us. If this becomes a rare and expensive expedition, so be it. For most holidays we desire comfort, relaxation, beautiful scenery and delicious food. All this is available closer to home. All we have to overcome is our innate feeling of unfairness that rich people can holiday regularly in places beyond the reach of our pockets. But the rich have always been able to afford locations and resorts that are beyond the means of the rest of us. It is irrational to use our envy of others to block the development of environmentally friendly flying.

Fixing the problems of aviation is a relatively easy task. Redesigning our cities is a far more complex challenge.

16 Cities for People

Cities in the developed world have evolved to suit the needs of the car. The expansion of car use is not only a major component of fossil-fuel consumption, but it also undermines community living and encourages urban sprawl. How well we deal with the problems arising from our dependence on the car will be a good measure of how willing we are to build a sustainable future for the world.[1]

For the sake of the environment and the health of our urban communities, we must unwind the spiral of car dependency. It can be replaced by the model of people-centric urban design. Making the required changes politically acceptable across all the world's societies will be a complex challenge. The developed world must be persuaded to lead the transformation. Meanwhile, the developing world has an opportunity to bypass investment in an extensive car infrastructure. The sooner that we begin the process of transformation, the better it will be for communities, and for the systems of planet Earth.

During the first half of the 20th century, city design was not influenced greatly by the car. Production of the first mass-produced car, the Model T Ford, started in 1908 but it was not until numbers increased significantly that the car started to impact on city design. The United States now has over 700 cars per 1,000 people. This has driven major change to the urban landscape, leading to 'suburbanization',[2] as suburbs expand unconstrained by the need to live within walking distance of a transport hub.

Cars are now universal across the developed world, and car ownership is one of the first aspirations of people in developing countries as income rises. China is a prime example. It has been characterized by images of roads thronged with bicycles. In 2008 there were only 9 cars per 1,000 people. But the Chinese are rapidly catching up as the urban middle class embrace the automobile, as the Americans did in the 1930s.[3] A huge populous country like China that follows the American model of car usage and the associated urban sprawl will increase dramatically the country's demand for resources – and the load on the global environment.

Car-centric urban design dominated the second half of the 20th century. We need to adopt a different paradigm for the 21st century.

The Environmental Imperative to Act

We now know, unequivocally, that we must cut carbon emissions right across society if we are to halt climate change. Forty per cent of world energy use is for transportation,[4] so this is a prime sector to target reductions in fossil-fuel consumption. One solution would be to switch our transportation to biofuels. On closer examination, it becomes clear that the potential supplies of such fuels are limited. To replace 5% of the current fuel used for transportation (gasoline and diesel being replaced by ethanol and biodiesel) would require 21% of cropland in the United States; in the EU the figure would be 20%.[5] This would be feasible, but increasing biofuel production to replace food crops beyond this level would risk precipitating a crisis over world food supplies.

We may have success in exploiting other renewable fuel sources for the transport fleet, but credible action, which leads to real reductions in the use of fossil fuels, must address the imbalance between demand and sustainable renewable supplies. This will require controlling the number of vehicles and reducing the distances travelled, as well as increasing the average fuel efficiency of the fleet.

Car-centric urban design is perpetuating the problems we face, making it very hard to reduce fossil carbon emissions. We need to understand the causal linkages that apply. Climate change is being driven by excess fossil carbon release; the transport sector is a major contributor to these emissions; and car-centric urban design is a major driver of the world's growing demand for transportation. If we are serious about addressing climate change, we must re-evaluate our policy for urban areas.

Car-Centric Urban Design

The cities of the world have become choked with vehicles and the fumes they emit. Gridlocked cars are a waste of time for the people caught up in them and delay the movement of freight. Traffic jams also exacerbate pollution as engines idle in stationary traffic, reducing the fuel-per-mile figure for each journey we make. This is a problem afflicting most cities across the world, from New York to London to Tokyo.

In the city centres, we are making progress. With tall buildings in close proximity, people can move around by foot between shops, offices and city centre apartments. Many cities have transformed these central areas – in particular the main shopping district – by making pedestrian zones. These car-free zones then come to life as communal areas where people can meet, informal markets can arise and street theatre and other entertainments can flourish. In good weather, people can sit drinking coffee and enjoy the fresh air (provided the fumes from the traffic a few streets away are not too intrusive).

Out of the city centres, the situation is different. Society is built around the vehicle infrastructure. The extensive road network will have a backbone of multi-lane roads, spreading out to a complex network connecting to each house, where there is space to park a car or two (or three). Shopping is concentrated in large malls with good road access and large car parks. Industrial areas require space for freight vehicles to park and load, and high capacity routes in and out to minimize delays – as well as car parks for their workers. This model of urban development means that everything is spread out to allow space for the required vehicle infrastructure. This, in turn, means that the distances we have to move to shop, to get to work and to live our lives are greater than we are willing to tackle on foot. We seldom encourage our city planners to turn this spiral of car dependency back on itself, by designing city communities that exclude cars.

The other driver of suburbanization is our individual desire for private space. The Western ideal of the perfect home is a large private plot with ample parking space. This is deeply ingrained in our culture, and such a property can be a very pleasant place to live. We are slow to realize that exclusive private access to a large space destroys community life.

If we all have a large plot for our own exclusive use, then straightforward spatial logic tells us that there will be fewer people within walking or cycling distance. We must, therefore, have a car, along with the infrastructure on which to drive it.

People-Centric Urban Design

When modern suburbs were built, they were designed around the car. A sound road network and sufficient parking are requisites of what we regard as good development. Suburbs have become sprawling areas consisting of patches of private space for each house which are connected by a road network that is dominated by cars. Each activity, whether it be shopping, going to work, playing sport or seeing a friend, requires a journey by car. However, there are alternative models of community urban living based around the needs of people.

When we focus on people, we are reminded that we are not just looking for a solution for the here and now. The decisions we take with regards to city design today will have implications long into the future. Our fixation with the car has lasted half a century, but with regard to city design it is a passing fad. People live longer than this, and have children and grandchildren about whom they care. Our cities will be their home into the long future. We must learn to manage our cities in a way that will be indefinitely sustainable.

Ecovillages show how sustainable community living can be achieved. They are settlements in which the major functions of life – housing, food provision, education, manufacturing, leisure, social life and commerce – are all present in balanced proportions.[6] However, very few ecovillages have been started in northern Europe over the last couple of decades.[7] The value of such community-based sustainable living has not been appreciated by policy makers or the general population. They are seen to be for those seeking an alternative lifestyle, hippies or others on the margins of society.

I believe that this attitude is set to change. We will see high-quality ecocommunities springing up, as the middle classes in the developed world seek to improve their lives and lessen their impact on the environment. Building such communities within cities will be challenging. It requires that we think of the city as a tessellated structure of communities which are largely self-contained. Within each human-scale urban village, people will be able to go about their daily lives without the need for a car.

If we rely on walking to get about these communities, this shrinks the radius of the area available for regular easy access. But, of course, communities can expand beyond this, with little detriment to society or the environment, by making use of the bicycle.

The bicycle will not be everyone's choice. Some people may not be able to cycle due to age or infirmity. Some journeys will require carrying more than fits easily on to a bike. Other people may be unwilling to cycle for whatever reason. For these situations, there are other options such as delivery bicycles and the rickshaw. But the rickshaw is little more than a summer tourist attraction in most Western cities. Cycling is efficient, low impact and healthy for everyone concerned (provided there is appropriate urban design). However, the bicycle is not an attractive option in most developed cities. Cycling is dangerous (one is at risk of being run over by a car) and unhealthy (one has to breathe in the fumes of motorized vehicles). With some notable exceptions – such as Amsterdam in the Netherlands, where the flat terrain facilitates cycling – developed countries have policies which inadvertently exclude the bicycle. We seldom give a high priority to ensuring a quality cycle infrastructure to support this personal travel option for local journeys.

The developed world has the choice to shift to people-centric urban design. This model leads to compact communities with ample shared space in which to build the community, and from which the car is largely excluded. I will explore this solution further, but first I want to look at the problems of car-centric urban design in the developing world.

The Developing World Following Behind

Many cities in the developing world are experiencing the same problems as they follow the developed world in adopting the car-centric model of urbanization. Policy makers push from the top down, seeking to improve the vehicle infrastructure. Those city residents who can now afford cars push from the bottom up, seeking better facilities for their vehicles.

The problems encountered are in some ways worse than in the developed world. The fleet of vehicles is less well maintained and more polluting. The road infrastructure lacks capacity so delays are longer and traffic gridlock a more regular occurrence. It is reported, for example, that weekday traffic speeds in Seoul and Shanghai average less than 9 km per hour.[8] Some cities are choked with vehicles from dawn to dusk, not just during the morning and evening rush hours. Many people cannot afford cars, so the number of people excluded from the spaces given over to the road network is greater than in the rich affluent world.

In looking to deal with these problems, it is easy to be drawn to the symptoms. We look for policies and investment to increase the capacity of the road network. We consider measures to improve the quality and maintenance of the vehicle fleet. We try to make car ownership and usage more affordable. In this way, countries in the developing world are striving to match the developed nations – to emulate their apparent success.

Few people advocate bouncing past the mistakes of the rich developed countries to develop cities which belong to people rather than cars.

Dealing with the Symptoms

Cities throughout the world are suffering from the effect of increasing car use. It is manifested in different ways in rich and poor countries, but the result is the same. Our cities and urban areas are less attractive places to live and work than they could be. We tackle the problem by addressing the symptoms. This is an instinctive first response deriving from the car culture which dominated the late 20th century.

To tackle the problem of delays and the excessive fuel consumption of urban journeys, we increase road capacity. To tackle the problem of pollution, we insist on emission standards leading to beneficial technical improvements, such as catalytic converters in car exhaust systems. In response to the poor fuel efficiency of our vehicles, we bring in differential taxation and place requirements on the car manufacturers to sell more efficient models. For the segment of the population who struggle to afford a car, manufacturers design smaller and cheaper models, and politicians court popular support by preventing fuel taxes and other charges from rising too high. This is especially true in poorer countries where those people who struggle to afford a car form a large section of the electorate.

To many people's thinking, this is the required (and only sensible) response. Within the narrow confines of the observed problems, this is logical. However, when these problems are examined carefully within the context of the environment and our desire to build sustainable cities, we see the negative long-term impact. We should move on from dealing with the symptoms to eliminating the causes, but the thinking required is more complex and the implementation is likely to be far more difficult.

Transport and Urban Design

People need to move about our cities. They require supplies of food and other consumables; they need a place of work and, of course, somewhere to live. There will be other reasons to travel, such as simple curiosity to see other places; but leaving those on one side, and defining the real need, provides a solid foundation to work with.

If we start from the cities we now have, our thinking leads to the concept of efficient mass-transit systems. It is clearly more efficient to transport one person than a person plus their car. However, I argue that this does not unwind our old 20th century thinking far enough. Instead of accepting the cities we now have, we should consider the cities we would like to have. The issue then becomes the migration from where we are now to where we want to be.

There is not a single concept of an ideal community. There are cultural and geographical differences and a range of workable models. I start with the assumption that we should aim at deliberately eliminating the car and penalizing car ownership. I do this to illustrate the effect and emphasize the point I make. When it comes to real-world policy formulation, it may be desirable for political reasons to make compromises. But, even so, the changes required will be dramatic. As the dangers of climate change become more apparent, and the fossil-fuel crunch drives up energy prices, we will be forced to act. Urban design is a slow process with long-term implications; we need to set policy early to start the process of change.

The ideal community is of a size which can be self-contained for most regular activities. It is small enough that all the services required, on a daily basis, are a walk or a cycle ride away. This should include shops, schools, leisure facilities and places of work. The people delivering the local services should also live within the community. Where the nature of the work requires a large workforce in one location, such as a factory or research facility, then the community should be designed around it. A support community consisting of houses, shops and leisure facilities should be close by, with all elements supporting one another.

It is natural for small town communities to be structured in this way. There is no reason why we cannot make our cities work in this way too. Our cities can be a tessellation of small self-contained communities linking together as one urban continuum, instead of areas with a single purpose, such as residential, retail or commercial.

A further progression of this model, which is interesting to note, is the way it can support urban agriculture. In open areas, or on roof tops, food can be grown for the residents. This is something many poor people in cities in the less developed world achieve, forced through circumstances to grow food where they can. But this is actually a very good model to adopt, through choice, to make best use of valuable open-to-sky space. In the developed world, concerns about the safety of vegetables and fruit grown under the influence of urban pollution will make this hard. But if we succeed in driving out the car – and the associated air pollution – then we can expect a resurgence in urban agriculture. Fresh local produce can be on sale in local shops – even in the world's largest, most affluent cities.

There will still be areas where certain specialist activities congregate. Despite broadband communications and teleconferencing, which reduce the need for face-to-face interaction, where regular personal interaction is required the close physical association of offices makes sense. There may also be clusters of similar retailers, where people can walk around comparing offers, and also clusters of complementary businesses. But even these specialist areas can keep their own support community of workers and services close by.

In this model, commuting – one of the greatest demands on a city's transport infrastructure – can be reduced. Instead of a daily migration of crowds of people from the suburbs into the city and back again in the evening, the flows of people can be much less. Instead of commercial areas being deserted spaces at night and at weekends, the whole city becomes a fully functioning and vibrant community. People will still need and want to be able to move around. We will need good transit systems, buses and taxis. Having removed any concept of a privately owned motorized vehicle as a necessity for general urban living, we have demoted the car to a more appropriate level in the hierarchy of society.

Driving the Car out of Urban Living

In the developed world in the early years of the 21st century, the car is viewed, almost universally, as a necessity. Our cities have evolved through the last century alongside the developments in cars. It is not until we make a conscious effort to redesign our cities around people that we understand that the car is, in many ways, an unnecessary intrusion.

Every time we consider policies to drive the car out of urban life we come up against the problem of unfairness. If we force up the cost of cars, and car use, then the poorer elements of society cannot afford them. If some people in a society are excluded from some activities, because they do not have a car and cannot travel to them, then this is unfair and is a political problem. If we take the converse approach, and exclude the car from many more places, this difficulty can be removed. A car-free urban policy does not need to be divisive once the car has become an unnecessary extravagance, and those who choose to indulge in owning one pay heavily for the privilege.

Let us first consider the land and space taken up by the car infrastructure. We tend to regard this as public land owned by the city for the general benefit of all, which we expect to remain as such into perpetuity and for which we require no financial return. This land is for vehicles and their drivers, with other residents excluded. It is not like a public park. We should charge road users a rent at full market rate. We should also raise taxes on transport fuel – as we will need to, in any case, to drive the world away from using fossil fuels.

Singapore, London and Oslo have all introduced congestion charges. This is a move in the right direction. In London, the congestion charge generates considerable revenue (£258 million annually[9]), which is then channelled into investment in public transport. These early schemes have also been useful in demonstrating, in a live system, that the technology for road charging works. The technology, such as digital cameras and roadside sensors, is robust, tested and its costs continue to fall. Every country has a car registration system which can be used to locate and charge the vehicle owner. More and more of the world's cities will find they can afford such systems.

Tax on parking spaces and garages is also easy to implement: the owners are easily identified, and there should be sanctions to ensure compliance. Driving up the cost of car ownership and usage is an easy task for the bureaucrats. Some countries will be more effective than others, some systems will be open to abuse, others tightly controlled. Despite the differences in implementation, it can be done. What is needed is the political will and majority public support.

Concerted action against the dominance of the car within our cities is required. Piecemeal policy focused on one area, such as pollution, safety or traffic congestion, has little chance of success. Such action could also lead to perverse outcomes, such as widening roads, taking yet more land from the community. There are challenges to be overcome in people's attitudes. People will resist measures which undermine their 'right' to have and use a car. We have to demonstrate that the results of these measures can lead to an improved city for the majority of its residents. It will require considerable upfront investment to start to build cohesive communities, and put in place the improved mass-transit infrastructure needed to connect them. City leaders in the developed world will find it hard to gain acceptance for the required changes. But we may find that policy makers in the developing world, if they recognize the shortcomings of the car-based urban model, bounce past the mistakes of the richer countries and show the world what the urban future should look like.

Striding Beyond the Mistakes of the Developed World

Telecommunications is a good example of the developing world missing out one of the stages which the developed world took in building its infrastructure. Through the last century, the richer nations built an extensive fixed-line communication network. This took a lot of effort and expense. It exists and we continue to use it. However, our engineers have now developed affordable mobile technology. Telecom providers in developing countries have realized that there is no need to copy the developed world. It is more cost-effective to bounce past this stage and go straight to a network consisting of base stations to serve mobile phones. Innovative charging models, with phones hired out for one call at a time, and phone-charging systems based on simple solar technology, make the technology affordable and accessible.

Power is another example. Many of the poorest countries have yet to build a network of power stations connected by a national grid. China, as it has developed, has copied the Western model and is building a new coal-fired power station almost every week. I argue that the model of a massive centralized power system is obsolescent.[10] In the coming era of fuel scarcity, and with growing pressure to act to bring climate change under control, we need a different system. Power systems based on localized supply, and making maximum use of renewable energy, is the next stage. The

West will be slow to accept the need for this policy reversal, and implementation will not be easy. It is hypocritical now for the West to urge China and other developing counties not to follow our development path. But as we, in the developed world, finally take the tough choices required to move on to this next stage in our development, the situation will change. The more enlightened policy makers in the developing world may be persuaded to miss out altogether the old industrial stage of power generation.

City design is another policy area where the developing world can stride past the mistakes of the West. The car-based city infrastructure model, which dominated 20th century cities, is not suitable for the 21st century. Cities in many developed countries will find the transition hard to make. The implications for infrastructure planning and design are colossal. There will be a long lead time between policy makers being persuaded and the delivery of substantive action. Policy makers for cities which have yet to build a massive car infrastructure have an opportunity to bypass this stage.

Cities which currently have a limited car infrastructure have the choice to focus policy on building a community-based model. It is likely that such cities have had low investment in the past and are already a patchwork of self-sufficient communities, arising from necessity. Effort should go into reinforcing this structure by making improvements – in clean water and sanitation for example – rather than following the example of the West and building the infrastructure required to support the car. The developing world has much of the expertise required in low technologies such as bicycles and rickshaws to show the developed world how it can be done. We should aim to make residents of cities in the rich world envious of the vibrant communities which the poorer nations can create, free from cars.

Learning from Informal Settlements

Informal settlements – such as the squatter camps of South Africa, villas miseria of Argentina or favelas of Brazil – arise as a natural consequence of people being drawn to cities but finding no place to live within the formal city structure. These informal settlements are not designed or planned, so they reflect humanity's basic needs rather than any imposed political or economic framework. They also suffer from a range of evident problems. One 'solution', tried by President Robert Mugabe in Zimbabwe in 2005, is to bulldoze such settlements so that the embarrassing problems are no longer visible. Obviously this could only form the basis of a solution if it were linked with specific action to rehouse the people displaced. Otherwise, another shanty town will arise spontaneously, on the original site or somewhere else. People need a place to live and a support community in order to survive.

If informal settlements are a natural model for human society, then we might want to build on the model rather than destroy it. I like Fred Pearce's article of 1992[11] on Rio de Janeiro's shanty towns which shows how such communities can develop. He describes the problems of Rosinha, a shanty town on the outskirts of Rio de Janeiro which is one of the largest shanty towns in South America, balanced with a positive view of living in such a community. In describing the community, he writes about walking along narrow 'streets' dodging wheelbarrows. This is the method the community has evolved for moving supplies. Fred Pearce makes the point that the lack of roads is a problem, in that the city's refuse trucks cannot gain access. But rather than jump to this conclusion, I would focus on the problem, which is the uncollected refuse (which is, of course, a serious health hazard). A solution that fits the context would be to organize refuse wheelbarrows to take the waste to a collection point – or direct to processing facilities, if these are nearby. The other part of Pearce's account which appeals to me is the single road to the centre used by a regular shuttle of buses. This would seem to be an ideal low-cost mass transit system.

My brief first-hand experience of observing life in shanty towns comes from Cameroon during the 1980s. I was there carrying out survey work and had a team of surveyors with me. I remember sitting in a 'restaurant' in one of the informal settlements surrounding the capital, Yaoundé. I suppose I have allowed my recollection of the drawbacks to fade, because my lasting memory is overwhelmingly positive. We arrived on foot; had a marvellous meal despite the ramshackle surroundings; and the whole bustling area was dominated by people, not cars.

I do not present shanty towns as the ideal model for the world's urban population. But we should recognize that the way they have evolved is a reflection of our humanity. In one sense they are a perfect model, because they have not been distorted by formal policy choices. We can then introduce formal policy that builds on our natural need for community life, focused on eliminating the negative aspects. Building community from the bottom up, within a policy framework that supports this approach, can lead to sustainable urban living.

The Challenge of Implementation

The concept of a car-free city is not new. These are the cities we had until the middle of the 20th century. It is also not hard to identify the policies needed to regain the car-free city. Joel Crawford, for example, describes a set of policies which could achieve a return to car-free cities.[12] The challenge is how to implement them across the range of the world's different societies.

All countries we classify as developed have car-centric city infrastructures to a greater or lesser extent. I keep returning to the United States for examples, because the commitment to the car is so profound. Whilst in Washington, DC, on business some years ago, I found that it was impossible to go for a run directly from my hotel at Tyson's Corner. Neither could I walk to the nearest shop or restaurant. There was no expectation that I might want to do this and no provision within the built environment to allow me do so, or to be able to do so safely. I was completely reliant on my hire car.

The United States has a high-capacity road network and cheap fuel. It is estimated that the average American commuter's journey takes 47 minutes by public transport but only 23 minutes by car.[13] There is little incentive for the American public to reduce their dependence on the car. This self-reinforcing cycle of high car dependency and high-quality provision will be hard to break.

The developing world will also find it difficult to loosen the stranglehold of the car. Karachi, for example, is probably the biggest city in the world without a rail network of any kind, and the buses are overloaded. Those who have the option of using a car take it.[14]

Top-down urban design must include integrated mass-transit systems that connect the city centre with a patchwork of urban communities (or villages). These should be of such a size and scale that making a journey within the community does not require a car. To travel between communities, there should be a mass-transit system with the capacity to cope. Having eliminated the 'need' to have a car, those people who would still like to use one – because they do not want to share transportation with other people, or for whatever reason – should be taxed heavily. This raises income to invest further in the mass-transit system. But there is another important benefit. If the smaller number of car drivers that remain are seen to be paying a disproportionately high price for the privilege, it should help to increase the political acceptability of the measures. But this will not work until we have sound alternatives to the car. So investment in the mass-transit systems will have to precede, or at least be in parallel with, driving up the cost of car use.

The other component of urban design required is support for building communities, led from the bottom up. As people, and the support functions upon which they rely, coalesce into urban villages this will eliminate many journeys altogether – particularly commuting. Such investment may well prove more cost-effective than investing in expansion to the mass-transit system.

Policy makers may be tempted to delay implementation in the expectation that during the 21st century we will learn to build cars that are better, cleaner, easier to recycle and which run on renewable fuels. I believe that this would be a mistake. The effect the car has had on urban design, in creating urban sprawl and taking land away from the community, is fundamentally negative. I am confident that our engineers can deliver zero-emission affordable cars. This would address the primary concern underlying this policy proposal: the environmental impact of the world's growing fleet of cars. But, on examination, the benefits of cities without cars seem so great that we should continue to exclude cars from everyday life even when cars become truly green.

The lack of potentially poisonous emissions will make it cheaper and easier to enclose our urban routes. During the course of the

21st century, I foresee the complete urban road network going underground. This will leave all our valuable open-to-sky space for other purposes. People, and people on bicycles, will be able to move around with ease; roofs and other open areas may support urban agriculture; any space not used will be covered with solar panels to capture renewable energy delivered direct to the point of use. Open-to-sky space is too valuable to allow cars to remain in possession of it – even the green models we will build in the future. There is, therefore, no excuse to delay the move away from car-centric city design.

Reclaiming Cites for People

If the whole world follows the path of the developed countries, and seeks to match current US levels of car ownership, then the global car fleet will be seven times larger than it is now.[15] This will put the global environment under enormous pressure. We need a new paradigm within which to craft policy that concentrates on the real needs of people, taking back the ownership of our cities from the car. As we escalate the costs of individual car usage, we can invest the receipts in improved mass-transportation systems for the population as a whole.

The conclusions I draw apply universally to all cities across the world. We should eliminate all subsidies for the use of cars, both direct and indirect, and drive up the costs of using cars in urban areas prohibitively high. This needs to be done carefully to ensure that we do not create an underclass of the car-less as we eliminate the concept of 'universal car ownership'. The changes required are immense and cover planning policy, taxation, incentives and restrictions. It will not be easy to flush out the ingrained aspiration of car ownership from our city dwellers around the globe, but, if we can, urban life will be so much richer and healthier as a result.

It is clear to me that the developed world should take back the ownership of our cities from the car. It will not be easy to gain acceptance for this policy. The car is so deeply ingrained in Western culture that we cannot easily be persuaded to part with it. Until we, in the developed world, admit to the negative influence of too many cars, we will not be able to start the process of changing our cities. Progress is delayed until this argument is won. Significant detrimental climate change and severe fuel shortages may finally persuade us.

Meanwhile, the developing world has the opportunity to learn from the mistakes of the developed nations and avoid becoming enslaved to a car culture. This is a choice only they can make. Advocates of car-free city living – who themselves live in cities of the West – seem like hypocrites when offering their views to the developing world. Whilst the West continues to fail to act, there is no moral authority to be taken seriously.

However, the message is clear, for all countries, both rich and poor. Cities must be designed for sustainable living in symbiosis with the surroundings. Above all, cities should be for people, not for cars.

17 Harness the Power of Community

Central to our humanity is the ability to build and maintain communities. This allows us to achieve far more than any of us could alone. Through social interaction we bring out the best in the individual for the common good. Within a community, resources are shared and cooperation takes place to deliver mutual benefit. When times are hard, we fall back on community for support, security and to share our concerns. It is unfortunate that, in our dash for economic development and expansion, we seem to have forgotten the importance of community.

When safety and security can be taken for granted, there is pleasure in escaping from the hustle and bustle of community life, to have the time to be alone. For example, a few years ago I spent two weeks with my family living in a small cottage on the edge of Lake Saima in southern Finland. We left the rest of society a long way away. We had no power or running water, but the lake water was so clean that we cooked with it. Using the dry toilet took a certain amount of courage, but it was hygienic and we could assure ourselves that it was completely natural. Heat for the sauna came from a wood-burning stove with a tank attached to make hot water. Drainage was through gaps between the floorboards down to the ground beneath. This was a simple life. During this wonderfully peaceful time we did not see another person except when we chose to visit the local town to replenish our supplies.

Our two-week holiday beside Lake Saima was an idyllic escape from the pace and pressure of the modern world. One evening after dinner we were sitting in the warm glow of the late evening sun listening to the natural sounds of the lake and the surrounding forest. I complained at the intrusive noise of the logging trucks on one of the forest roads. The loggers were working late and interrupting our peace. My wife got me to look at the map. The road in question was over 10 km away. It is not often in this modern world that escape is possible to such a place of utter peace that the noise of a truck from 10 km away seems like an intrusion.

On my own, I have been in many more remote and wild places. On such trips I have always felt secure because I can hide if I feel threatened, run fast if I have to, and if cornered can defend myself. With a young family it is different. We are potentially vulnerable. In our remote cottage we had no security, weapons or defences. However, at no point during those two weeks did I feel threatened or insecure. We could relax in total confidence that we were safe. Within a stable, prosperous country this is possible. In such situations, community does not seem to matter much, but the truth is that community matters very much indeed.

In a world where the structure of society starts to disintegrate, we will need strong communities in order to survive. Anyone living alone or in a small family group will be vulnerable. Those people with possessions and resources will be most at risk. An increasingly desperate and lawless population will want these resources and will be willing to fight to get them. We, too, will have to fight back to defend what we have.

To be sure of surviving we should ensure we live in, and are accepted by, a strong community. This must be large enough to defend itself but small enough that people feel they belong.

If society does collapse, we can build gated communities protected by a defended perimeter. To travel outside our home base we will need an armoured vehicle, guards and protection. This will allow us to travel from the safety of 'home' to another community with equally strong defences – if they agree to let us in. If you can afford it, joining such a community will be the best individual response to such a crisis. It is a depressing thought that the world is heading in the direction described. The dystopian society depicted in the film *Mad Max*[1] may come off the cinema screen and into our lives.

Falling back on community is a good defence in uncertain times. There is also a much more important role for community.

By harnessing the power of community, society can be strengthened and improved to the point where there is no need to live in small heavily defended enclaves.

Community Is . . .

Community is hard to define and no two communities are the same. Each of us is a member of a number of overlapping communities: family, work, hobby or sport, local and, of course, the biggest community of all, our country. For the purposes of this discussion, the focus is on physical communities, being careful not to focus on infrastructure. For this, we can have a top-down design and a formal plan. But communities are not designed in the same way as infrastructure. They are built from within. Communities grow, evolve and die subject to complex and hard-to-define interactions. The world has many different cultures, attitudes and religions, all of which influence the structure and dynamics of communities.

How a community is today reflects the historical path it has followed. Where the community goes in the future is affected by external factors, but the more powerful factors are the internal forces arising from people's desires, priorities and beliefs.

It is worth pausing to ask the question whether we would want all the world's communities to be clones of one international 'ideal' community template. This is where the strongest proponents of globalization would like to take us. To me, the answer is definitely 'no'. We should take pleasure in the variety of humankind and not seek to standardize our societies. This is not just romanticism. The world needs a variety of community models to ensure the health of global society, as I will go on to show.

Each community has its set of rules, expected behaviours, aims and priorities. These may be explicit, as in the laws that govern the conduct of the affairs of a country, or implicit, as in behavioural norms that have arisen without any formal process or written rules. The strength of a community is not determined by the formality of the rules. A state has considerable legislative power, but without the concept of 'nation' will struggle to work as a community. Conversely, most families do not need written guidelines to be a close supportive community.

The words that I choose to define an effective community are: allegiance, loyalty and commitment. Members offer allegiance to the group, loyalty to each other and commitment to working for the common good. There will be disputes and disagreements, as there always are; within a community these can be solved by compromise, acceptance and sacrifice. Members are willing to compromise to reach agreement, accept decisions taken and sacrifice personal benefit for the common good. In such communities, self-worth is defined by pride in one's place in the community and respect for others.

Community and Democracy

Where people in a community come together to make a decision, all aspects will be discussed and the wider impacts of possible solutions considered. There is a shared commitment to focus on community outcomes. The process will identify the solution that is acceptable to the majority of people. If there are strong community values, then decision making goes deeper than this, ensuring that no one is unfairly penalized.

Community-based decisions will not always lead to the 'best' solution, particularly where short-term negative effects have to be tolerated to deliver long-term outcomes. There is also the problem of slow process. This is where we have learnt to delegate community power to leaders who are then entrusted with making timely or unpopular decisions on the community's behalf. This is democracy.

The members of a democratic government are elected for a fixed term. Our representatives are given the power to make decisions on behalf of the community. The community will choose people that they believe will be good leaders and make sound decisions. The person elected is also aware that, as their term expires, they will be assessed on their actions. If they want to be re-elected they will have to make decisions for the community, not just to the benefit of their own group of cronies. People in power for a fixed term are also aware that they will still be living in the community when their time in power expires. There is, therefore, a very strong incentive to behave for the public good.

We believe democracy to be a good system, but this is only true if it is implemented by people who live by community values. We can have the process of representation, fixed terms in office and elections without leading to decisions that are good for society as a whole. Zimbabwe under Robert Mugabe is a case in point. Mugabe's Zimbabwe still has a democratic process but it has become a total sham. The world has to be vigilant that our democracies are true democracies in which community is put before self.

Western democracies are also far from perfect. For example, political elites may take control of the democratic process. These power brokers can have enormous influence over who is elected. Candidates that senior party officials want in power can be 'parachuted' into safe seats, even if they have very little connection with the area. Democracies will always be subject to such manipulation. The system relies upon people, and relationships between people. This is democracy's strength, and its weakness. Despite these shortcomings, democracy is the closest we can get to a political system based on community values.

Community as a Driver for Change

Inclusive community decision making is a good process that not only leads to sustainable policies but also makes implementation easier. A decision arrived at through the process of a genuine community dialogue is then owned by the community. It does not need to be sold, in the way that a top-down decision does.

The concept of using community dialogue to drive change can be taken a stage further. When a problem is encountered, instead of focusing on the problem, effort can be directed at mobilizing the relevant community. At the outset, the shape of a possible solution may not even be considered. The method relies on the community to generate a solution. This approach will not suit every problem but the method gives a useful insight into the power of community thinking.

Take a factory facing a crisis, for example. The workforce is complaining that wages are too low; the products made at the factory are not selling well; and the business is losing money. If nothing is done it will go out of business. In such a crisis, the owners may decide to close the factory down and cut their losses, getting what they can for the assets. Another approach is to activate the power of community thinking – if there is time.

Let us define the community as the owner(s), management, workers and customers. If the facility is a major local employer then local government might also be involved. If all these stakeholders can be connected in a community dialogue with everyone listening, contributing and willing to compromise, then favourable circumstances have been established to find a solution. The key to success would be to build a shared vision built on shared values. Achieve this and a solution – if one is possible – will fall out of the process.

Another example is a failing school. The school is running a financial deficit, pupils are achieving below-average results and parents are in open revolt against the head teacher. There are likely to be numerous corrective actions required. Community thinking would lead us to focus on building an effective dialogue between local government officials, teachers and parents. If trust has completely broken down, there may be no alternative to sacking the head teacher (deserved or not) in order to be able to restart the dialogue. Once the groups trust each other and develop a shared vision, there is every chance that a solution will emerge. It is in the self-interest of all parties to succeed.

Using communities as drivers of change can be highly effective, but we need to be aware of the destructive forces that work against community.

Destructive Forces

There are all sorts of reasons that communities suffer. We tend to cite lawlessness, unemployment and lack of facilities; but these are symptoms not causes. Dealing with symptoms leads us to increase police numbers, set up job-creation schemes and increase government social-support schemes. Such measures can be expected to make improvements, of course, but tackling causes is where the real long-term solution lies – if we can identify the causes correctly.

Before looking for the fundamental causes, it is worth noting a problem undermining modern democracy. The problem is that economics has been elevated to the status of a religion. It is heresy to question whether there might be values other than economic efficiency. If a decision is good for the economy, then it is regarded as the right decision, even if it results in negative impacts on communities. Instead of tying our politicians to measuring progress in economic terms, we should measure success by community outcomes. This lays a foundation for building sustainable communities.

The fundamental causes of community decline arise from three destructive forces: the pursuit of wealth, automation and lack of resources.

The Pursuit of Wealth – Reframe the Basis of Wealth

All of us aspire to wealth in one way or another. This is natural, normal and not to be despised. However, a narrow focus on material wealth is deeply damaging. Often what we really desire is relative wealth. We want to be seen to have more than others in our community. We want to own two cows rather than one; a two-bedroom apartment rather than a bedsit; a large detached house rather than a small semi. This soon gets out of hand in a spiral of conspicuous consumption. A swimming pool becomes a 'necessity' when others in your social group have one. When a private 9-hole golf course is no longer enough because the neighbour has a full 18-hole course, it is clear that our pursuit of wealth has gone too far.

When choosing a job, salary is a factor. When this is used as the prime factor, it leads us into ridiculous situations. 'I don't like the job but it pays the mortgage,' is often heard. It would be sad if this is the only positive comment we can make about our employment. It is not unusual to come across people with a large house, large mortgage and large salary who are deeply unhappy.

When employers take on staff, high salary can be used to attract the best candidates. The people employed then stay until another company makes them a better cash offer. It is not unusual to find employers who pay high salaries and suffer from high staff turnover.

Society works so much better if we give money a lower priority. Cash is a useful tool to grease the wheels of commerce and provide a mechanism to purchase the resources we require. But that is all it is. Jobs should be chosen on the basis of interest, challenge, satisfaction and sense of community. Jobs should be offered on the same basis. Companies can get loyal employees for less than the market rate and employees can find a 'home' where they feel valued, appreciated and supported. Salary becomes a base requirement, and an administrative detail, rather than a prime driving factor. This is a two-way street. Employers and employees have to behave differently. Companies have to become like communities. There are very successful examples, such as the John Lewis Partnership in the UK.[2] This should be the norm rather than the exception.

The wealth that I desire is health, family, friends and money – in that order. If everyone were to reframe the basis of wealth in this way, the pursuit of wealth can become a force for good in building community.

Automation – Make It Our Slave

Society is fast approaching the point in human progress when we can automate anything and everything. We do not even need to copulate to have children: scientists with test tubes can do it for us. Replace the scientist by a robot, and then that most basic of human functions will be completely automated. The role of men in reproduction becomes irrelevant. Technology has to develop further before women too can be eliminated. It is just a matter of time. We can be sure the technologies will be developed to grow embryos to babies inside machines.

Current thinking is that if a machine can do a job, then the job should be given to a machine. This is making society run ever more efficiently. We need less people for the same set of activities. This causes slack in the labour market, so we increase consumption to compensate. Ultimately, when we have automated everything, further increases in consumption will require more robots and more resources sucked out of the planet, but no more jobs. It is unsustainable to counter unemployment caused by automation by increasing consumption.

In the West, the concept that automation is good is deeply ingrained. I had a discussion with a business-school colleague who is concerned at the plight of people in the poorer countries, and highly committed to improving their lot. He spoke out against a scheme to provide treadmill water pumps to poor rural communities. These were designed to replace diesel pumps – an obvious environmental benefit. They also allowed fathers to stay at home on the land with their families, rather than move to the cities to look for work in order to be able to pay for the fuel. There is considerable evidence of the positive effect they have on rural communities.[3] However, my well-meaning colleague argued that it is demeaning to ask a person to do a job that could be done by a machine. If we take this as a principle in developing policy, we will box ourselves into a corner from which there is no escape.

Reducing the head count is often the basis of the business case for investing in machinery and IT. The opposite thought process, of investing in employing more people to make savings in capital investment, is alien to most managers. It will take some time to win converts away from the blind faith we have in the god of automation. The option to employ people to replace automation should be equally valid as alternative courses of action are compared.

In the developed world, more and more activities are being automated: cash machines instead of bank clerks; ticket machines in place of staffed ticket offices; vending machines in place of the company tea lady. We can go much further. For example, RFID[4] tags are a step beyond bar-codes. They can be read automatically by sensors in close proximity even when hidden from view. As the price of RFID tags continues to reduce, it will become cost-effective to attach one to almost every item sold. The process of paying for your shopping can then be completely automated. All we will have to do is fill up the shopping trolley and wheel it past automatic sensors. Pay desk and check-out staff will become obsolete. It is not just manual labour that can be axed. As IT systems become more advanced, the bulk of the work of doctors, lawyers and other professionals can be replaced by computers and robots.

Automation is taking away regular close human interaction. It will become possible to live without needing to engage with another human being. Already there are examples of people dying in their homes with the automated world carrying on around their dead body for years.[5] Pension paid automatically, bills paid by direct debit, post piling up and no one noticing – until someone is offended by the bad smell emanating from the home on hot summer days.[6]

We are at a very fortunate stage in human development, being able to use technology in a myriad of ways. This brings with it new responsibilities. We must not allow automation to take over and destroy the cohesion of society.

In many areas of business, government and service industries there has been a strong focus on automation to eliminate people and jobs. To turn this thinking around, we need to realize that we can automate almost anything. Automation is no longer special. Automation is a commodity; we can use it in any way we choose. If we want something automated, the technology can deliver.

Once we regard automation as a commodity, we can turn our attention to the more important task of building community. It should be quite normal for people to do tasks that could be done by machine. We inflict repetitive physical activity on ourselves when we go to the gym, to jog on a treadmill or ride a static exercise bike. We do this because it is good for us and we feel better afterwards. Some of us enjoy the mental relaxation that comes with such activity. There is no need to use automation to design physical activity out of our lives. This means being selective in what we automate and how we implement automation. The aim becomes to design society in a way that engages all its members in useful and enjoyable activity. Building a strong community in this way is more important and challenging than the simple process of delivering automation.

Shortage of Resources – Sharing Instead of Fighting

When there is a shortage of resources, people retreat into defensive mode. The behaviour is instinctive. Such hardship can reinforce the tight community to which we belong, as people need to rely on each other. However, it can also be damaging in that we will fight other communities to protect the resources that our community needs.

The threat to resources does not even need to be real to activate the instinctive human defensive response. A rumour that something may be in short supply is enough to set off panic buying. On average, each car is driven around with its fuel tank half full. If everyone decides to keep their tanks full then there is a huge spike in demand to fill this capacity. In 2005, in the UK, a rumour circulated that blockades were being planned similar to those that had caused the fuel crisis of 2000. Three thousand petrol stations were emptied even though the rumour turned out to be false. I remember an interview with one driver who had queued for more than an hour and then could only squeeze two litres into an already very full tank. Such irrational behaviour is part of the human condition.

Another example is the severe shortage of basmati rice that occurred in the United States in April 2008. Rumours of shortages set off panic buying and emptied the shelves in stores across the country. Despite assurances from the stores that supplies were coming through as normal, each person was protecting their position by buying a stockpile. For each individual, this is a reasonable response. For society as a whole, such behaviour is a problem.

Shortages caused by panic buying are mere inconveniences. When the shortages of resources are real, and threaten the basis of survival, then our defensive mode has no bounds. People retreat back into family and tribe to defend their resource base. Graphic illustrations of this come on our television screens from the Darfur region of Somalia. People are fighting other tribes and ethnic groups over a diminishing resource base. In Darfur there are also other factors at work, but there is no hiding the uncomfortable truth that humans will kill each other to defend their own survival.

In Europe we have a secure and affluent society (despite economic ups and downs). People are content to allow the European Commission to spend money to improve the circumstances of the newer and poorer members. If Europe were to descend into a severe and prolonged depression with a shortage of fundamental resources such as food and fuel, then the cohesion of the EU would be put at risk. Nationalistic tendencies would come to the fore as each country sought to secure the resources it needs.

The severity of conflict will correlate with the severity of the resource squeeze. When shortages result in inconvenience, people will complain vocally and loudly. When survival is put at risk in a very cold winter or when food starts to run low, this will erupt into violence. We will kill, if this is the only way to feed our children. That is our nature.

Relying on an open global market in which demand outstrips supply is dangerous. When the world has been stripped bare, there will be no more capacity to exploit. The crunch will come sooner. As people start to worry that soon there will not be enough, they will start to hoard resources rather than allow exports. There will be an unseemly scramble to control the world's resources that remain. The prospect of a conflict over resources is already influencing the behaviour of some countries. China, for example, is seeking to strengthen alliances with resource-rich countries to provide the commodities it needs to support its continued development. The global struggle for resources has begun.

Over-consuming the world's resources is leading us towards destroying society. Learning to live within the resources available is how we will rebuild safe and strong communities. The defensive human mechanism to control and safeguard the resources we need becomes a virtue when it leads to careful husbandry and sharing resources in a sustainable manner within our community.

Unless we learn to understand the forces that undermine community, we are entering a very dangerous period. There is a very good way to test the strength of your support community. Imagine that all your physical possessions have been taken from you. All the investments you have made are now worthless. Your bank has folded without paying compensation. You are completely and totally bankrupt. The question to ask is, what have you now got left? If the answer is 'nothing', then this is a deeply sad situation. A rich and powerful person in today's world, who has built an empire without building a circle of true friends and supporters, may well be in this category. However, someone, rich or poor, who has contributed to the community by being a good team player will find a strong community of people who will rally around to help.

Putting Community First

It is obvious that community is important and that building community is effective in improving society. It is less clear, but equally true, that the way modern society has been run in recent decades has undermined community values. This is the unintended consequence of adopting a narrow economic focus. This is effective economics, but it has left politicians to deal with the resulting problems that afflict communities. We need to turn this around by recognizing the limitations of economics.

Economics alone is a sterile subject; powerful and effective but without soul. Economics is only brought alive when used to deliver social outcomes that improve society and enhance our lives. Economics has to be demoted from master to servant.

Putting community first is the way to refocus our efforts, and is the fundamental basis on which to build a sustainable society. The aim should be to deliver social outcomes whilst reinforcing the integrity of the environment, using the power of economic tools to do so. Decisions taken by communities naturally fit this way of thinking.

The concept of 'community first' has more resonance with the small-scale structures of society. For example, within a family the willingness to act for the common good is almost boundless (or should be). Small communities in which people know each other can work in a similar way. Rising up through the administrative levels of society, interaction becomes more impersonal and collective ownership of decisions harder to achieve. This leads to the principle of subsidiarity (power should be exercised by the smallest or least central unit of government).

There are limits to subsidiarity, of course. A patchwork of small communities, each free and independent, would lead to a number of problems and inefficiencies. Coordination is required at higher levels, being careful to take control of only those issues that are dealt with better at that level. This is where linking social provision, the environment and the economy is not automatic. Cross-function connections are required and these are often lacking. It is a complex challenge for governments to learn to think sustainably.

The state has ultimate responsibility for the sustainability of its society. The state also has the most capability, with the power to set and enforce fundamental rules and regulations. A strong state can also draw upon national identity and national pride to gain acceptance for the measures required. By 'strong' I am not referring to military power or economic performance. I mean a country that works as a community, with a society held together by a shared vision and shared values.

States that are merely a legal structure containing different nations do not work as strong communities. This is where a federal structure which gives considerable autonomy can strengthen a state by reintroducing community behaviours. The former Yugoslavia is an example where state and nationhood did not coincide. Yugoslavia worked, because of the vision of Ataturk. After his death, when the vision started to fade, it was only a matter of time before each nation reasserted itself. It is a shame that so much blood had to be shed to reimpose the natural order. Slovenia, Macedonia, Croatia, Serbia and Montenegro and Bosnia are now nation states with control of their own affairs, and with stronger communities as a result. The problem now is how to live in peace with the neighbouring communities.

To achieve world peace and security, we need global institutions such as the UN Security Council and the International Court of Justice (ICJ). Such organizations are vital but limited in scope. This is quite right. According to the principle of subsidiarity, we should only control at world level that which is best dealt with at world level.

At world level, the concept of loyalty or commitment to a global tribe is non-existent. This means that the power of community thinking does not operate at global level. It is important to realize this and recognize the primacy of the nation state in world-level affairs. People identify with their nation and are willing to accept restrictions and constraints for the sake of the nation to an extent that they will not accept when asked to make sacrifices for the sake of the world community.

Efforts are being made to reinforce regional communities such as the EU. As a cooperation of loosely coupled nation states, the

EU works. The extent to which a sense of European identity can be developed for closer ties is doubtful. Loyalty to Europe is soon overridden by national loyalty when compromise is required for decisions that benefit Europe as a whole.

When international leaders negotiate, it is hard to reach agreements that benefit the world community as a whole. Countries find it hard to accept constraints and limitations for the good of humanity. Countries send negotiators with the brief to achieve the best outcome for the country's national interest. It is rare that any politician would willingly give ground for the sake of the world without winning a corresponding concession.

The lack of community thinking at world level is dangerous – particularly when global capitalism is allowed free rein.

Capitalism and Community

Capitalism has proved to be a most effective economic system. It provides an unbiased economic mechanism to allocate resources efficiently. However, capitalist thinking leads to commitment, loyalty and allegiance to self. Own interest will always win out. Self-worth is defined by ownership and property. Capitalism is not the problem. Capitalism disconnected from community is.

More than 200 years ago, Adam Smith provided the fundamental foundations of capitalism.[7] He wrote 'It is the maxim of every prudent master of a family, never to attempt to make at home what it will cost him more to make than to buy . . .'. He wrote these words from within a society built on community. He could not have foreseen that his ideas on the division of labour would become disconnected from the community values that to him where second nature.

The most enthusiastic proponent of capitalism is the United States. Even so, the internal politics of the United States take community into account. Despite a strong economic focus, domestic decisions by the US government have to balance social, environmental and economic issues. The problem arises on the world stage, where the United States unashamedly behaves to suit its own national interests. When the United States champions capitalist mechanisms such as free trade and the liberalization of capital markets, it does so to the extent that the United States will benefit. I do not believe that the United States is wilfully deceiving the world. The US attitude is to allow capitalism free rein. Within the United States there is the balancing force of the electorate, forcing politicians to think beyond the economy. At world level such forces for restraint are very weak.

It could be argued that global organizations such as the UN, International Monetary Fund (IMF) and World Trade Organization (WTO) are the true representatives of the global community. These organizations have vital roles but they do not have the power that national governments have. They also do not have the support of a global tribe. Improving the operation of the UN and other global organizations is important, but we should not expect to be able to build a strong and committed world community.

The Myth of a Global Village

Communications have connected the globe as never before. Everyone is only a click away from one another, whether down the street or on the other side of the Earth. Capital flows are simply a string of numbers passed over the Internet. Huge sums can be transferred almost instantaneously. Business puts together supply chains that reach around the globe, matching cheapest production with the most lucrative markets. International teams come together in cyberspace to deliver global solutions. Global call centres and help desks are formed by linking offices in the United States, Europe and Asia so that someone is always in the office to provide 24-hour cover.

The world has a huge range and variety of community values. Economic globalization has tended to ignore these. Without the checks and balances of a true world community, naked capitalism has been allowed to take hold. Globalization has brought economic benefit to many places and countries in the short term, but the negative consequences are starting to show through. Populations are being exploited and the environment is being put under increased pressure. The failure of globalization is its role in disconnecting economics from community.

Some people, such as the economist Joseph Stiglitz,[8] argue that world-level decision making has to become orientated towards thinking of the world as one community. Certainly better cross-functional coordination is required. For example, WTO rules can prevent countries acting to protect the environment. The WTO and the United Nations Environment Programme (UNEP) need much closer alignment. I support this view strongly, but I do not believe that one globalized world community is feasible, or desirable. We need a minimum of global rules covering only those things that need world policy, such as protection of the shared resources of the oceans and atmosphere, and key elements of a fundamental charter of human rights.

A world that came together as one community with a shared vision and shared values would be a dangerous world. This is counter-intuitive. Such a world should, in theory, be able to resolve any and all disputes. The problem would be that any flaw or fault in such a world community would be amplified right across the globe. For example, a high-consumption lifestyle adopted by every country and every person would destroy the planet. It would also be dangerous not to have alternative models of society to observe and copy (or avoid). Each way to run society has its day. As it runs out of steam, we need alternatives to borrow, improve and implement.

Variety in society is both a pleasure and a source of security and stability (from a world perspective). There will, of course, be misalignments and conflicts between societies. These small disputes will act as a safety valve, diffusing tension as each society takes pride in, and ownership of, its vision and values. Each country will influence the other, borrowing good attributes and observing weaknesses to avoid. The most dangerous conflict arises when self-determination is taken away and external values are imposed on a society. This is, of course, resisted and risks destabilizing the country as people feel they do not have the power to control their own destiny. Terrorism is likely to be the result.

The United States, in particular, is slow to appreciate that a world in its own image is a dangerous aspiration. The United States is a beacon of democracy and freedom. There is also much to admire about American capabilities and the country's implementation of capitalism. But the US model is not the model to impose on the world. The United States might do better to look at the strengths of other cultures in Europe and elsewhere to make its own society better than it is. But it is quite right that Americans will fiercely defend their right to decide this for themselves. The United States should not be surprised when other nations do the same.

The importance of community has been submerged as the world has embraced global capitalism. We need to redress this imbalance in order to concentrate on harnessing the power of community to build a better global society. A sustainable world will consist of communities taking control. Balancing social, environmental and economic issues will then come naturally.

There is one area where communities will want to take close control. This is agriculture. People want to be sure that they have enough food to eat, and that the food is safe. This will be hard in a period of soaring demand for other agricultural outputs such as biofuel.

18 No Compromise over Food

Food is fundamental to survival and food production is one of the most important activities we undertake. It is odd that industrial processes have been allowed to take over in an area that is so vital to human health. Regarding agriculture as merely another industry, to be run on commercial lines, is undermining the Earth's ecosystem. The time has come to stop sacrificing the health of us, and the planet, for the sake of economic efficiency. We must speak out to insist on safe food and a sustainable system of agriculture.

To be reading this book you must have sufficient supplies of food. Otherwise, you would be out foraging for food. When we are hungry, our inbuilt instinct is to concentrate on the search for food. When food supplies are secure, we have time for higher pursuits. We look forward to the pleasure of a delicious meal, in good company, but it is entertainment and pleasure we seek, not nutrition and calories.

Imagine that you are destitute, with no money and all your credit cards cancelled. Food would then matter an awful lot. We might start by sneaking into a neighbour's garden or nearby allotments to scrump fruit from the trees, or dig out a carrot or two. Those of us with a bit more know-how might set a snare to catch a rabbit. Once caught, it could be roasted over an open camp fire. Such food would be fresh and nutritious. Being penniless could turn out to be a rather healthy option. Fresh food in moderate quantities is what we all need.

Impoverishment for city dwellers may mean scavenging around the rubbish bins, looking for morsels of discarded food. The rubbish bins of a good restaurant (if they are emptied daily) would be a good place to start. The peelings, offcuts and half-eaten portions should be of high quality. This is a stomach-churning thought. Of course, it would be better to be able to afford the smart packaged foods available in supermarkets – or so we think. If you could see what goes into many sausages, you would far rather eat barbequed rabbit or second-hand food from a top-class restaurant.

Within the industrial food system, the focus of effort is on packaging, marketing and looks. There is an assumption that regulations ensure food safety, but the current system is loaded with incentives to bend the rules. For example, meat condemned for human consumption is cheap. It is tempting to divert such meat back into the supply chain. After a rinse and cutting out of any evidence of bad or stained meat, it can be repackaged and sold on. This is illegal, of course, but the profits are huge. From 1993–6, a multimillion-pound operation sold 1,300 tonnes of condemned meat to butchers, supermarkets and restaurants across the UK.[1] In 2000, those responsible were caught and prosecuted, but there may be many more that are never caught.[2]

When food is an industrial commodity for remote faceless consumers, such gross activities are inevitable. There is no one in the supply chain who will have to suffer eating the product, or meet those who do, so there is no natural oversight. Reliance is placed on regulations enforced by inspectors. But inspectors are fallible and cannot be everywhere. Shifting to a transparent sustainable system based on short supply chains is inherently safe and requires very little oversight from officialdom.

The Food Crisis

During 2008, world food prices rocketed. Wheat doubled in price; maize was 50% and rice 20% more expensive.

The demand for biofuel was quoted as one reason. Up to one third of US maize in 2008 went for ethanol production. This pushed prices up, so that a bowl of cornflakes in the morning cost 10c more than the year before. Such price rises are cause for discussion in the United States but no one feels the need to panic. The United States produces far more corn than it needs for its own food requirements. From the US perspective, diverting this surplus corn into biofuel is entirely reasonable.

Withdrawing so much maize from the world market had the knock-on effect of making the world's poorest people hungrier. Americans were accused of continuing their love affair with the car on the back of the poorest nations. No matter how unfair the accusation, this was the impression given by US policy. The EU was no better. Its biofuel targets reduced EU exports of staple foods onto the world market.

It is not just the demand for biofuel that is putting agriculture under pressure. As poorer countries develop, and families have more wealth, they aspire to a richer diet. Instead of being vegetarians by force of circumstance, they now want to eat meat. This linkage between affluence and increased food consumption is far more profound than a desire for improved diet. Some populations are going from subsisting on a meagre diet short in nutrients to suffering the problems of obesity in one generation.[3]

The food crisis will not be solved early or quickly. The UN predicts high world food prices for at least the next decade.[4] The world response to the crisis is logical, predictable and deeply flawed. The declaration made at the end of the UN Conference on World Food Security held in Rome, June 2008, shows how the world is thinking. On the face of it, it seems sound policy.

> *We firmly resolve to use all means to alleviate the suffering caused by the current crisis to stimulate food production and to increase investment in agriculture, to address obstacles to food access and to use the planet's resources sustainably, for present and future generations. We commit to eliminating hunger and to securing food for all today and tomorrow.*[5]

Of course, this is what we must do, but many policy makers have trouble understanding the word 'sustainably'. Those that do understand sustainable agriculture struggle to be heard.

Within the declaration, it is stated explicitly that 'We encourage the international community to continue its efforts in liberalizing international trade in agriculture by reducing trade barriers and market distorting policies.' This is presented as a cornerstone of agricultural policy at world level. This leads us to avoid questioning whether it is the thinking needed for a sustainable world. I argue that, although liberalizing world trade is good economics, it undermines the ability of the world to feed itself into the long future. We are sacrificing the concept of self-sufficiency of food supplies on the altar of improved economic efficiency.

The discussions that followed through the second half of 2008 concentrated on the logic of increasing food production. The measures discussed included increased use of fertilizer, more irrigation, investment in more mechanization and the potential role of genetically modified (GM) crops. Proponents of GM crops were delighted. The food crisis helped them to argue their case. The world needs the food; let's stop worrying about the dangers and push ahead.

The focus on increasing output also leads to bringing non-productive land into cultivation. In the search for maximum efficiency, hedgerows are being ripped out to increase the area of fields, transforming the countryside into huge fields of monoculture tended entirely by machines. The limited amount of biodiversity that still remains in the developed world is being squeezed out of the way.

In the developing world, the logical response to the need to produce more food is to clear virgin forest for agriculture. For the health of the planet, it is vital that these forests are saved, but in a country where the population is hungry, growing food will always be the priority. This fact is used to justify further industrialization of farming to wring the maximum possible output from the agricultural land we already have. It is important to realize that this will never be enough whilst we ignore the issue of self-sufficiency. In fact, industrialization of farming is a major cause of the problems we face now. Over many years, the industrial farm lobby of Western countries has won subsidies to be able to dump excess capacity onto the world market, undermining agriculture and self-sufficiency in many poorer countries.

The world's response to the 2008 food crisis was based on the industrial view that has been allowed to dominate agricultural policy. It is hard to argue against such logic until you realize that the flaw lies in the basis of the thought processes. Agriculture is not just another industrial process operating in isolation. Agriculture is an integral part of our ecosystem. Improvements must be made with this in mind, or we will find that our logical response is the wrong response. The thinking that has brought us to the current food crisis is not the thinking that will find the solution. We must start again, and look at agricultural issues in a different way.

Define the Problem

Before looking for solutions, let us define the problem underlying the food crisis. It is not a lack of food we face but an imbalance between supply and demand. Put simply, we have two choices: to increase supply or reduce demand. It would be sensible to look at both.

Controlling the human population is one obvious measure as discussed in Chapter 12. Two centuries back, a world of one billion was easier to feed than the six billion we have now, which in turn will be easier to feed than the projected nine billion mouths by 2050.[6] The food crisis demonstrates the urgency of finding an acceptable control mechanism for human population. Connecting people with the carrying capacity of their locality is one of the key factors. This applies to land, energy, water and, of course, food.

Implementing a connection between the world population and agricultural capacity is not simple. To balance one with the other, we have to consider lifestyle, food choices and availability. There might be enough food, but in the wrong place. There might be enough food, if only people ate less. There might be enough food, if we did not allocate agricultural land to biofuel. The arguments soon get wrapped around each other in a mess of conflicting priorities that becomes impossible to untangle. The problem is that we are looking for something that does not exist. In our globalized world there is no self-regulating mechanism between hunger and food capacity – except the coarse mechanism of price, and on its own price is not an effective policy.

If we rely on an open global market to feed us, the relatively rich will always have enough food to eat. Food can double or triple in price without causing starvation in the developed world. We can reduce consumption and eat meat less often. For the world's very poor, who spend a high proportion of a small income on the minimum staple diet to survive, rising world food prices cause real hardship.

Sustainable agriculture requires a connection between supply and demand. This has to be at a local or regional level because it gives people confidence that there will be continuation of supply. It also helps to constrain choices people make over family size when an area's agricultural capacity is running close to its limits. There is also direct feedback from the consequences of driving for more capacity, such as water stress brought on by excessive irrigation or pollution caused by the inappropriate use of fertilizer.

Not all agriculture has to be localized. There are long-life staple food items that can be produced anywhere and stored, shipped and consumed at some time in the future. But we need to be careful: becoming over-reliant on such supplies undermines the sustainability of world agriculture. It would be better if local communities, countries or regions maintained their own stockpiles of long-life food (such as grain and maize) to deal with fluctuations in crop yields that will always occur from year to year. Such local planning is far better than reliance on the vagaries of a poorly regulated world market.

Sustainable agriculture requires that food is grown or reared close to the consumer. This provides transparency in production and an inherent guarantee of quality. Local food also minimizes food miles, thereby reducing the carbon footprint of agriculture. The most important aspect of a local food policy is that it connects a population with its resource base.

It is useful to look back at the problems of the 2008 food crisis from a different perspective. The problem is not US and EU policy which diverted agricultural capacity to biofuel. The problem goes back further than this policy shift. The problem is the subsidized exports from the industrialized agriculture of the developed world. These exports have been undermining agricultural self-sufficiency elsewhere in the world for a decade or more. When the developed world pulls these subsidized supplies off the market, over the long term there will be a return to more sustainable agriculture. Over the short term, the world has a crisis.

The developed world has been wrong to protect its farmers by dumping excess food on to the world market, depressing prices and encouraging countries to live beyond their agricultural capacity. We should be very sensitive to the needs of countries that can no longer feed their populations from their own resources due to our mistaken policy. Countries should be helped to become self-sufficient in food once more.

Policy makers in the major industrialized countries do not intend to undermine the agriculture of other countries, but their narrow economic focus often means that they do. Markets are forced open, destroying the delicate balance of poorer countries' rural economies. If countries have a sustainable, but inefficient, agricultural sector (viewed from a capitalist perspective), we should not undermine it. Sustainability is more important than industrial efficiency. It would be far safer for our world if many countries chose a low-impact agrarian society. Those that do make this choice should be helped, not forced to change.

Let us look afresh at agriculture from a new perspective.

Food Is . . .

Food is necessary to survive but it would be a sad world if this dominated our decisions. This would lead to working out what are the most nutritious foods that can be grown the most easily, and consumed in the smallest quantities required to sustain human life.

These are the calculations that are used in industrial-scale farming to feed battery hens or penned pigs. Keeping the animal immobile is another way of ensuring that calories are not wasted running about. This highly economic thinking is how the business of farming fattens up stock for the abattoir at the least possible cost. The same sort of calculations could be used to maximize the size of the human population. Maize porridge or boiled potatoes supplemented by a daily vitamin pill should be enough to keep each of us alive.

A world with a ballooning human population, in which each person is allowed only the minimum ration of food to survive, is not a pleasant prospect. Food should be a pleasure. Taking time to eat good food with friends and family is one of the most enjoyable pursuits in life. Destroying this aspect of our civilization just to be able to have yet more people crowded on to planet Earth makes no sense.

At the other extreme, many people in the developed world have taken the joy of food too far. Over 30% of adults in the developed world are obese. The World Health Organization estimates that in Europe there will be 150 million obese adults and 15 million obese children by 2010.[7] It is hard to believe that people choose to be obese. There is something about modern society that is leading people in a direction they do not want to go. The role that bad diet plays in illnesses such as diabetes, heart disease and cancer is understood – but people seem to take little notice. The positive benefits of a good diet are also understood, but not many people go out of their way to get the freshest and best ingredients. It is not just that people are being lazy or complacent about their health; we have set up a food system that is inherently unhealthy. It takes considerable extra effort and expense to eat a healthy diet. The current system should be replaced by one in which the affordable default option is to eat healthily. One thing that prevents this is that food is regarded as just another commodity.

The Danger of Food as a Commodity

In dealing with agriculture as a commodity business, decisions are taken on purely economic grounds. The assumption is that consumers make their choice based on price. For the producer, cost is the deciding factor in all aspects of production to ensure that the product is produced at the lowest possible cost. For the supply chain from producer to customer, price is again the key factor. This is a simple economic model and the basis of the world market.

Such a commoditized market works well for substances such as salt and sugar. These are long lasting, and easily stored and shipped. Despite concern at their high levels in many processed foods, salt and sugar are simple, pure substances. It should matter little where they are produced. It will have the same healthy (or unhealthy) properties regardless of the place of origin. The only danger would be contamination with other substances and this should be easy to test. It does not matter where sugar and salt enter the market and there is no need to be concerned about its origins.

Applying raw economics to other agricultural products does not work so well. Take the market for beef, for example. This is a high-value product with correspondingly high profit potential. Transportation and storage requires refrigeration, which is expensive, but with a high value-to-weight ratio this is a manageable overhead. It is economically viable to shift consignments of frozen beef across continents and across the world. The world market in beef works – in economic terms.

Looking beyond the economics, there are other factors to consider. One drawback is that beef requires a much larger area of land to rear each tonne than to produce protein from other sources, such as soya beans. There are also concerns that red meat in large quantities is bad for the health. Beef should therefore be consumed in moderation, but small amounts of beef are good for us. Cattle are herbivores and, provided their pastures are not polluted, the meat is a healthy food. It is a good source of both iron and high-grade protein.

In the global beef market, we put our trust in each link of the global supply chain. It starts with the farmer, but he/she has no direct link with, or responsibility to, the end consumer. The farmer wants the best price for the cattle by whatever means the market allows. An example is the use of antibiotic drugs. These have been found to increase growth rates so are added to cattle feed. The increasing human resistance to these therapeutic drugs does not directly affect the farmer or the local community, so no one cares enough to stop it. The animals enter an industrial system of factories and middlemen. At the other end, the consumer buys a pack of meat off the shelves of the supermarket knowing little about the route it has taken. At each stage, people are thinking about maximizing their share of the profit.

In looking for efficiency, farmers have taken cattle off the free range and into feeding lots. Fodder is selected to provide rapid weight gain. It has been found that high-protein cattle feed made from grinding up the remains of other animals fattens cattle well. This process has gone further, to the extent that the remains of cattle are fed back to cattle. We have converted a herbivore into a cannibal, all in the name of industrial efficiency. This was allowed by inspectors because there was no proof that this was bad for people's health – until BSE.

The exact origins of Bovine Spongiform Encephalopathy (BSE) are unclear. Some research has explored the theory that it originated in man and then crossed into cattle. One hypothesis is particularly gruesome and suggests that human remains of victims of Creutzfeldt-Jakob disease (CJD) ended up in cattle feed.[8] Another theory, which has more support but is no less appalling, is that the remains of sheep carcasses infected with scrapie (a closely related disease) were fed into the animal-feed production process. We know as fact that once BSE appeared in cattle, infected animals were themselves reprocessed into animal feed before regulations were tightened.

The prion that causes BSE is tough and resilient. A high temperature is needed to kill it. I find it worrying that much comment and analysis has been directed at the temperatures used in the process of making cattle feed. The implicit understanding is that processing animal carcasses into animal feed is an acceptable practice, provided the temperatures used are high enough. The specific concerns about BSE have been countered. There is no proof that continuing to feed animal remains to cattle is dangerous, so the industrial machinery of modern agriculture continues as before. Common sense would say we should ban all mammalian tissues in animal feed. It is foolish that we don't.

Regarding beef as a commodity means that beef is produced as cheaply as possible. This is not a fail-safe system. There is always the temptation to push hard against the limits provided by the regulations – and beyond, when inspectors are not on site.

Safe, healthy beef is for sale. There are farmers who raise cattle on open grass pastures and the animals are bought by butchers who select their meat with care. Such beef is hard to find and more expensive. If we change the system so that we don't compromise over food (as I will go on to explain), beef can be healthy and safe by default.

Vegetables are another example. We have come to expect our supermarket shelves to be well stocked with a wide range of fresh produce throughout the year. To achieve this, supermarkets purchase from around the world. The fruit or vegetables are picked raw so that they appear ripe when they reach the point of sale. The nutritional value of such 'old' fruit and vegetables is impaired compared with truly fresh items.

To get our vegetables to look just right, and pass the visual inspection by buyers, may require the use of pesticides to ensure that bugs do not leave unsightly nibble marks. The supermarket personnel examining the incoming boxes are looking for perfect shape, uniform size and saleability. They are not generally looking for pesticide residue. It is assumed that regulations in the country of origin keep the most dangerous pesticides off the fruit. But the commercial pressure is to use whatever means available to ensure compliance with supermarket requirements.

There is also the question of the number of food miles clocked up by the food in our supermarkets. Cheap fossil fuel has made us blind to this cost overhead. As fuel prices rise, the knock-on increase in the price of food brings food miles to our attention. Prices will be higher in the short term as retailers have no choice but to pass transport costs on to consumers.

Once the food retailers realize that the cost of transportation is firmly entrenched at a much higher level, they will change the system. Farmers, wholesalers and retailers will work hard at exploiting the new parameters. The system will readjust into a new structure that requires far fewer food miles. Economics will be working its magic, as our servant, to implement a more localized agriculture driven by the simple lever of higher transportation costs. By understanding this, we realize that fighting transportation cost increases to keep food prices down is simply delaying real progress. We need unequivocal policy that transport costs will rise substantially to ensure that the system changes. There will then be the right circumstances for affordable and sustainable food.

Regarding food as a commodity, where every stage from harvest to consumption is driven by economic decisions, relies on regulations to keep it safe. Each time a new risk to health emerges, we bring in more legislation to counter it. This process is always a step behind the people dreaming up the next efficiency improvement. Reactive regulation, enforced by random inspection, is not enough for such an important aspect of human well being.

Misplaced Trust

Supermarkets have transformed the way we buy and consume food. Large out-of-town supermarkets have been allowed to become the dominant food retailers. A huge range of foods are neatly packaged and lined up on the shelves. These range from basic ingredients and 'fresh' vegetables to microwave-ready dishes and complete meals. We can fill up the trolley quickly and take it through the checkout and out into the car park. The process is fast, clean and leaves a very good impression. This is what the store designers are paid to achieve. This is the system we trust for our own health and that of our children.

I remember a conversation I had with an engineering undergraduate. His first job had been with one of the large bakery companies. The first task he had been given was working on sliced bread. It worried me that an engineer, not a nutritionist, was deciding upon the recipe. The reason, apparently, was that the slicing machines were not producing uniform, neat slices. The solution being pursued was to improve the structure of the bread to match the capabilities of the machine. It may be that he was using entirely healthy ingredients to solve the task he was given, but this is often not the case.

We know what goes into packaged food because labelling regulations are very precise. This is not the same as being informative. The long list of ingredients in tiny lettering includes chemicals we know nothing about. Anything proven to be poisonous will not be allowed, of course, but this is not the same as assessing the nutritional value. A chemical added primarily to improve the engineering properties of bread is not likely to make a positive contribution to health. This is certainly true of preservatives, the use of which is widespread.

Date marking is one the reassurances we have of the freshness of our food. We carefully look for the sell-by date and then reach into the back of the shelf for the longest date. Alternatively, our attention is drawn to the bright orange money-off sticker. These are used by stores to clear out produce reaching its sell-by date. We are happy to take the discount because we have complete trust that the food will be safe until this date.

Some bread will stay 'fresh' for up to two weeks before visible signs of mould make it inedible. Bread we make at home cannot achieve such a feat. This is because all it contains is pure food ingredients such as flour, yeast, water, vegetable oil and salt. It would not last long enough to be put into the delivery system operated by the big industrial bakeries.

Date markings are a useful mechanism, but all they tell is the date until which the food will be edible. They seldom indicate the date of manufacture or, for example, the date that the fruit was picked from the tree. Showing the packing date is an improvement in information provision, but means nothing. The food could have been in bulk transit for a long time before being packed into its final wrapper.

The trust placed on the food supply system is based on the impression we get from a shop's appearance, the list of ingredients that we do not understand and a sell-by date that tells us nothing about how long the food has taken to reach us. These are poor measures. Failing all else, we can fall back on the reassurance that comes with a well-known brand. We are led to believe that a good brand is a guarantee of quality. Marketing executives spend heavily to build up the image with advertising and promotions. In some cases, this is little more than a layer of deceit. In other cases, companies work hard to ensure that quality matches the image of the brand. For the consumer, it can be hard to separate the spin from the truth.

Bernard Matthews is a well-known brand for poultry products in the UK. The growth of the company reflects the changes that have taken place over the last half century. Bernard Matthews started his poultry business in 1950 with the purchase of 20 turkey eggs and a second-hand incubator from a local auction. The company history gives an insight into the early years of the company:

> *In 1955 [Bernard Matthews] bought a new home for him and his turkeys, the then neglected Great Witchingham Hall near Norwich for only £3,000. The Hall has 80 rooms and when he moved in, Bernard and his wife Joyce occupied one whilst the turkeys had the run of the other 79!*[9]

Bernard Matthews Farms Ltd grew out of the localized agricultural system that still existed in the 1950s to become, by 1968, the largest turkey farmer in Europe. It is a multimillion-pound business and a leader within the UK food industry. This growth took place in tandem with changes to the agricultural industry. Oven-ready products, convenience food and frozen food products were developed and marketed.

In the 1980s Bernard Matthews featured in television adverts to become a famous household name. We want our food to be safe and we want to deal with someone we can trust. With local butchers going out of business, unable to match the efficiency and prices of the supermarkets, people still hankered after a personal guarantee of quality. In the era of mass media, Bernard Matthews could provide it.

By the 1990s Bernard Matthews was recognized in the food industry as a leading innovator. Pre-packed sliced cooked meats was one innovation, moving on to complete pre-packed meals. The company is now the biggest cooked meats brand in the UK. The way the company operates reflects the changes that have taken place in the industry. The large supermarket chains wield considerable power. Their buyers push prices as low as possible, putting huge pressure on the profit margins of suppliers. Industrial-scale production is required to stay in business and cost reduction is a prime focus of management.

It was in this new business environment that the bird flu crisis of 2007 struck the industry. The first outbreak occurred in February on a Bernard Matthews farm at Holton in Suffolk. Pictures of buildings housing thousands of birds in close proximity were brought to our television screens. These were disturbing pictures. We do not like to be shown the realities of the food industry. Further alarming information was brought to the public's attention by the investigations carried out by the Department for Environment, Food and Rural Affairs (DEFRA). It was found that the H5N1 strain of avian flu virus identified was almost identical to the virus that had caused an outbreak of bird flu in geese in Hungary the month before. *The Times* reported that Bernard Matthews had been importing 37 tonnes of partly-processed turkey meat from Hungary every week.[10] A connection between the imports and the infection was never proved but the DEFRA report concluded that 'infection was most likely introduced to GB via the importation of turkey meat from Hungary'.[11]

The DEFRA investigation looked closely at the fact that imported meat was being processed on the same site that turkeys were being raised. It was found that wild birds, notably gull species in large numbers, had access to waste material from the meat-processing plant. The investigation also found that the building in which the live turkeys were kept, and where the outbreak occurred, was in poor condition (unlike other buildings on the site). This meant that rats and mice had access, so could have transported infected material into the building. The report also identified the possibility of the introduction of infection from infected bird droppings via a leaking roof.

The graphic images of factory farming that emerged in the press coverage of the crisis did not fit easily with the image of its brand. Until this incident, it was not widely known that Bernard Matthews had been importing huge quantities of poultry meat from Hungary. Bernard Matthews was found not to have contravened any regulations and was not prosecuted. The company was not at fault. We have allowed a system to arise in which industrial farming is the norm. It is our attitudes that have to change. If we decide that we will not compromise over the safety and quality of our food, we can transform industrial agriculture. Bernard Matthews is a commercial company that can change direction very quickly but only if we, the consumers, demand it.

> *Bernard Matthews Farms knows that it has not always made the best decisions in recent years but we have listened and we are changing.*
> Bernard Matthews Farms Ltd statement 2008[12]

Bernard Matthews Ltd is a reputable company operating within the law and it implements diligently the regulations that are placed on the industry. When we find that the official reports of the bird flu outbreak are disturbing reading, we should remember that Bernard Matthews is one of our better companies. Our concern should be for the practices that have become normal, and our stupidity in allowing them. We have to change our expectation and insist on a better system.

Sustainable Quality Food

Agriculture must be reintegrated into the ecosystem in a way that is sustainable indefinitely. To do this requires making a connection between consumption and the means of production. Localization and self-sufficiency should be the default option. Fresh and local food is good for the health and good for the planet. In designing such a system, unusual or out-of-season produce will become much more expensive. This should not hold us back. The people who desire such produce are also the people who can afford to pay.

High transport costs work in favour of local produce and local producers. Governments can go further and introduce a distance-to-market tax. This need not be a bureaucratic nightmare. It could easily be incorporated into the systems of the large supermarkets. For practical reasons, small shops and local markets would have to be exempt. This is also beneficial, in that their competitive position would be reinforced by helping to counter the economies of scale enjoyed by the supermarkets.

Packaging is another area where bold action can make progress. The food industry will object strongly but the battle is worth fighting. There are huge quantities of food packaging going into landfill. This is a stream of waste that we can stop. The minimum action is to ban all non-biodegradable packaging. In an industrialized food system, which is totally reliant on secure bar-coded packaging, this proposal will meet with intense resistance. If forced to act, greater use will be made of biodegradable plastics. More progressive thinkers within the industry will realize that more localized production and consumption leads to other potential solutions.

Greater use of paper bags and reusable containers becomes feasible within a localized system.

Planning regulations and property taxes is another area where governments can score big wins for little outlay. Once again, the big supermarkets will object strongly. Already there are restrictions on new out-of-town stores as politicians have seen the effect on town centres. Policy should go further to bring in swingeing property taxes on the existing out-of-town stores. Smaller retail outlets situated within the communities will then benefit. There is likely to be an overall increase in shopping bills for us all. However, this is a small price to pay compared with the financial and environmental benefits of helping society to pull back from a heavy reliance on the car.

The actions required to ensure that we have a sustainable supply of quality food is entirely compatible with the other changes we need to make in society. Until the system is changed, we have a problem. Many places no longer have local shops, and where there are shops they are not very good. Convenience stores, as they are often called, are surviving by selling small quantities at premium prices to people without cars or people who do their main weekly shop by car and need to top up during the week. Changing this system will not be easy.

I want good value local shops selling quality food, with local produce being the cheapest option. These are not like the expensive organic shops with low turnover that can survive only within affluent communities. The result will be to bring organic and local produce to the mass market. The high turnover will mean fresher food, even fresher than today's organic shops. This is an aspiration worth fighting for. There is no need to compromise over the quality of our food.

One source of food that has not been covered in this chapter is fish from the open ocean. The reason for this omission is that such fish will not be on the menu for long unless human society learns to show more respect for the ocean.

I spoke with the Director of a Finnish research organization that regularly monitors the Baltic Sea. He explained that their research ship was often at sea for a week at a time. One aspect he enjoyed was the diet of fresh fish straight from fishing line to pan. He lamented that many of the fish now contained levels of pollutants that exceed EU guidelines for safe human consumption.[13] He personally still enjoyed eating the fresh fish but he was required to inform the crew of the risks and provide alternative meal choices. This is just the start. Unless we ease the guidelines, first the Baltic Sea and then the other oceans will all be off-limits to fishing for human consumption.

Fish higher up the food chain will be the first to be banned, such as shark, swordfish and marlin, followed soon after by tuna.[14] It is only a matter of time before fishing bans will end up applying to the entire ocean, unless we drop our food safety standards.

Discussing fishing regulations, quotas and methods is, on the face of it, useful work, but in reality is as useful as a dentist attending to the teeth of a man on death row the evening before his execution.

19 Rescue Poseidon

In Greek mythology, Poseidon, the god of the sea, is invincible. The ancient Greeks would have found it hard to believe that man could bring the immortal god to his knees.

The wasteful and careless way that we are running modern society will destroy the natural heritage of the oceans. Fundamental change in human behaviour must start now or the oceans seen today will not exist in the 22nd century. Aquarium managers will try to save examples of marine life but it will be a losing battle. Once the marine ecosystem has been destroyed, it will be many thousands of years before the complex biodiversity can be rebuilt.

From a human perspective, sitting on the beach will still be safe but swimming in the sea will become a universal danger to health, as it already is in close proximity to some centres of population and industrial activity.[1] Sailing will still be a safe leisure pursuit but capsizing will become a more serious hazard than simply a cold drenching. If any sea water is swallowed then emergency medical attention will be required.

We are converting the oceans of the world from a biodiverse reservoir to a cesspool. Anything we no longer need gets chucked into the ocean. We allow dangerous substances passage on the oceans with little oversight. There is no one there to see if such material is 'lost' in transit. The oceans belong to us all, but no one accepts responsibility.

It is obvious that we must leap into action – except that, as land animals, living selfish introverted lives, we do not notice the consequences of the damage. We care even less. This puts the oceans in great peril. The oceans will not be safe until we find a way to stop humans from polluting the environment. Without direct and immediate impacts to the society of today, inaction and procrastination is likely to be the human response. This is a shame because action to save the oceans is possible and feasible.

Pollution and the Ocean

Pollution of the seas can make headlines but only if the effects are visible on shore: filthy beaches, sea birds caked in oil or dead fish washed up on beaches. For the water for human consumption there is no need to worry. No matter how filthy the oceans become, the Earth's ecosystem will evaporate the water and deposit it on the land as clean rain. Provided the atmosphere is kept clean, and our watersheds protected, then we will have clean water to drink.

When the land becomes polluted it is possible to backtrack on our mistakes. By stopping releasing damaging chemicals and long-life pollutants, over time the land will be washed clean by the natural hydrological cycle. The rain falls and carries pollution away. When it ends up in rivers these take it quickly away from our locality. Where the pollution is carried down into the groundwater it may take decades or even centuries to wash through, but eventually it will. Some people use these observations of the recovery possible after we stop polluting to argue that the oceans, too, are self-cleansing. This is a triumph of hope over logic. It is true that the oceans are so vast that any one incident of pollution is diluted to such an extent that it is hard to detect. However, the sum total of all the myriad of discharges over many decades is adding up, and is measurable. Not all these 'pollutants' are an immediate danger, for example, CO_2.

Elevated levels of CO_2 in the atmosphere, and the associated changes to the climate, are widely discussed. Little attention is given to the effects in the oceans. The CO_2 dissolves into sea water. For decades, this has been seen as an environmental plus in helping to extract carbon from the atmosphere and mitigate climate change. From the ocean's perspective, increased levels of CO_2 are hugely negative. The CO_2 dissolves to become carbonic acid. This increases the acidity of the ocean, making it harder for many species to survive. For example, the great coral reefs of the world are under threat. These beautiful and complex ecosystems may disappear entirely. But the damage is more fundamental than a loss of pretty habitats and colourful fish. All the marine creatures that need calcium carbonate to build their shells and skeletons will find it increasingly hard to build the body parts they need.

Long-life plastics are another man-made scourge of the oceans. Over the decades, since plastic was invented, bits of plastic have ended up in the oceans, where it stays. The plastic is churned around and around, broken into ever smaller pieces. There is now a microscopic haze of tiny plastic particles spread throughout all the oceans of the world.[2] Fish 'breathe' the water and with it comes these plastic particles. They get stuck in the gills and can bring an early death. This is the only mechanism that nature has to rid the oceans of this menace. Over thousands of years, dying fish sinking to the bottom will take the plastic down with them into the sediment to join the other pollutants that will mark humankind's place in geological time.

Heavy metals are another problem. Concentrations of these pollutants have been steadily increasing in step with industrialization. For example, burning coal releases mercury compounds into the environment. Natural processes, such as rainfall, wash the pollution away to end up in the ocean. Heavy metal residues accumulate within fish, concentrating in the fish at the top of the food chain. Swordfish, marlin and tuna already have dangerous levels of heavy metals. It is recommended that such fish should be eaten only occasionally and not at all by pregnant women. Whether the mercury is harmful to the fish is not widely discussed; we feel that it has no direct relevance to humans.

Radioactive waste is another pollutant that finds its way into the sea. The Irish Sea now has a radioactive layer in the sediments at the bottom of the sea that coincides with the period of operation of the UK's Sellafield[3] nuclear reprocessing plant in Cumbria. It is estimated that 200–250 kg of plutonium has been discharged into the Irish Sea since the plant started operating in 1952. The UK now has much tighter controls, but as more and more countries seek nuclear power with varying degrees of control and oversight, more radioactive material will end up in the ocean. Responsible governments argue that such waste should be stored on land where it can be monitored. As the decades pass, and the toxic stockpiles grow, the temptation will increase to dump the radioactive waste into the deep ocean trenches, out of sight and out of mind.

Poseidon is being hit from all sides by pollution from man with no end to the onslaught in sight. On the issue of climate change, we are talking about taking action. Eventually we will respond as we experience the negative effects. Whether our actions are enough to halt further acidification of the oceans is doubtful. We may even make it worse. Some of humankind's 'solutions' include enhancing the role of oceans in trapping CO_2 from the atmosphere.

The atmosphere could be scrubbed clean by natural processes within a timescale that we understand. If we were to stop releasing excess CO_2 into the atmosphere, then over a period of 50 years levels of atmospheric CO_2 could start to drop back to safer levels. It is within one person's lifetime that progress could be made.

Cleansing the oceans would take much longer. This is why it is vital that we stop polluting the oceans. This includes stopping indirect pollution from human activities on land, as it is only a matter of time before this too is washed down into the ocean. The case for action is bulletproof. Even so, there are many more issues to grab the world's attention. Breaking down human complacency over the state of the oceans will be hard, but we must try.

Overcoming Human Complacency

The oceans are vast remote regions of the Earth, much of which has not even been explored. To most humans, these oceans are out of sight and out of mind. Any concern goes no deeper than ensuring the holiday beach is clean and safe. An exception is the late Jacques Cousteau (1910–1997). He cared very much about the ocean. We remember the beautiful photography he brought to our television screens but we tend to forget the warnings contained in the commentary. Since his death, few of us would be able to name a living oceanographer. We behave as if the oceans do not matter and treat oceanography as an obscure academic discipline. If humans were sea creatures it would be very different. If we relied for survival on breathing through gills we would be very worried, and insist on change. But we live on the land so the warnings from Jacques Cousteau fell on deaf ears.

Saving the oceans will be difficult if this is made the focus of effort. First, success would require complex coordinated global policy reaching across a number of areas, ranging from emission control and waste handling to the regulations for manufacturing processes. Second, there are more pressing issues for world leaders to worry about. Third, few people care enough to bother. These are high hurdles to overcome.

Fortunately, saving the oceans is entirely compatible with many other improvements that need to be made in society. Public health requires that chemicals that nature cannot break down should be eliminated from society. Arresting climate change requires that we stop burning fossil fuels. The world trade system needs a complete overhaul, so that it reinforces the integrity of the shared global environment rather than undermining it. These are all measures that we should take for the sake of human society; the fact that they will also save the oceans should reinforce our resolve to shift quickly from talk to action.

Human Needs

The human need for water is tiny compared with the water available on the planet. There is far more ocean (70 %) than land (30%), and the deep ocean reaches nearly 11 km deep. If Mount Everest was chopped off at sea level and dropped into the Marianas Trench in the South Pacific, it would disappear with over a kilometre of water above its peak. It is impossible that we would ever run out of water.

The water from the oceans is of little direct use to humankind. The salt content is too high. Fortunately, out of this vast salty reservoir, water evaporates into the atmosphere leaving the salt behind. Any other pollutants in the oceans will also be left behind. This water then condenses into clouds to fall as rain. Rain will always be clean provided the atmosphere is clean. Humans can be certain of regular supplies of fresh clean water falling onto the land – whatever we do to the ocean. We could have an ocean that is a chemical soup of dangerous pollutants devoid of all life and nature would still feed humans with fresh water. It is more than we deserve. Mother Nature treats us kindly; it is time we returned the favour.

Humans in most parts of the world take water for granted. It can be drawn from the nearest lake or stream. If surface water is not available locally, digging or drilling will tap into subterranean supplies. If pumping water out of the aquifers still does not produce enough, desalination plants can be used to extract fresh water from the sea. Water seems to be a limitless resource and this perception influences our behaviour.

One problem related to water is the need to keep clear of our own waste. There is a deeply ingrained aversion in humans to other people's bodily waste. Even where there is no risk, such as in the use of dry compost toilets, we cringe at the sight and smell of other people's excrement. This instinct has served us well. Primitive man would take water to drink from a sweet-smelling spring or stream and defecate somewhere else, away from the living area. In the modern world we want our waste flushed away, out of sight, out of mind and out of smelling distance. We do not care much where it goes as long as it goes away.

For most of human existence there has been no need to think deeply about waste, and the processing of waste. In a world where all waste was biodegradable, natural processes soon cleaned it up. Human waste simply became nutrients for other organisms. Without needing to make a conscious effort, waste handling was a fully integrated component of the natural system. This is how it was, how it always should have been and how it should be again. In the industrialized world this requires special effort.

Industry and Water

Over the last two hundred years, scientists have made discoveries at an astonishing rate. These have led to new chemicals and materials with amazing properties. For each discovery, new applications are found. New products become possible as these novel materials reach the market. For example, the family of plastics has led to a whole range of products and components that were not feasible before their invention in the 20th century.

The way we exploit the fruits of invention is to try out the new chemicals and materials in any number of ways. We look for new uses, not potential dangers.

The exception is for chemicals that we plan to put into our bodies, such as new drugs. The regulations require extensive and laborious trials. Even so, some drugs drop through the safety net. Thalidomide was one such drug. It is estimated that 10,000 deformed children were born in Europe and Africa in the late 1950s and early 1960s as a result. The United States only suffered a handful of cases due to the good work of Frances Kelsey, a pharmacist working for the US Food and Drug Administration (FDA). It was her job to assess Thalidomide. In 1960 she refused to grant a licence. At the time there was no proof of dangerous side effects. She came under intense pressure from the drug's manufacturer to change her opinion. When she was vindicated by the emergence of the large number of deformed births in other countries, she was hailed as a hero.[4] This example shows that even where chemicals are directly ingested by humans, we require proof of the damage that can be caused before holding back. It is fortunate that there are scientists such as Frances Kelsey who insist on a fail-safe approach, but they have to work hard to be heard.

Where chemicals are proven to be safe for human use, such as the hormones used in birth-control pills, they are judged to be safe compounds. The fact that such hormones are entering rivers and streams in increasing quantities does not bother us much. Changes to the reproductive organs of fish have been detected. Such research is tucked away in obscure publications such as the *Journal of Aquatic Animal Health*.[5] This journal is not high on the list of essential reading for world leaders.

Chemicals for industrial processes have less stringent controls. The de facto principle applied is that any chemical can be used until evidence comes to light that the chemical is hazardous. Regulation then focuses on the dangers to the health of workers and, if the chemical is included in the product, on the health of customers. Effects that the chemical has on the ecosystem are considered to be secondary. Pressure to protect the ecosystem only becomes strong when there are knock-on effects that impact on human health or agriculture.

Lead-based additives to petrol are a good example of society's slow response. Early last century it was discovered that tetra-ethyl lead was effective in preventing 'knocking'. This is the damaging action of pre-ignition in engines. Adding tetra-ethyl lead to the fuel allowed a higher compression ratio and more powerful engines. The lead ended up in the exhaust fumes and spread widely throughout the environment. It was well known that lead was a poisonous substance and it should have been obvious that this was not a good idea. Even so, lead additives in fuel became widespread through the 1920s and continued right up until the 1980s, when research proved that lead exposure was linked with IQ deficits in children. The European Union did not ban lead additives until 2000.

It is odd that we tolerated 80 years of poisonous lead emissions from our vehicles before we called a halt. The principles that I put forward would not allow such stupidity to take hold.

Asbestos provides another example. The asbestos group of minerals are naturally occurring. It is a tough and flexible fibrous material resistant to heat, electricity and strong chemicals. These properties make asbestos almost indestructible and good for applications that require resistance to fire, insulation from high voltages or that may be subject to chemical attack. It should come as no surprise that the human body finds it difficult to cope when particles of asbestos dust end up in the lungs. However, asbestos was used widely until there was documented evidence of the deaths it caused. The human body's defence system attacks the tiny indestructible fibres trapped in the lungs. Because this fails to eliminate the asbestos, scar tissue grows around the foreign particles. This scar tissue spreads slowly, taking away the capacity of the lungs and, in effect, suffocating the person. It may take decades from the exposure to asbestos before death from asbestosis.

The human habit is to try out any substance or chemical and to continue using it until evidence is produced that it is harmful. This is a dangerous habit. The new paradigm should be not to release into the environment any substance that is alien to nature and which nature cannot break down. Where we have followed this principle, often it has proved not to be difficult. We have found that we do not need to add lead to fuel to stop engines knocking. We have also found other ways to fireproof buildings without using asbestos. It has been possible to live without these inventions. The common problem is a lack of effort to find substitutes, driven by a concern that it might cost more.

The way that the world dealt with the problem of CFCs can be viewed as an example of very good, fast decisive action. Scientists of the British Antarctic Survey (BAS) reported the ozone hole in 1985. A series of meetings led to an agreement for coordinated global action under the Montreal Protocol. In just four years, effective actions were taken and the ozone layer appears to be no longer under threat.

CFCs can also been seen as an example of humankind's bad habit of experimenting without considering the consequences. When CFCs were discovered, scientists looked for a use. They found that CFCs are good refrigerants. The fact that they are highly stable long-life compounds, not found in nature, was ignored. If the world had adopted the way of thinking I champion in this chapter, these compounds would have been left where they belong, in the laboratory as curiosities. So although the world responded quickly to evidence of damage to the ozone layer, it was incompetent that the world ever reached that position. It is like praising a driver who has just run over a child at a pedestrian crossing and bundled the child into the car and off to hospital. Muted praise is due for the response, but it would have been far better if the driver had been more attentive in the first instance.

The way we speed our progress, allowing any substance into industrial processes until there is unequivocal evidence of damage, is courting disaster on a massive scale.

Imagine being stuck in a lift with a chemist who had just discovered an exciting new compound. A sample of the compound is in a test tube in his pocket. He takes it out as a topic of discussion whilst waiting for the lift to be repaired. In the confined and airless space within the lift, he offers to open the test tube to share his discovery. Are we delighted to be part of the experiment or scared of being poisoned? Out in the fresh air, we would be less concerned. It is easy to forget that the world is one shared sealed life-support capsule floating out in the emptiness of space. There is no other place where our dangerous chemicals can be shunted off to. Once they are made, they remain with us, within one shared atmosphere, within one shared ocean.

All industrial processes should be run such that we would not be worried if they were humming away in the front room at home. Processes should be tuned into the ecosystem, reinforcing the shared environment and eliminating the concept of industrial waste. This is possible, although very different to the way the world runs now.

Current Production Processes

Current processes make use of whatever chemicals will deliver production outcomes as cheaply as possible. Dangerous chemicals need to be kept safe within closed systems. Regulations focus on protective measures for workers. When the chemicals are exhausted and no longer useful, they are passed to a contractor for disposal. Having won the contract through competitive tender, the contractor has to work out the cheapest way to dispose of the waste. In well-run countries with tight rules and effective enforcement, this approach can be made to work.

Worldwide, production processes tend to follow the lead of the developed nations. Factories and facilities are set up based on the same processes and the same technology. Often regulations are less stringent and enforcement is less rigorous. If corruption is pervasive, the system of oversight may become completely ineffective. The world's most corrupt countries, Somalia, Myanmar and Iraq,[6] have little chance of implementing effective controls. A badly maintained and leaking plant is a common sight in such countries. The extractive industries can be particularly damaging. These are located wherever the mineral is to be found, often in remote and poor communities. The combination of huge profits, weak oversight and corruption leads to environmental destruction on a scale that developed Western countries would not allow within their own borders. It should concern us that many resource-rich African countries, such as the Democratic Republic of the Congo,[7] are in the group of the world's most corrupt countries according to the world corruption index. Particularly worrying is Russia,[8] where corruption is rife and the capability to pollute the world environment is huge.

Replicating 20th-century industrial processes around the world may not be polluting our own backyard. Such facilities are beyond our control and, we believe, not our responsibility. However, the resultant pollution belongs to the world. Over time, the pollution finds its way into the one ocean that we all share.

Poor control of processes in other parts of the world should be of concern, but this is not the only problem. Factories in the developed world produce waste that is stored and handled in full accordance with the regulations. The responsibility of management ends when this has been handed over to a contractor who can provide the paperwork required by national regulations. Often this contractor can then ship the waste abroad, provided paperwork can be supplied that guarantees safe disposal. As the waste moves further from our jurisdiction, it enters the grey world of weak and corrupt governments. Written guarantees of safe disposal may be available, for a fee that may have no connection with any sort of processing. At the final destination, the people receiving the waste may not even understand what is being delivered, let alone have the expertise to dispose of it safely.

Disposing of ships at the end of their life is an example. The older ships especially contain oil, toxins and materials such as asbestos. Safe dismantling is a specialist and expensive process when carried out in the shipyards of Europe. The alternative is to sell the ship on the world market without asking too many questions about the buyer's intentions. The ship might then join the many hundreds of ships that are run aground each year on beaches in Turkey, India, Pakistan and Bangladesh. This is big business: Bangladesh derives 80–90 % of its steel from end-of-life ships.[9] The workers suffer appalling conditions in extracting the metal and components with value, leaving all the toxins to be washed away by the sea.

It is near impossible to insist that ships be broken up in yards with the correct facilities. Ships have a number of owners through their working lives and usually end up operating under the flag of a country with weak enforcement. The way to deal with this problem is at source. Ships built in our shipyards, or purchased by our companies, should by law be designed for easy recycling with all toxic substances and materials banned. The ship-building industry is the correct place to take action to prevent environmental damage from ship-breaking in poorer countries.

The simplest of all disposal methods – in the murky world of international trade in waste – is to lose it in transit. A cargo of waste can be loaded at one port and appropriate paperwork purchased from corrupt officials in another country. The cargo can then be dumped at sea and the papers filed away. The waste is then out of sight and out of mind. The human instinct, to remove waste from our direct proximity, wins again, but we are all losers in such a game.

The world has one shared ocean. It is so vast that any one incident will be spread wide across the world's oceans and hardly detectable. All the ships dismantled on the beaches of Bangladesh, all the chemicals dumped in Côte d'Ivoire,[10] and all the toxic stockpiles of the world have not yet caused severe lasting damage to the ocean, but it is only a matter of time before the oceans succumb.

The way we operate industrial processes is flawed. Processes are designed around minimizing the cost of each stage with waste regarded as an unavoidable overhead. Thinking about the whole chain of processes together, and the relationship with the ecosystem, is too much bother. The overall result is more wasteful and inefficient than it could be.

Ecological Industrial Processes

Technical innovation should be focused on working with the ecosystem, not against it. Ecological industrial processes are feasible and sensible. Tighter regulations and improved oversight will have a place, but the industrial world I have in mind is inherently safe.

If the right principles are adopted at the design stage, the whole concept of waste can be eliminated. This requires more thought, uses less resources and need not be more expensive – especially if the levies charged on pollution and waste continue to rise.

Implementing ecological industrial processes requires more research into biodegradable chemicals and processes that mimic nature. Each stage, from the source of input resources to the final destination of the product, need to be examined together. There may be resource savings to be made within the whole life cycle that are not apparent when looking at a single process. Often these resource savings are also cost savings. Where this is not so, and costs are higher, this should not prevent progress. Businesses that develop an ecological process, which is not economically competitive, should campaign for adoption in the home market. Governments should be willing to introduce regulation to favour such processes, handing an advantage to home industry. Die-hard defenders of the old model of free trade may object, but such objections must be faced down.

The example that the developed nations can set in proving the concept of ecological industry is a triple win. First, the next generation of standard processes to be rolled out worldwide, for other nations follow, will be kind on the environment. Poor execution of ecological processes will not have the same dire consequences as poor execution of 20th-century industrial processes. Second, taking the technical lead in developing the processes will be highly profitable. Third, the long-term damage being inflicted on the world's oceans will be alleviated.

Adopting ecological industrial practices will stop a lot of pollution, but on its own it is not enough. Progress is also needed in tackling throwaway society.

Throwaway Society

In modern society, throwing away anything that is no longer needed or wanted is regarded as normal behaviour. The expectation is that municipal authorities will get rid of it. It is their responsibility, not ours. As landfill sites become filled to capacity, it is the responsibility of local government to find more. We overlook the fact that ballooning quantities of mixed rubbish in landfill will corrode and decay, leaching their contents into the ground. Over time, all this pollution will be washed down to its final destination in the shared global ocean. These landfill sites are pollution time bombs that will be with us for centuries. The throwaway culture has to be reversed for the sake of human society, and for the survival of the marine ecosystem.

As manufacturing becomes more automated, and goods get ever cheaper, we can afford more stuff. Unwanted presents, little-used gadgets and other junk build up in every corner of the house. When the pile gets too high we make a trip to the refuse tip, recycling centre or car boot sale. White goods, if we are lucky, give 20 years' service. A quality car might last as long. Each family is responsible for throwing out a fridge, a cooker, a washing machine and one (or two) cars every two decades. This is a massive stream of junk, very little of which has been designed for true recycling.

Recycling systems have been set up to deal with such massive flows of rubbish. Where I live in southern England, a new system has just been put in place. I have a green wheelie bin, a black wheelie bin, two green boxes and a large green bag, each for a different category of waste. The system seems advanced, but it is dealing only with symptoms, leaving the culture of a throwaway society intact.

The new recycling system for our household replaced the old system of two plastic baskets, one for paper and one for bottles and cans. I phoned the council offices to ask what should now be done with the old recycling containers. I received the reply that they were now surplus to requirement. If I did not want them the council would send a vehicle around to collect them. I found this interesting and pressed for a fuller answer: 'So what will you do with the two baskets when you pick them up?' I asked. 'We have no use for them', the council official repeated over the phone. I asked again, 'What will you do with the sturdy black plastic baskets from the old recycling system?' There was a pause on the end of the line. Perhaps the lady had realized that the answer she was about to give was ridiculous. She said, 'We no longer need them. We just chuck them away.'

I found it astounding that at the heart of well-intentioned efforts to improve recycling, the throwaway society was alive and thriving. The process intended to reduce the amount of rubbish going into landfill was contributing to yet more unwanted junk.

Life-Cycle Design and True Recycling

Saving the world's oceans requires humankind to live within the natural water cycles of the planet without poisoning the system with pollution. Nature shows how. All natural processes are closed loops that repeat again and again and again. The waste from one organism is food for another. Society has to operate in the same way.

The challenge is working out how to deal with man-made material that does not fit inside one of nature's cycles. Simply to ban such substances is not a realistic option. We have come to like many of these new substances and materials, and we would like to continue using them. The problem is that new materials are discovered, and applications found for them, but then the inventors lose interest. The invention should not be regarded as complete until a closed lifecycle has also been designed for the material.

Nature does this by trial and error. The apparently stable cycles observed in the study of ecology have had millions of years to settle down. For humankind also to use the method of trial and error would be to inflict huge uncontrollable change on the ecosystem that may take millions of years to settle into a new global equilibrium. Life is very robust and will adapt to the new conditions with new species evolving as others become extinct. This is a dangerous experiment in which the species Homo sapiens may be one of the losers.

In dealing with man-made materials, it is important that we ignore the haphazard ways of nature and use deliberate design to define the lifecycle of products and materials. In this way we can ensure that nature's cycles will not be disrupted. This stage may be tougher than the initial discovery. If it cannot be done, then there should be no place for the substance in industry or society.

Full life-cycle design encompasses the initial production, a schedule of refurbishment and decommissioning plans for end-of-life disposal. For this to work, design has to deal with two material cycles: 'bio' and 'technical'. The bio cycle is used for biodegradable material (in effect using the cycles of nature). The technical cycle is used for man-made materials. These two recycling loops are different and must remain separated. Components can be made of either biodegradable material or technical material. Complex products can include components from both cycles but must be designed for easy disassembly. This means at end-of-life they can be processed within the correct cycle.

Biodegradable materials are the easiest to deal with. These can usually be passed back to nature in safety. Decomposition should be either automatic or initiated easily. For example, some rubbish bags are designed to start to decompose when exposed to sunlight. Provided that the compounds left after the decomposition are natural and safe, biodegradable material can be disposed of almost at will. Nature's biorecycling loop will then take over.

Technical material needs special handling. The initial production draws inputs from nature, such as an ore from which metals can be extracted. For example, iron is extracted by smelting the ore hematite. Most of the world's iron is then converted into steel with a range of additives giving special properties. Products made from steel range from buildings and cars to watches and nails. When these products reach the end of their useful life they should be recycled.

Crude recycling involves remanufacturing the steel, perhaps through including a proportion of scrap in the process of converting pig iron to steel. We can do better than this. Clever design ensures that components can be reconditioned, to go back into new products or used to repair existing products.

The highest standard of 'recycling' is to increase the life of products to prevent waste. Making better products with much longer lifespans is the easiest and most effective action. The challenge is persuading purchasers that the higher initial investment is justified.

The prime requirement is to design products for long reliable service. The secondary design requirement is to facilitate reuse and refurbishment. When, finally, the product has reached the end of a long life, the technical material must be recycled. This does not mean downcycling to a secondary use. Examples of this are bottles smashed as an ingredient in concrete, or plastics mixed with other ingredients to make roof tiles which cannot be further recycled. Single stage reuse that delays the arrival in landfill by one or two further stages is not true recycling.

One category of material that must be avoided in life-cycle design is 'monstrous hybrids'.[11] These are components that include a mixture of materials that cannot easily be separated. Formica-surfaced tables are one example. Huge quantities of cheap furniture are made in this way. But the economics become different when using life-cycle design in a society that puts a high charge against waste. The decommissioning costs of these 'cheap' products would make the production uneconomic.

Europe has made a start in making the required transition with the Waste Framework Directive (WFD) that was finalized in 2008 after lengthy argument. It sets a five-stage waste hierarchy:[12]

1 waste prevention (preferred option);
2 re-use;
3 recycling;
4 recovery (including energy recovery); and
5 safe disposal, as a last resort.

The huge resistance from EU governments as the WFD was hammered out shows how hard it will be to learn the new way of thinking and implement real change. The WFD is progress, but we need to go much further than EU politicians and EU governments have discussed so far.

The only solution for materials that we use now, but for which we cannot design a safe life cycle, is to ban them. On this basis, CFCs would never have been used as refrigerants. CFCs are highly stable compounds that are alien to nature and tough to conserve safely when equipment is decommissioned. There was no need to wait for evidence of the ozone hole; such substances should have been banned on principle. When a potential material does not have a safe and affordable life cycle design, a permit to manufacture should not be issued.

This fail-safe approach should apply even when there is no proof of toxicity. If nature cannot break the material down, it will hang around and quantities will build up. There is bound to be a problem eventually. Long-life plastics are an example. They are not toxic, but we now know how damaging decades of plastic waste are in the oceans, where they are broken into smaller and smaller pieces without being eliminated.

The implications of adopting full life-cycle design go beyond manufacturing. Clever life-cycle design is near impossible for durable goods that are made in countries outside our control and shipped halfway around the world. A natural consequence of this is that the trade in manufactured products would become more localized. This is how to implement a model of full responsibility for the life cycle of physical goods, all the way from initial production through to decommissioning.

Adopting life-cycle design becomes a central plank in moving beyond the damaging aspects of globalization to building truly sustainable economies. Indirectly, this will also be part of the protection required to save the oceans.

The Final Destination

The final destination for all our long-life pollutants is the ocean. Once they reach the ocean there is no other place for them to go. The damage caused is irreversible. Even if there were no more industrial pollution starting from tomorrow, there is all the waste buried in landfill that will slowly leak over the next century or more. The toxic brew we have been mixing through the era of industrialization will remain with mankind for thousands of years.

There is a glimmer of hope in this depressing tale. If humankind is exceedingly patient, then over geological time there will be an improvement. The current geological epoch has been termed the Anthropocene, starting from the second half of the 18th century when humankind's influence started to become significant.[13]

The excesses of the 20th and early 21st centuries may get confined to a narrow toxic band in the sedimentary rock of the Anthropocene period. Unfortunately, it will take millions of years for this process of sedimentation to work its magic.

As our grandchildren sit on the beach in their old age, they will reflect on how it might have been. Their electronic books and virtual reality systems will be able to show how it was. They will see that back in the early years of the 21st century, it was still possible to swim in the sea and snorkel over coral reefs. Future generations will not have such leisure options available to them.

The beaches of the future will be artificial, the original beaches having been submerged by rising sea levels. The romantic sunset will be real enough, but the water off which the light reflects will be devoid of all but the most robust forms of aquatic life. Those that can survive may be horribly deformed due to mutations brought on by pollution. The coral reefs will have died and acidification of the oceans will prevent the formation of new coral.

Whilst contemplating the state of the oceans, our grandchildren will regret that their ancestors did not take action sooner. They will wonder why human society in the early years of the 21st century ignored the oceans and did so little to save them.

We are on a track that will lead ever so slowly to the death of the oceans. This does not seem to bother us much. There are too many other issues to grab our attention. Fortunately, the changes required to become a sustainable society will reduce markedly our negative impact on the oceans. Rather than worry about the oceans, we should worry about the continuation of civilization. It is time to support real change.

20 Support Real Change

The concept that we are just one generation within the expanse of human existence has been lost. This is the era of selfish overindulgence, and it is dangerous. We want it here, we want it now, and we do not care what it takes. Our generation shoulders a heavy responsibility to rebel against the values that have brought us such wealth and economic success. Civilization must be turned onto a safer path – whilst there is still time.

We can be sure, using advanced measurement and imaging technology that we can record accurately the world we now have. There are growing archives of satellite imagery, photographs, film and video. Our descendents should be able to view the Earth as it used to be, with a vast reservoir of biodiversity in the rainforests and oceans. Whether we will have any live examples of nature to accompany the archives depends on what we do now.

The world in 2009 is still hoping to continue without a revolution. It is hoped that oil prices will remain affordable, house prices will stabilize, the banking system will be saved by government intervention and carbon trading will stop climate change – in that order of priority. The measures we are prepared to take are little more than papering over the cracks. We need much more substantial change. The Sustainable Revolution is necessary, urgently needed and unavoidable. The longer the period of denial, the greater will be the resulting disruption.

One aspect of our denial is being rectified. Few people now deny the role of human society in changing the climate. The scientists of the IPCC have done an excellent job in assessing the damage that humans are causing. The efforts to respond to this good work have been dismal. Politicians and officials have attended many conferences, taken a lot of flights and had tons of paper printed to record their deliberations. The only substantive result is to have proved that negotiating around the periphery of the issues does not work.

The long drawn-out discussions and arguments over a successor to the Kyoto Protocol on climate change are not hitting the issues head on. There is a reluctance to take the measures required to phase out fossil fuels. Of even greater significance, the ineffective discussions over carbon dioxide emissions have been a smokescreen hiding other more dangerous long-term impacts to the environment. These include a slow ratcheting up of background radiation from the poorly regulated parts of the world nuclear industry and the slow death of the oceans.

Other initiatives have been struggling to make headway. For example, the rules of world trade, administered by the WTO, prevent governments from taking sensible action to protect the environment. This was acknowledged as far back as 1992 at the Earth Summit in Rio de Janeiro.[1] The discussion that followed led to the Marrakesh Declaration of 1994 and the setting up of the Trade and Environment Committee of the WTO. The committee has achieved little. Some useful discussion has taken place, but the committee has been put into a straightjacket. Wholesale reform of the system of world trade is clearly needed, but this has been explicitly kept off the committee's agenda. Where the committee identifies problems, its solutions must continue to uphold the principles of the WTO trading system.[2]

A decade later, in 2002, the World Summit on Sustainable Development in Johannesburg kicked off another series of initiatives. We are now approaching the end of this programme of work, called the 10-year framework, to promote sustainable consumption and production patterns. An example of some good work that has come out of this framework is the UNEP's Life Cycle Initiative. This programme produced a report in 2007 titled 'Life Cycle Management: A Business Guide to Sustainability'.[3] It is a very useful publication but it is not well known, or widely read, by business leaders.

In other areas, the problems go deeper than indifference and procrastination. A good deal of drive and effort has been going into dubious policies in the mistaken belief that they are the right policies. Policies in favour of deregulation, a commitment to open markets and the use of GDP as the prime measure of progress are examples. These policy choices were worth trying. In a narrow economic sense, they delivered what was expected of them. Now that we understand how damaging such policies are to the social structure of society and the way they undermine environmental policy, we must back off, and back off quickly.

The challenge for politicians is to make the difficult and unpopular decisions to start the transformation. If the Sustainable Revolution is to get going, they will need our support. We should give it willingly, not only because it would be the right thing to do, but also because it will protect our future and ensure the cohesion and safety of the local community around us.

Persuading people to be good world citizens and make unilateral changes to consumption patterns and lifestyle is a lost cause. This is not the way to build the majority call for action that the politicians need. A better mechanism is to tap into people's selfish desire to protect what they have, and improve the quality of their own lives.

It is sad that, in order to start the Sustainable Revolution, it is necessary to take a jaundiced view of human nature. For my generation, I see no alternative. I hope that future generations will learn the concepts of sustainability at primary school so that appropriate behaviour becomes second nature.

The Sustainable Revolution will bring huge disruption. There will be winners and losers. In my book *Adapt and Thrive*,[4] I encouraged corporations to exploit the opportunities of the Sustainable Revolution. I now encourage everyone to reconfigure their personal affairs to survive and prosper from the coming revolution. There is no need to feel guilty. Acting in this way will be self-fulfilling. The more of us who are ready to live well within a sustainable society, the more likely it is that the future we want comes about.

Put Quality of Life before Quantity

Strong communities are the building blocks of a sustainable world (see Chapter 17). The first defence against the coming disruption is to be sure that you are embedded within such a community. This will ensure that you have security and mutual support around you in any eventuality. As people relearn the importance of community values, you will be well placed to share in the success of the community.

In looking for employment, a high priority should be given to job security to provide protection during the uncertain times ahead. A wage or salary is required to pay the bills, of course, but chasing after a big pay cheque will make less sense within a world that embraces the values of sustainability. With less emphasis on material consumption, we will be free to place 'satisfaction' and 'contentment' in our job-search criteria. As community spirit and interdependence increase, status will be defined as the standing you hold within the community. Within a sustainable community, displays of material wealth and conspicuous consumption will come to be regarded as ridiculous.

Corporations looking to hire workers would do well to pay their staff with a high quality of life in preference to a high salary. This will generate commitment and loyalty that works both ways. Companies should regard employees as long-term assets to be carefully nurtured. Employees will value a place in a corporate 'family' that invests in their future. Companies will have to plan for long-term success – instead of exploiting short-term opportunities – in order to be able to adopt this strategy. This is how business in a sustainable world should operate. Treating employees in this way need not cost more. It should be quite the opposite, with a lower wage bill being the result of pulling back from financial incentives as the prime staff incentive.

Choosing Where to Live

Sustainable societies will be dominated by dense developments clustered around good public-transport hubs. We will come to accept that less space for our exclusive use is the price we must pay for communities that work. The late 20th-century model of urban sprawl will have to be dismantled. Already, whole neighbourhoods of houses on the periphery of some cities are in danger of becoming ghost towns as a result of the collapse in property prices in 2008. Poorly built houses in sprawling suburbs that are not served by public transport may never recover their former value. When the housing market picks up, it will be led by energy-efficient homes located within developments that are designed around people and community (Chapter 16).

If you own a large, poorly insulated house in a suburb where the car is the only transport option, you should try to sell it whilst it still has value. Owning such a house was the aspiration of many people during the years of the housing boom and cheap fuel. In the short term, there may still be people who cling to this dream. As more people become supporters of the Sustainable Revolution, such houses will become nearly worthless.

In buying a property, ensure that it has been designed to minimize fuel bills through good insulation and is fitted with the technology to capture solar energy. Location will be the prime factor (some things don't change). Access to a good transport hub (by foot or a safe bicycle route) will be important. Community services and shops located close by is another requirement.

Flying

Flying in conventional aircraft is one of the most unsustainable activities we indulge in. We expect to be able to fly and we like it to be cheap. There are many excuses trotted out to defend the airline industry. None of these arguments survives scrutiny.

People who fly are not the vulnerable and poor. Passengers can afford to pay the full cost. One argument against this – that it would be unfair to the poorer people in the developed world – is ridiculous. Until we replace the current fleet of planes with one that has a low environmental impact, flying should be exorbitantly expensive. There are a small number of senior people in government and industry whose time is so valuable, and whose presence at high-level meetings so crucial, that flying is the best solution. These people do not need subsidies. The cost of their ticket should fully reflect the environmental damage caused. The rich will also be able to afford to fly, and they will have to pay heavily for the privilege. Those of us in neither category will have to accept that flying is an occasional and expensive special journey until the next generation planes are brought into service.

In Chapter 15, I predicted a major shake-out in the airline industry. There can be little doubt that my analysis is correct. As the impacts of climate change become more severe, the political climate will be right to raise taxes on aviation fuel to match or exceed the taxes levied on other fossil fuels. Flying will contract and become much more expensive until a new generation of 'green' aircraft can be designed, developed and brought into service.

If you have a desire to go on a long-haul holiday, do it soon. There are cheap seats to be had. There is no point in holding back; the scheduled flight will fly in any case. At the same time, speak out for increases in taxation on flying and aviation fuel. This may sound cynical and selfish but this is what the world needs. For any one person to choose not to fly is one empty seat on a plane flying from A to B. Campaigning for dramatic increases in costs that apply to every person, every country and every airline will help to cut the number of flights significantly. It will also remove the restraints we have applied to our aero-engineers, giving them the freedom to design new aircraft fit for the 21st century.

In addition to booking one last long-haul holiday, sell any shares you have in airlines, particularly those that own large old aircraft. You will then be well placed to observe the huge contraction in capacity as sustainability is finally and belatedly taken seriously by those with influence over the aviation industry.

Buying Goods

The way we shop can have a huge influence over the growth of a sustainable society. So-called 'green' and 'fair-trade' products are examples of using marketing to influence customer choice. Where these products are less effective and/or more expensive, the retailer is simply appealing to our charitable nature. We need to move beyond this, to products that are the best choice because of their quality and value for money.

Look for producers that are committed to the development of sustainable green products. If you are attracted to one of their new green products, then purchase it. If not, continue buying the old conventional product, but from this same supplier. Indirectly, you will be supporting their progress. Avoid buying from companies without a plan to reform. Such companies will not be around for long once the Sustainable Revolution bites, and any on-going product support will fold with the company.

I recommend sticking with conventional products until the green alternative is shown to be better. This will ensure proper commercial discipline in the growth of companies for the future. Wasting charitable intentions by buying substandard goods helps no one. Once a green alternative technology has been shown to deliver real benefit, I urge people to lead the change and adopt it quickly. Such leadership will set a fashion for less proactive people to follow.

Solar water heating is an example where the business case is very strong, but inertia has been holding people back. Every house should be fitted with such a system. Solar photovoltaic (PV) panels are different. These will become standard fittings in the future, but the payback periods at current energy prices can extend beyond 100 years. Energy prices have to increase further and cheaper PV technology has to become available before this market will boom. But boom it will. It is only the timing that is unclear.

In a sustainable society, products will be built to last. They will also be built to be refurbished at regular intervals and totally recycled at the end of a long life. It is worth getting into the habit of buying products for long-term usage. Instead of buying the cheapest, and expecting to replace it in a few years time, consider buying the best quality and save money through longevity.

'Made in China' is a label to avoid. One reason is that the huge growth in Chinese manufacturing has brought massive environmental damage to China. That is not just a Chinese problem; it is a problem of global scale. We are complicit in having so much made in China without looking too closely at the methods of production. A second reason not to buy Chinese products is that true recycling requires a close relationship between the manufacturer and the consumer. This will usually involve physical production being close to the end-user. A sustainable world will close down the extended supply chains that have shaped global manufacturing over the last decade.

It makes sense to support those local producers who make high-quality, long-lasting products that can be repaired, refurbished and recycled within the local area. Over the long term this will be cheaper, as well as better for the environment by replacing the steady stream of short-life products that are filling up landfill across the developed world.

Support Tough Immigration Rules

The UK has a population of 61 million people.[5] This is more than the UK has the natural resources to support. We consume over three times more than the capacity of our island's agriculture, forestry and fisheries. This total reliance on spare capacity elsewhere in the world's ecosystem is a risk and a danger. It is time for the UK to commit to living more within its means.

The UK has been a trading nation for centuries. We could hope to continue. Over the short term, there is no choice. We have 61 million mouths to feed and 61 million consumers to satisfy. Unless we negotiate cast-iron guarantees with countries with spare capacity, the UK will struggle in the future.

In building a sustainable society on the small islands of the UK, it will be important to hold population down to a sustainable level. We can then invest properly in the future of the people we have. Immigration must be brought under control. The economy may suffer without new immigrants willing to work for low wages. This is the price of building a secure society that is fit for the future.

It is important that we move fast to control immigration whilst the economy is in reasonable shape. If we delay and the economy collapses, the extreme right may take matters into their own hands with a huge backlash against anyone who looks foreign. This risk of social division is serious. We should force through an illiberal immigration policy now before there is a real crisis. Those well-meaning people and organizations whose first reaction is to resist will need to think carefully about their actions. It would be better that they help to frame an effective and compassionate policy than to oppose it. Politicians will need our support. This is not about bashing foreigners; it is about investing in a sustainable future for the population we now have.

Once steps have been taken to control the influx of yet more people, the UK can consider measures to reduce population. Fiscal policy should be planned around a slowly contracting population. Decisions over incentives, allowances, child support and other social measures should be taken with this aim in mind.

Preserving Natural Habitats

If all of the actions required in the developed world are initiated, a big hole will remain. The world's prime remaining natural habitats are in the underdeveloped world. These do not belong to us. We can reduce the pressure we are placing on them by insisting that resources such as timber and biofuels only come from sustainable sources. This indirect protection will be vital, but on its own will not be enough.

The rich world will have to accept that natural habitats have value. Without such acceptance, it will be hard to persuade the owners to agree to robust long-term protection. Saving the Amazon rainforest is vital to the health of the Earth's ecosystem. The world has to find a way to preserve it. A system that rewards countries for preserving natural habitats is required. We can argue over the methods, incentives and payments, but if we genuinely value our natural heritage then controlling and carefully preserving natural habitats will be a source of wealth in the new world order.

It is vital that we find a sustainable future for the world which meshes the needs of human society with the protection of the planet. The measures outlined in this book seem like a dramatic transformation. This is the minimum action required. How well we tackle this challenge will dictate the future for human society.

Part Three
The Future

21 Living Sustainably

Working with nature, not against it, is how to be prosperous into the long future. People used to know and understand this. We adopted behaviours that suited our geographic location and climate. Our buildings were constructed from local materials and we dressed according to need. We lived with the seasons, wearing warm clothes in the winter and loose, cool clothes in the summer.

In the modern world, we have come to believe that we are no longer constrained by nature. We can have any building design we desire – and bolt on heating or cooling plants as required. Indoor ski slopes in the desert,[1] or tropical spas inside the Arctic Circle,[2] are all possible. For agricultural produce, there is no need to carefully nurture natural habitats and hunt for food. Humankind's industrial agriculture can deliver far more food per hectare than Mother Nature. Nature has become little more than a curiosity, to be visited at the weekend by a car journey to the nearest nature reserve.

Believing that our technology and organization is superior to nature is a dangerous delusion. Anyone caught in a storm is reminded that we humans are puny creatures in comparison with the raw power of the Earth's ecosystem. When nature turns on us, as it will, it is certain that we will lose. Nature must be respected. Living sustainably is how humans will secure a safe future. Such a future can also be a rich and enjoyable life.

Planet Earth can be a paradise for a human population of an appropriate size. A high-consumption society would have to be small. A low-consumption society could be bigger. The overall load on the ecosystem must remain within safe limits. Western Europe shows how this could be possible. If immigration is taken out of the equation, the populations of most western European countries are stable or declining. Some people choose not to have children. Most parents accept that two children are enough. In the prosperous developed world, it is not difficult to design fiscal policy to discourage large families in a way that is fair and equitable, leading to a declining population.

In a sustainable world, each country has the responsibility to link the size of its population with its resource capacity. If each community is tuned into the carrying capacity of the locality, the circumstances are right for people to choose to bring into the world only the number of children that can live healthy and fulfilling lives. This is a part of the attitude needed for a sustainable world.

Where some populations expand out of control, people will suffer discomfort and a lower quality of life. This is a natural consequence. We should hold back from interfering. Assuming that a coherent policy framework is adopted, such as that described in Chapter 12, resource constraint can suppress population growth in an acceptable way before the point at which starvation takes over.

In the globalized world of the 20th century, it was assumed that the global market could always deliver enough of everything we need. This attitude has disconnected populations from their local resource base. It will take time to rebuild the linkages. Each time that a drought threatens, and the harvest is poor, a population comes under pressure. This situation requires careful stewardship of food supplies, including plans to safeguard the seed needed to plant next year's crop. These can be complex challenges, which draw communities together in a shared sense of purpose and mutual reliance. When the crisis is past, people remember what happened. People learn to store long-life food, such as grain and maize, whilst times are good. People also learn to be wary of growing the population larger than that which can survive the next poor harvest.

In a sustainable world, governments and aid agencies must be dissuaded from dumping food on a region in response to each potential crisis. The food typically goes to central locations with good transport links to the outside world. People are drawn in from the surrounding regions to reside in camps where food is provided. But these relatively well-nourished people are surviving with their dignity and pride taken away. Communities can be destroyed as a result of well-intended but misdirected Western aid. In destroying community we also undermine the sustainability of the region.

Pictures of people scrabbling for food prompt the West to send yet more food and more aid. Where the country wants to deal with the crisis within its own resources, we often resist. We prefer to force access for our logistic capabilities so that we can bypass inefficient and potentially corrupt local officials to deliver food directly to those we judge to be in need. Holding back, to ensure that the local community is not undermined, is hard to do in the modern world of live television coverage. Western sensitivity to disturbing television pictures should not force aid agencies to deliver short-term fixes. Such agencies should be free to make their expert assessment, including talking with local leaders, in order to deliver appropriate long-term solutions.

Where cycles of plenty followed by scarcity are normal, careful thought is needed to break the cycle of population growth followed by starvation. Providing food during the starvation phase of the cycle provides little real help. Aid would be better applied during the upside of the cycle to reinforce local arrangements to conserve stocks for lean periods. Aid should also be directed at holding population growth in check when times are good. At such times there are no powerful images to activate our charitable intentions, but this is when real long-lasting improvement can be made.

Living within the world's agricultural capacity is vital, and the way to achieve this is to entwine people's lives with nature. This applies to the developed world just as much as to poorer regions. Even within cities, agriculture close to where we live should be normal. In sustainable cities without toxic traffic fumes, such food is healthy, fresh and grown at the point of need.

All open-to-sky space in cities is valuable. Some can be used for rooftop agriculture. All other roof areas should be covered with solar panels to generate energy. The other use for open-to-sky space is for people to sit, walk or cycle. Roads are a wasteful use of such space. As our transport fleet goes electric, eliminating toxic fumes, it will be safe to put the whole transport network underground.

Sustainable living is a very attractive future. It is also a very different future. The corrosive properties of selfish individualism have to be recognized and countered. The attitudes that must take over can still demand a lot from life but will be configured differently.

Each person, and each family, requires sufficient high-quality private space. It does not need to be large or to consume high amounts of energy. Around these modest private dwellings there needs to be shared space – shared with other people and shared with nature. The blending of leisure space, agriculture and nature can support vibrant and happy communities. Each person has the facilities that only a millionaire can afford, but shared with the community rather than fenced off into large private gardens or estates. Some communities will choose to be exclusive gated communities shared by a select group; other countries will develop such a stable and safe society that fences and gates are generally not required.[3]

Instead of a concrete jungle taking over from nature, human communities can include nature, agriculture, living space and places of work all within one highly self-sufficient community. Such communities are the fundamental building block of sustainable human society. The concept also applies to cities. These can be a tessellation of urban villages, each clustered around a transport hub.

For these communities to work well, all its members need to be drawn into active engagement. Society should be designed around people and useful activity for people. Respect and high standing should derive from serving the community. Rich people can show off by donating facilities to the community or owning large spaces that they share with the community. The traditional use of old manor houses in England is an example. The owner was the lord of the manor and had considerable power, but many such owners understood that respect was in the gift of the community. The grounds of the manor house would be used for local events on a regular basis. The house was run by a community of servants and other people providing employment and contributing to social cohesion. Since the 20th century many such manor houses have been bought by rich celebrities or entrepreneurs who have fitted high-security systems to keep people out.

People who cling to the 20th-century wish for large private spaces and high-consumption lifestyles should be taxed heavily. This is a measure that some people support out of envy and a wish to redistribute wealth. The much better reason is to counter, and then eliminate, the attitude that conspicuous consumption is to be admired. Grand lives do not require great consumption.

Rubbish is a plague of our time, but it will not exist in a sustainable world. There will be equipment that has reached the end if its life, clothes that are worn out, food scraps, out-of-date publications and all sorts of surplus stuff, but none of it will be rubbish. All of it will have a useful next purpose. Combustible material such as paper and wood will be burnt for energy; other biodegradable material will be composted to generate methane. The by-products will be fertilizer for agriculture and, of course, CO_2.

CO_2 is a normal output of a sustainable biomaterial cycle. The CO_2 emitted should cause no concern as it is taken up by the next crop. The problem that we now have of excessive CO_2 levels in the atmosphere will be solved in a sustainable world by banning the exploitation of fossil fuels (Chapter 14).

All components that are not biodegradable will be reconditioned, or the material will be reclaimed and made into new components. Mining will only be required on a small scale to expand the total amount of technical material in circulation. Another type of mining will focus on the legacy rubbish in disused landfill sites. The toxic mix of 20th century rubbish will be hard to deal with, but the metals and materials will have value, and will be worth reclaiming.

As we clear up the mess of industrialization, many of the worst sites will be reinstated and given back to nature. Scientists are finding plants that take up pollution as they grow.[4] These can be harvested to extract polluting substances. The particular plant can be highly selective in what it pulls out of the soil. Over many growing seasons the ground can be cleansed. It may also prove possible to process the crops to reclaim valuable substances, such as heavy metals. Once again, inviting nature back into sites occupied by human society delivers positive outcomes.

The protection of natural habitats becomes a different challenge. Instead of seeking solely to keep mankind off protected nature reserves, we should combine the world of humans with that of nature. An example is the firing ranges used by the military. A more extreme example of mankind not caring a damn for nature is hard to find. These sites are littered with bomb craters and unexploded munitions. But they also act as a haven for many kinds of wildlife which are free from disturbance except for the low risk of being hit by a missile. This is accidental nature conservancy, and it works.

Deliberate design to bring natural habitats into the area occupied by humans can reinforce the ecosystem and also help it to adjust to the climate change that humans have caused. Farmland should include space for nature so that there are corridors for species to move between nature reserves. The mix of crops should be selected to work with nature. In this way, the need for artificial fertilizer can be reduced or eliminated. Working to reinforce the natural ecosystem can also encourage natural predators, such as ladybirds, to reduce the need for pesticides. Sustainable agriculture uses less material resources; the quality of the produce is higher – measured by taste and health benefits rather than looks; and overall yields do not need to suffer when considering the whole balance of food, fuel and fertilizer.

The downside to sustainable agriculture (from the viewpoint of the industrial agriculture lobby) is that it requires a lot more care, thought and human involvement. As we bring nature back into farming, we also bring people back to the land. This can be enjoyable and healthy employment, providing a lifestyle that does not need high pay. To run agriculture in this way in the developed world requires a major reversal of policy and a fundamental shift in the attitudes of both policy makers and workers. The benefits to the world ecosystem will be amplified beyond the improvements we observe in our local environment. Developing countries will have a different example to aspire to. Many of the least developed countries could choose to miss out the stage of industrialized farming and bounce forward to 21st-century green agriculture, building on and improving their own traditional methods.

The remaining big challenges for the planet, such as protecting the remaining rainforests, can also be solved by inviting people to take ownership. This has more chance of success than seeking to exclude humans entirely. Local people can be stewards of the forest and harvest the fruits of the forest in a sustainable manner. It is clearly in their self-interest to work to retain the forest for their children and future generations.[5]

Where a fence defines the boundary between a nature reserve and land occupied by man, we often see a dramatic change. On one side there may be cleared farmland; on the other, a forest struggling to survive. There will not be such sharp distinctions using sustainable agricultural practices. For example, oil-palm plantations in places such as Indonesia are currently a major threat to the rainforest. The high demand for biofuel causes commercial pressure to clear more virgin forest and replace it with oil-palm plantations. It is seen as a zero-sum game where the land is either forest or straight rows of monoculture oil palms. This situation can be changed by allowing other species and wildlife to grow alongside the oil palms. Plantations can become forests with a high density of oil palm. Operated in this way, the commercial forest can be a useful extension to the nature reserves nestling within. Indonesia's place in the world ecosystem could be protected, and the micro-climate of the rainforest preserved – in conjunction with exploiting it. Such palm oil plantations will be more complex to manage. It will be harder to use automation, so more people will need to be employed. In a sustainable world, less machinery, more employment and a healthy ecosystem all work hand-in-hand together, providing a better lifestyle for local people and preserving the environment.

This is my vision of a sustainable world. The general themes are not hard to identify but the detail is far from clear. Human society and the ecosystem working together is a very complex interrelationship. How it turns out will not be the result of top-down design. A sustainable world will evolve as we adopt sustainable behaviours. By changing attitudes, a sustainable world becomes possible. It may look like the idyllic world I describe or something rather tougher and rougher.

Let us not be fooled into thinking that a sustainable world will be Utopia. A sustainable society will still reflect human nature. Choosing to live sustainably requires that we adopt a different attitude, but we cannot change the way we are. All people will not suddenly become kind and caring. To shift to a sustainable lifestyle, and insist that other people do the same, will require robust and resolute action.

22 Fight for the Future

Humans are born into the world with nothing. As they grow into children, they learn from adults that possessions matter, but all they really need, and truly value, is security and love. Many children go on to be young adults who enjoy the pleasures of life without caring much for possessions. 'Youth' and 'freedom' are their defining attributes as they leave home. Young humans are naturally receptive to the concept of sustainable living, but we will have to fight hard to change the ingrained attitudes of modern Western society.

Humans are competitive creatures, competing for girlfriends or boyfriends and participating in sport and games. Parents have to drum into their offspring the need to direct their competitive instincts towards a successful career. Finally, most young people stop rebelling against their parents and come to accept the attitude that society expects of them. In the West, the usual requirement is material success, and that success is gauged in relative terms. Having enough is not enough if our neighbour has more. We 'need' ever more possessions to hold our place in the hierarchy of society.

When resources run low, we fight to keep what we see as our share. In a materialist world, this has to be more than other people around us. This attitude is setting up the human race for an unpleasant struggle for survival in which we will all be losers.

The wealth accrued during the current era of unsustainable consumption will count for nothing as society collapses under the weight of its own success. The sooner this is understood, the sooner we will be willing to give our competitive nature a new challenge. The prize that is worth fighting for is a sustainable society.

The prime difference between the society we have now and a sustainable society is that the ecosystem is safeguarded. This matters more than short-term issues of suffering, unfairness or economic hardship. These are acute problems that we can overcome. A failing ecosystem is a chronic condition that has no easy fix. Humankind will suffer for many generations from damage to the ecosystem, long after the particular problems of today's society have been forgotten.

Concentrating on the prime aim of protecting the ecosystem is the route to success. This means that we should not group all the problems of the world under the umbrella of sustainability. A sustainable world will not be fair; it will not be peaceful. There will be beacons of success for other countries to aspire to, but there will also be sinks of despair. This is an imperfect world we inhabit. The selfish human instinct is an irresistible force. Rather than seek to combat it, it should be redirected towards building a sustainable society. There will be losers and people who suffer, but the short-term pain is a price worth paying.

The focus on economic success is part of the problem the world faces. Laissez-faire capitalism and support for globalization has dominated economic policy since 1990. The policy of deregulation, privatization and free trade has come to be known as the 'Washington Consensus'.[1] From a narrow economic perspective, this policy prescription has been shown to work. Those crafting the policies did not foresee the problems that would arise in the 21st century as globalization brought huge expansion to the world's demand for resources.

The Washington Consensus has been the basis of the advice coming out of the IMF and the World Bank over the last two decades. In many cases, this has been a prescriptive policy with which countries have had to comply in order to receive loans and financial support. Where there was sound government and transparent mechanisms, it worked well. The UK, for example, has done well using such policies. Opening up to world trade has led to the closure of some industries but other economic activity has taken its place. Privatization has brought improvements to services and driven down prices to consumers. Deregulation has made the City of London a leading financial centre and major income earner.

Other countries have found that the policies of the Washington Consensus have not served them well. Mexico, for example, has had trouble implementing the policies.[2] Some argue that the problem is failure in implementation, but the problem is more fundamental. The policy prescription does not suit all countries, which have different cultures and different circumstances. Joe Stiglitz, the World Bank's Chief Economist 1997–2000, has been an outspoken critic. He argues that policy has focused too narrowly on pursuing economic growth and that a new paradigm is required for development.[3]

The financial crisis of 2008 moved the argument from a few dissenters to mainstream discussion as weaknesses in deregulated markets were exposed. World leaders have been prompted to act. The G20 group of nations met in Washington in November 2008 to start discussion about reforming the financial system. They pledged to work together to 'achieve needed reforms in the world's financial systems'. This could be the start of a policy review as fundamental as the process that led to the Bretton Woods agreements signed in 1944.[4] These agreements were drafted whilst the Second World War was still raging and were designed to rebuild the international economic system when the war was over. This has been the basis of the world economic system ever since. The system is now out of date and needs fundamental reform.

As world leaders start the debate for change, the examination of policy should be much broader than the aim expressed by the G20 to 'restore global growth'. Making this explicit aim the prime focus for the discussion illustrates just how blinkered world leaders and their advisors have become. Our policy focus should be on social outcomes whilst reinforcing the integrity of the environment. Economics is one of the most powerful tools we have. But making economic outcomes the prime objective is like concentrating on the toolbox, rather than the task in hand.

The debate the world needs to pull out of the current crisis must include the environmental consequences of world trade and other problems that undermine the sustainability of society. Such a broad debate could lead to a new economic policy framework, as radical as Bretton Woods was in its day, but fit for the circumstances of the 21st century.

As the US President, Barack Obama, and other world leaders shape policy, they should realize the depth of change required. The world needs a fundamental shift in attitude. It cannot happen overnight. It will take time to understand what is required and to craft policy that suits.

Smaller countries are already setting the pace. Counties such as Sweden and New Zealand have made substantial commitments towards sustainability. Such small affluent countries, with ample natural resources, will find it relatively easy to become sustainable. It may not be a simple task, but it is clearly feasible. Those countries that lead in developing and implementing policies for a sustainable society will become beacons for the rest of the world to copy. For many other countries, the challenge will be immense.

How the world's biggest economies respond will be crucial. Interestingly, the headline figures indicate that the United States would find it relatively easy to become a sustainable society. As discussed in Chapter 1, if the United States were to reduce average consumption per person from 9.4 gha to the European average of 4.7 gha, the US population would be living within its ecological capacity.

If the United States adopted policy to become a sustainable society, it would earn the admiration of the world – and cause considerable hardship elsewhere. The United States is currently a huge exporter of agricultural produce. It would be no surprise if a sustainable US society directed this capacity towards US needs. Agricultural capacity can be switched quickly to the production of biofuels and biodegradable materials. The transition period, as US food supplies are pulled off the world market, would be hard. Other countries can hope that the United States chooses to adopt methods and technologies that allow the country to continue to export food. But this is a choice for the United States. Objecting to US decisions that solve the country's excessive load on the planet would be unjustified.

In a sustainable world, countries will have to fight hard to develop, protect and preserve the capabilities they require. Specific arrangements for sustainable trade will evolve, but this will be different to the concept of an open world market. The Earth is running out of capacity and, as we reach the limits, the policy of free trade will have to be rewritten.

One country will find the change to a sustainable future particularly hard. China has a large ecological capacity of over one billion gha. However, its huge population (1.3 billion) currently consumes more than twice this amount. It is running a massive deficit of 1.6 billion gha, overtaking the United States (–1.3 billion gha).[5] The difference compared with the United States is that the Chinese deficit is deeply entrenched. Each Chinese person is not a big consumer. The average ecological footprint is 2.1 gha per person. This matches the figure that each resident of the world would have if the entire ecological capacity of the planet were shared out equally to each person. But the world does not operate on the basis of sharing all we have. The world is a selfish place. For China to find ways of living within its capacity will require either reductions in consumption or action to reduce the size of the population.

From a Western perspective, the problems of China seem insoluble. We make the assumption that the Chinese people aspire to the lifestyles we now have. If that means matching our current levels of consumption, then China cannot possibly cope. We already see China building relationships with resource-rich countries to secure supplies. There is a very real danger that the Chinese will cause lasting environmental damage not only by exploiting their own resources but also by reaching out to plunder the resources of every country to which they can gain access.

For example, the continent of Africa is at risk. Chinese influence is growing through the country's investment in many poor African countries. This can be seen in a positive light by those still locked into the narrow view that growing the economy is the main component of development. But the Chinese are not in Africa with charitable intent. It is doubtful that the new colonialists will be any better than the Europeans were in centuries past. In Europe, we have learnt the error of our ways, put history behind us, and now support Africa to find African solutions. We owe it to African countries to be robust in doing what we can to defend Africa from Chinese exploitation.

How China decides to continue its progress will have a huge impact on the world, but the power of Western influence is limited. China needs a Chinese solution, and only the Chinese can decide how to run their country. The West should back off from trying to persuade China to reform along Western lines. It is more important that China reduces its load on the world ecosystem. China has to consume less, or have a smaller population. Where the Chinese use methods that we do not like, such as the one-child policy, we should be careful not to criticize. China has a massive problem; the Chinese should be supported in trying to tackle it.

It is feasible that China will decide not to follow the Western development path and will bounce forward to a sustainable future based on advanced green technology. China may also decide to return to some of the values of its recent past by encouraging low-consumption rural communities. If China can show the world that its huge population can live sustainably, then it would take the moral high ground, and it would be right to expect other countries to follow.

Converting the United States to the cause of sustainability is the big prize. Until it was overtaken by China, it was the most unsustainable large country in the world. It is also the country with the most influence. If the United States can be converted, then the world would have a different example to follow. We can expect the concept of sustainability to be taken seriously once the most powerful country in the world champions it. From a European perspective, the United States can become sustainable simply by consuming resources at the same rate as us. When US tourists visit Europe, they often miss the luxuries of home, but people in Europe do not generally live deprived lifestyles. We live well; but we live differently. There is no reason for the United States not to continue to live well but according to a different set of priorities.

Real progress in reconfiguring the world economy requires that at least one of the world's main national economies adopts policy for a sustainable future. Smaller countries can show the way, but the tipping point will come when large countries like the United States or China decide to act. If both China and the United States delay action and attempt to continue the policies of the 20th century, the impact on planet Earth would be calamitous. Conversely, if both great countries compete to be the first to reach sustainability, this would be a superpower struggle that is worthy of the 21st century.

With Barack Obama in the White House, the United States and the world have an opportunity. One man cannot possibly solve such a difficult and complex set of challenges. We should not expect too much. However, one man can start the change of attitude required. President Obama's rhetoric sets the required tone. During the election campaign of 2008, he talked about investing in a clean energy future, the promotion of grass-roots social engagement and building liveable and sustainable communities. President Obama will have to fight hard to convert the rhetoric into policy.

The people now in power have been brought up in a political climate, and according to a set of values, that are now out of date. Resistance to change will come from those who have done well out of raw capitalism, and are reluctant to try another way. There will also be simple inertia. People do not like to have their lives disrupted, even if this is what is required to shape a better long-term future. Change makes people worried and edgy. This is not surprising, as there are difficult and potentially unpleasant times ahead.

It is relatively easy to say what needs to be done – as this book has outlined. It will be fiendishly difficult to make it happen. There is no avoiding the fact that many people's accustomed lifestyles will change. This must not be used as an excuse for inaction. We must fight hard to defend the future, despite the difficulties, against those who continue to deny the need for change.

23 My Generation: Villains or Heroes?

Presidents, prime ministers, chief executives and senior managers of today come from the generation born in the 1950s and 1960s. This is my generation. We have presided over the greatest economic boom that the world has ever seen. We have also watched from the sidelines as the ecosystem has come under intolerable pressure.

The financial crash of 2008–9 marks the end of an era. If we concentrate on kick-starting the world economy to get one last surge of unsustainable growth, we may be able to force the world economy into another boom that lasts long enough to take us through to retirement. Our generation will then go down in history as the selfish generation that put material success before the health of the planet. If we recognize the problems of 2009 as a warning, and accept the need to take painful and dramatic action, then we can become the generation that changed the direction of society and set a different path for humanity in the 21st century.

Our material success is there for all to see. The developed world has a huge road network packed with gleaming cars, shopping malls stocked with all manner of goods and large houses full of possessions. These range from designer clothes that will remain in fashion for just a few months to gadgets so cheap that we can chuck them away when the novelty has worn off.

Our pride in possessions has gone to extraordinary lengths. The Audi RS6 estate car, launched in 2008, has an engine that delivers 572 bhp. This is more power than Jackie Stewart had at his disposal when he won the Formula One World Championships when I was a boy in 1973. In a sports car, such power has a purpose. In an estate, the only reason can be to have more power than the family next door. By the time this book appears in print, Mercedes or BMW may have increased the power of their estate car to retake the top position.[1] The game of measuring success through having relatively more than others is running out of control.

The generation before us did not have such material wealth. They started their careers in austerity following the destruction of World War II. They can take pride in having rebuilt the world order, once again putting humankind on the path to success. A pinnacle of their achievement was to put a man on the moon in 1969. John F. Kennedy set the vision in his address to the US congress in 1961:

> *I believe that this nation should commit itself to achieving the goal, before this decade is out, of landing a man on the moon and returning him safely to the Earth.*

Just eight years later, Kennedy's vision was delivered as Apollo 11 returned to Earth after taking the first astronauts to the moon. The engineers and scientists manning NASA mission control had an average age of 32 years.[2] These young people will have been, on average, just 24 years old when they listened to Kennedy's speech.

I detect a feeling amongst young people today that they are receptive to change. They are open-minded and can be persuaded to change their lifestyle. If world leaders were to set them the objective of building a sustainable society, I believe that they could rise to the challenge – and make progress as quickly as the Apollo project. Our generation must start the process of changing attitudes and setting different policy objectives to give the younger generation this opportunity.

Building a sustainable society will require drive and innovation, but also a return to old, enduring values. The way that we treat planet Earth should not be negotiable or subject to the whim of the next economist with a new theory on how to increase economic growth. When Neil Armstrong stepped on the moon he said the famous words, 'One small step for man; one giant leap for mankind.' Looking up at the blue planet, he was not to know how humankind would make such wasteful use of our technical progress over the next four decades.

The leap for humankind that the Apollo flights heralded is the exploration of the solar system and beyond. This will only be possible if we have a vibrant, secure and sustainable human society back on Earth from which to mount future missions.

The first permanently manned space outpost is the international space station. This has been manned continuously since November 2000. The second outpost is likely to be on the moon, living in domed structures with special glass to filter out harmful radiation. Inside, a sustainable life cycle can be established, using the sun to grow food and with all waste recycled. Space-age geologists will prospect on the moon for minerals to use in construction, to reduce the amount that has to be flown from Earth. Once the technology to manufacture such structures from minerals mined on the moon is operational, the circumstances are set for a huge expansion across the surface of the moon (and under the lunar surface). The people trailblazing this stage of human progress will not be far from home. If it goes wrong and all systems fail, they can hop back to Earth relatively easily.

Once enough equipment and robots have been established on the moon, it can become the launch site to explore further into the solar system. When the technology of off-Earth living is perfected, and can be relied upon, colonies further afield can be established in the same way. I am confident that humankind can build permanents outposts on Mars. We already have sufficient technology: we just need to apply enough investment. We will also need a reason to try. Our curiosity may be enough. Our natural inquisitiveness leads us to explore new frontiers on our planet, in science and into space. Beyond Mars, the next big leap will be out of this solar system to another sun and another set of planets.

When the human species has a number of colonies on a number of planets, we could then afford to allow our inquisitiveness free rein to experiment with changing the atmosphere and climate of these new settlements. We could try to manipulate the atmosphere to become more like that on Earth. We could try introducing life with the idea of establishing an ecosystem. The organisms that we transplant, if they can survive the alien conditions, may, over the centuries, settle into an environment that will support life. An Earth-like environment suitable for humans to walk in without breathing equipment may be too ambitious a target. The construction of an environment suitable for growing crops harvested by robots would be much more feasible.

Where attempts to convert a planet to human needs fail, we can abandon it and move to another. Some planets may be destroyed as they are stripped bare of the minerals that human civilization requires. In a universe full of barren planets, that would be acceptable.

Back on planet Earth, we would hope that our unique planet has become a cosmic nature reserve, off-limits for all destructive and polluting activities – the cradle of human civilization preserved in all its perfection. This is how it should be, but only if Earth survives intact from the onslaught of humankind in the 21st century.

I fear that the technology we need to live on Mars and other planets will also be required on Earth: living domes with filtered air to keep humans safe from the pollution and radiation of a damaged planet. Planetary engineers will try to use the experience they gain with other planets to try to rebuild the ecosystem of planet Earth. They would find it impossible to rebuild the incredible biodiversity that we have now if, in the meantime, we have destroyed it.

Humankind is at a dangerous junction. If we can learn respect for the ecosystem, bring population under control and become much more careful with the way we exploit the resources of the planet, then the future is bright. Our descendants will explore the universe. If we fail to act, civilization could collapse before developing the technology for routine long-distance space travel. The knowledge base required is huge and complex. Now, we have the foundations of a technically advanced civilization that can explore the universe, but it could so easily be lost.

Historians cannot help us now. We do not have evidence of the results of humankind's grand experiment with our special planet. We have to move beyond the impulsive brilliance that has made humans so successful. This time, instead of trying, failing, picking up the pieces and rising again, we need to act before circumstances force us to. There is no time to watch the experiment we are running with planet Earth to completion; we must stop it whilst there is still time.

My generation have the interim results. These show deeply worrying changes to the environment. It is also quite obvious that our dash for progress is the cause. Our success has brought us to the position we face. The combination of our material aspirations and unfettered drive for growth will destroy us. It is our responsibility to change the parameters we use to measure progress and set the way for the next generation to build a sustainable future.

First, we must plan for a sustainable future. Currently, there is widespread denial that sustainability matters. This is self-serving ignorance in the same vein as not thinking about death. We don't think about death very much because it worries us, and there is nothing we can do to stop it. There is no point in spending every day wondering where, when and by what means we will die. This is a rational way to retain our sanity. We are behaving with regard to sustainability in much the same way. We are ignoring an obvious truth in order to make our lives easier. Admitting that we need a sustainable society risks undermining all we have. But sustainability is not like death. Destroying our world is not inevitable; it can be stopped. We have to grasp the difficulty of planning for a sustainable future in order that future generations can also live fulfilling lives.

Second, we must push past those people who will resist a sustainable future for the world. People who choose to live a sustainable life should be free, of course, to do so in their own way without external interference. But the majority of people will not compromise over their material demands unless forced to do so. People who are wastefully over-consuming should be forced to change through financial and social pressure. Their pockets should be hit with heavy taxation and their behaviours changed by adopting different measures of relative worth. Excessively big cars should cost a lot to drive and should lead to their owners being shunned by peers within their social group. Taxation and fashion are unlikely allies, but, if the combination can be brought together, they become a powerful duo. Sustainability becomes automatic when it is both the cheaper and the fashionable option.

My generation faces a complex set of issues, ranging from climate change and population growth to threats to the cohesion of society and economic meltdown. These issues intertwine, with every issue impinging on every other. Solutions are hard to find, but an overall solution is possible if we change attitudes.

If we dare not – or cannot – change society we will become victim of our own success.

Epilogue

The first draft of this book was built around the concept that humankind had inadvertently sentenced the world to death. The sentence of execution had been passed and we had to lodge an appeal if we were to earn a reprieve. This was a dark and depressing theme around which to build my argument. The first draft title 'Stuck on Death Row' was just as depressing and had to change.

An insight into my black thoughts is provided by this quotation from the first draft:

> *If we fail to act now, whilst there is still time, we sentence our descendants to a life of despair, or worse . . .*
>
> *Capitalism is bringing great material wealth to many people across the world. The party is in full swing and there is plenty for everyone. There are no barriers – we can all join this celebration of mankind's industry. It is clear that over-indulgence is rampant but we do not want to risk spoiling the party mood. The heady cocktail of our economic success is clouding our vision.*
>
> *In full view of us all, other forces are at work. These are constructing a scaffold within our midst. It may not have the normal components of steps, platform, rope, trapdoor and lever; but it will be just as effective. Most of the party-goers do not know what is being built, or, if they do, they believe it is not being built for them. Some other wretched criminal will be marched in and hanged in full view.*
>
> *For me, the party has lost its shine . . .*

As I sat and wrote the detail within each chapter, two things changed. The first was that I started to see that the decisions we need to take are straightforward. There are few practical difficulties to overcome. Each of the ways I propose to save the world is feasible and achievable. All we need is the will.

The second change was how people's reactions have altered. Some years ago, my ideas met with scepticism and sometimes outright resistance. Now, people listen and engage with the debate. People are at least willing to discuss the changes required. The ideas are much the same, but the reception they receive is different. These are hugely encouraging signs.

I have pulled out of my deep dark mood to one of optimism and excitement for the future. We really can set up a future for our descendants that will make them proud of us. These are dangerous words, when all we have is a tiny spark trying to set alight a wholesale attitude shift. Unless we feed the small flickering flame with the fuel of true action, it will splutter out before it has really taken hold.

I have included the quotation from my early draft lest we forget what is at stake. People want a happy ending; so do I. But this is not a story. This is real life, and there will only be a happy ending if we are willing to work hard to make it so.

Notes

1 ONE EARTH, ONE CHANCE

1. Population Division, Department of Economic and Social Affairs, *The World at Six Billion* (United Nations, 1999).

2. Global hectares (gha) are hectares with world-average biological productivity (1 hectare = 2.47 acres). Footprint calculations use yield factors to take into account national differences in biological productivity. Footprint and biocapacity results for nations are calculated annually by the Global Footprint Network. The continuing methodological development of these National Footprint Accounts is overseen by a formal review committee (www.footprintstandards.org/committees).

3. *Living Planet Report 2008* (WWF).

4. Global Footprint Network, *Annual Report 2007*.

5. Prof. Stephen Tinsley and Heather George, *Ecological Footprint of the Findhorn Foundation and Community* (Sustainable Development Research Centre, 2006).

6. Global Footprint Network, *Ecological Footprint and Biocapacity* (2008 edn), spreadsheet accessed from www.footprintnetwork.org.

7. Brazil has a surplus of 0.9 billion gha; Russia a surplus of 0.6 billion gha. Figures derived from Global Footprint Network, *Ecological Footprint and Biocapacity* (2008 edn), spreadsheet accessed from www.footprintnetwork.org.

8. The biggest deficits are: China 1.6 billion gha, United States 1.3 billion gha, Japan 0.6 billion gha and India 0.6 gha. Figures derived from Global Footprint Network, *Ecological Footprint and Biocapacity* (2006 edn), spreadsheet accessed from www.footprintnetwork.org.

9 China's consumption is 2.1 gha and capacity is 0.9 gha; India's consumption is 0.9 gha and capacity is 0.4 gha (all figures are per person).

3 THE SELFISHNESS OF HUMAN NATURE

1 *Fullsize Truck Question . . . an odd one*, Hunting Net Forum, http://www.huntingnet.com/forum, posted 16 Apr. 2008.

2 Tony Blair speaking at a press conference and reported by the BBC, 'Blair green views "muddle-headed"', www.bbc.co.uk, 9 Jan. 2007.

3 D. Chandler, 'Footprint', *MIT TechTalk*, Vol. 52, No. 23, 16 Apr. 2008, p. 4.

4 CHOICES

1 Nicholas Stern, *A Blueprint for a Safer Planet* (The Bodley Head, 2009).

2 The World Bank defines living on less than $1.25 a day as extreme poverty; less than $2 a day as very poor (at 2005 prices).

5 BREAKING THE STALEMATE

1 John McCain speaking in Pittsburgh 15 Apr. 2008 called for a summer gas-tax holiday that would suspend the 18.4¢ federal gas tax and 24.4¢ diesel tax. This was on the same day the oil price hit a record high of $113 per barrel.

2 P. J. McManners, 'Business should plan now for the day when energy costs are much higher', *Sustainable Business*, Feb. 2009.

6 CLIMATE CHANGE HITS HOME

1 Scientists at the Mauna Loa observatory in Hawaii measure CO_2 levels in the atmosphere. In 2008 they recorded 387 parts per million (ppm). Source: Dr. Pieter Tans, NOAA/ESRL (www.esrl.noaa.gov/gmd/ccgg/trends/).

2   Jane G. Ferrigno, Kevin M. Foley, Charles Swithinbank and Richard S. Williams, 'Coastal-Change and Glaciological Map of the Northern Ross Ice Shelf Area, Antarctica: 1962–2004' (USGS publication, 2007).

3   British Antarctic Survey (BAS), 'Antarctic Factsheet Geographical Statistics' (Aug. 2008).

4   Vicky Pope, 'Climate Change: latest UK Forecasts of Regional Impacts Around the World', speaking at the 'Climate Security: the Policy Challenges seminar' at the British Embassy in Helsinki, 15 May 2008.

5   J. T. Houghton, Y. Ding, D. J. Griggs, M. Noguer et al (eds) *Climate Change 2001: The Scientific Basis.* Contribution of Working Group I to the Third Assessment Report of the Intergovernmental Panel on Climate Change (IPCC) (Cambridge University Press, 2001).

6   S. Charbit, D. Paillard and G. Ramstein, 'Amount of CO_2 emissions irreversibly leading to the total melting of Greenland', *Geophysical Research Letters*, 26 Jun. 2008.

7   The World Glacier Monitoring Service, *Global Glacier Changes: Facts and Figures* (WGMS, 2008).

8   Intergovernmental Panel on Climate Change, *Climate Change 2007: Synthesis Report* (IPCC, 2007).

7 THE BOOM BEFORE THE BUST

1   The extent of Arctic sea ice in Sep. 2008 was the second lowest ever recorded (4.67 million sq km). The lowest was in Sep. 2007 (4.28 million sq km). Source: National Snow and Ice Data Centre, http://www.nsidc.org.

8 SCRAPING THE BOTTOM OF THE BARREL

1   The cost of extraction ranges from C$14 to C$40 (converted to US$ at an exchange rate of 0.85). Source: National Energy Board (Canada), *Canada's Oil Sands: Opportunities and Challenges to 2015: An Update* (2006).

2   The nominal average price of oil in 1999 was $16.6 per barrel. This is $21.3 per barrel adjusted for inflation 2007. Source: www.inflationdata.com/inflation/inflation_rate/Historical_Oil_Prices_Table.asp.

3   US Environmental Protection Agency, 'Green Power Equivalency Calculator Methodologies', http://www.epa.gov/grnpower/pubs/calcmeth.htm#oil.

10 ALTERING THE FUTURE

1   James Lovelock, *The Vanishing Face of Gaia: A Final Warning* (Allen Lane, 2009).

2   George Monbiot, *Bring on the Apocalypse* (Atlantic Books, 2008).

3   John McManners, *Fusilier. Recollections and Reflections 1939–1945* (Michael Russell (Publishing) Ltd, 2002).

11 SHOW RESPECT FOR THE EARTH

1   Jonathan Loh (ed.), *2010 and Beyond: Rising to the Biodiversity Challenge* (WWF, 2008).

2   The lesser known Juan Sebastián Elcano led the Magellan expedition back to Spain in 1522 after a voyage lasting over three years and which was the first complete circumnavigation of the Earth.

3   55.8 million years ago, the Paleocene-Eocene boundary was marked by a sudden global warming event termed the Paleocene-Eocene Thermal Maximum (PETM). Global temperatures rose by around 6°C.

4   P. J. McManners, *Adapt and Thrive: The Sustainable Revolution* (Susta Press, 2008).

12 STOP BREEDING

1   Thomas Robert Malthus, *An Essay on the Principle of Population* (J. Johnson, London, 1798).

2 Population Division, Department of Economic and Social Affairs, *The World at Six Billion* (United Nations, 1999).

3 The term 'survival and the fittest' was coined by Herbert Spencer in his book *Principles of Biology* (1864). Charles Darwin adopted the term for later editions of his book *On the Origin of Species by Means of Natural Selection* (first published 1859).

4 Jane Elliott, 'I was too fat to have a baby,' 22 Oct. 2006, www.news.bbc.co.uk.

5 Nancy Riley, 'China's Population: New Trends and Challenges', *Population Bulletin* (publication of the Population Reference Bureau), Vol. 59, No. 2, Jun. 2004.

6 G. Hardin, 'The Tragedy of the Commons', *Science*, Vol. 162, Issue 3859, Dec. 1968, pp. 1243–8.

7 Arjun Adlakha, *International Brief Population Trends: India* (US Bureau of the Census, 1997).

8 The average age of the UK population in 2006 was 39 years old. Source: UK Office for National Statistics, www.statistics.gov.uk.

9 Population Reference Bureau, '2007 World Population Data Sheet'.

10 United Nations Statistics Division, *Demographic Yearbook 2005*.

13 THE THREE-WAY BALANCING ACT

1 Stephen H. Schneider, 'Geoengineering: could we or should we make it work?' *Philosophical Transactions of the Royal Society*, Vol. 366, Issue 1882, 13 Nov. 2008.

2 The term 'sustainable development' was described in this way in the report of the World Commission on Environment and Development (WCED), *Our Common Future* (United Nations General Assembly document A/42/427, Aug. 1987), often referred to by the name of its chairman as the Bruntland Report.

3 J. Alan Pounds, Martín R. Bustamante, Luis A. Coloma, 'Widespread Amphibian Extinctions from Epidemic Disease Driven by Global Warming', *Nature*, 439, 161–7, 12 Jan. 2006.

4   The production of biofuels requires energy. Often this comes from fossil fuel sources. We must subtract this processing energy to get a true figure. We can end up in the situation where there is very little net fossil fuel reduction. The fossil fuel used is from low-tax sources and the resulting biofuel can then dodge the high taxes on transport fuels. So the producer makes a profit, the government loses tax revenue, little carbon reduction is achieved and, on top of all this, good agricultural land is taken away from food production.

5   Ed Diener and Robert Biswas-Diener, *Happiness: Unlocking the Mysteries of Psychological Wealth* (Blackwell Publishing, 2008).

14 PLAN TO BAN FOSSIL FUEL

1   The Montreal Protocol on Substances that Deplete the Ozone Layer (UNEP, 2000).

2   Ozone Secretariat, *Our Story* (UNEP, 2005).

3   Calculating how much land would be required to harvest energy to replace fossil fuel in agriculture is difficult. This rough estimate is based on the assumption that a farmer uses 80 litres of fuel per hectare to plough, plant, tend and harvest a crop. It is assumed that 1,000 litres of rapeseed oil can be produced per hectare for conversion into biodiesel. Producing the biodiesel requires energy that is usually from a fossil-fuel source. This energy must be taken out of the equation, It is assumed that energy equivalent to 20% of the biodiesel is used in production. On these figures, 10% of the land under cultivation is required to produce the fuel used by the farmer. This ignores other indirect energy inputs from fossil fuel, notably any artificial fertilizer that might be used.

4   Oil was trading at $3.60 a barrel before the 1973–4 oil crisis. After the crisis it was trading at $12 a barrel. Adjusted to 2007 prices, this was equivalent to a rise from $20 to $48.

5   Oil prices in brackets are adjusted for inflation to 2007 prices. Source:www.inflationdata.com/inflation/Inflation_Rate/Historical _Oil_Prices_Table.asp.

6 *Stern Review Report on the Economics of Climate Change*, commissioned by the UK government and launched Oct. 2006 (Cambridge University Press, 2006).

7 B. D. Hong and E. R. Slatick, 'Carbon Dioxide Emission Factors for Coal', *Quarterly Coal Report*, Energy Information Administration, Jan.–Apr. 1994.

8 'United Kingdom Fuel Duty Escalator, Domestic Best Practices Addressing Climate Change', survey carried out autumn 1999 by the Environment Agency of Japan for the G8 Environmental Futures Forum in Feb. 2000. Source: www.env.go.jp/earth/g8_2000/forum/g8bp/report.html.

15 MELTING THE WINGS OF ICARUS

1 The Convention on International Civil Aviation (also known as the Chicago Convention), was signed 7 Dec. 1944 by 52 states. It was ratified 5 Mar. 1947. (9th edn, Doc 7300/9, 2006).

2 The emphases placed on the words 'fuel' and 'shall be exempt from customs duty' have been added to support the point made here and is not in the original text of the Chicago Convention.

3 *Meeting External Costs in the Aviation Industry*, Annex B (UK Commission for Integrated Transport, 2003).

4 P. J. McManners, *Adapt and Thrive: the Sustainable Revolution* (Susta Press, 2008).

16 CITIES FOR PEOPLE

1 This chapter is based on 'Cities for People: Removing Cars from Urban Life', a paper I presented at the World Institute for Development Economics Research of the United Nations University (UNU-WIDER) project workshop on 'Beyond the Tipping Point: Development in an Urban World' held at the London School of Economics and Political Science, 19–20 October 2007.

2 'Suburbanization' is the term used in *Mobility 2001: World Mobility at the End of the Twentieth century and its Sustainability*, report for the World Business Council for Sustainable Development.

3 N. Wei-Shiuen and L. Schipper, 'China Motorization Trends', *Growing in the Greenhouse: Protecting the Climate by Putting Development First* (World Resources Institute, 2005), ch. 4.

4 Approximate figures extracted from *World Energy, Technology and Climate Policies Outlook 2030 – WETO* (European Commission, 2003).

5 *Biofuels for Transport: An International Perspective* (OECD/IEA, 2004).

6 D. Gilman and R. Gilman, *Ecovillages and Sustainable Communities* (Gaia Trust, 1991).

7 J. Dawson, *Ecovillages: New Frontiers for Sustainability*, Schumacher Briefing No. 12 (Green Books, 2006).

8 *Mobility 2001: World mobility at the End of theTwentieth Century and its Sustainability*, report for the World Business Council for Sustainable Development.

9 Transport For London, *Operational and Financial Report: Third Quarter 2006–7*.

10 P. J. McManners, *Adapt and Thrive: The Sustainable Revolution* (Susta Press, 2008).

11 F. Pearce, 'A Shanty Town That's Here to Stay', *New Scientist*, Issue 1837, 5 Sep. 1992, p. 22.

12 J. H. Crawford, *Carfree Cities* (International Books, 2000).

13 E. L. Glaeser and J. D. Gottlieb, 'Urban Resurgence and the Consumer City', *Discussion Paper No. 2109*, Feb. 2006, Harvard Institute of Economic Research.

14 'Thronged, Creaking and Filthy', *The Economist*, 3 May 2007.

15 There are approximately 600 million cars in the world and a world population of six billion. If the whole world were to have seven cars per ten people (as in the United States), the world car fleet would be seven times larger.

17 HARNESS THE POWER OF COMMUNITY

1 *Mad Max* (1979) is an Australian apocalyptic action thriller film directed by George Miller and written by Miller and Byron Kennedy.

2 The John Lewis Partnership is an example in the UK. Its founder, John Spedan Lewis, set up the Partnership with a governance system and constitution that put the welfare of the workers at the heart of the business. The combination of commercial acumen and corporate conscience was ahead of its time. He placed the company into a trust run for the benefit of the workers in 1929. John Lewis continues to be one of the UK's largest and most successful retailers with 69,000 owner-workers.

3 International Development Enterprises (India) (IDEI) is an Indian not-for-profit organization that has successfully deployed a range of simple, affordable and sustainable technologies to small farmers in India. http:www.ide-india.org.

4 Radio-frequency identification (RFID) tags, or transponders, are small objects that can be applied to or incorporated into a product for the purpose of identification and tracking using radio waves. These tags can be read beyond the line of sight of the reader and up to several metres away.

5 Ilkka Malmberg, 'Life and Death of an Urban Recluse', *Helsingin Sanomat*, 9 Mar. 2008.

6 Andy Newman, 'Neighbours Reflect on a Death No One Noticed', *The New York Times*, 5 Dec. 2007.

7 Adam Smith, *The Wealth of Nations*, Book IV, Ch. II (Edinburgh, 1776).

8 Joseph E. Stiglitz, *Making Globalization Work* (W. W. Norton and Company, 2006).

18 NO COMPROMISE OVER FOOD

1 'Condemned meat conspiracy exposed', reported on BBC News, 21 Dec. 2000.

2 Nicola Carslaw, 'Protection from plough to plate', reported on BBC News, 21 Dec. 2000.

3 Yangfeng Wu, 'Overweight and Obesity in China', *British Medical Journal*, Vol. 333, No. 7564, pp. 362–3, 19 Aug. 2006.

4 *The OECD-FAO Agricultural Outlook 2008–2017* (Food and Agriculture Organization of the United Nations, 2008).

5 Extract from the 'Declaration of the High-Level Conference on World Food Security: the Challenges of Climate Change and Bioenergy', Rome, 5 Jun. 2008.

6 Population Division, Department of Economic and Social Affairs, *The World at Six Billion* (United Nations, 1999).

7 Francesco Branca, Haik Nikogosian and Tim Lobstein, *The Challenge of Obesity in the WHO European Region and the Strategies for Response: Summary* (World Health Organization, 2007).

8 A. Colchester and N. Colchester, 'The Origin of Bovine Spongiform Encephalopathy: the Human Prion Disease Hypothesis', *The Lancet*, 3 Sep. 2005.

9 http://www.bernardmatthewsfarms.com/history, accessed 5 Oct. 2008.

10 'Bernard Matthews admits "possible" Hungarian bird flu link', *Times Online*, 9 Feb. 2007. Source: http://www.timesonline.co.uk/tol/news/uk/article1358254.ece, accessed 4 Oct. 2008.

11 'Outbreak of Highly Pathogenic H5n1 Avian Influenza In Suffolk In January 2007: A Report of The Epidemiological Findings By The National Emergency Epidemiology Group' (Defra, 5 Apr. 2007).

12 '2000s Back to Basics', statement on Bernard Mathews Ltd corporate website, http://www.bernardmatthewsfarms.com/history, accessed 6 Oct. 2008.

13 'Salmon and herring caught in the Baltic Sea, particularly in the Gulf of Bothnia and the Gulf of Finland, may subject consumers to higher than normal levels of dioxins and PCB compounds which are harmful to health.' Advice from the Finnish Food Safety Authority, 2006 (www.evira.fi).

14 A report for the UK Food Standards Agency (FSA) advises that shark, swordfish and marlin were found to exceed acceptable levels of mercury and should not be eaten. It also found high levels in tuna (but within EU guidelines) and advised that pregnant women and children should not eat it. 'Statement on a Survey of Mercury in Fish and Shellfish' from the Committee on Toxicity of Chemicals in Food, Consumer Products and the Environment (Dec. 2002).

19 RESCUE POSEIDON

1 'The oceans are very adaptable but through our endless exploitation of the oceans we've pushed their limits. In parts of the world it is not safe to swim in the seas and the possibility of enjoying swimming, surfing, windsurfing or fishing is ever decreasing'. Global Forum for Sports and Environment, Mar. 2007 (www.g-forse.com).

2 C. Moore, S. Moore, M. Leecaster and S. Weisberg, 'A Comparison of Plastic and Plankton in the North Pacific Central', *Marine Pollution Bulletin* (Dec. 2001).

3 The Sellafield reprocessing plant was originally named 'Windscale' but it was renamed in 1981 to try to disassociate the plant from its past, including the infamous fire of 1957 that released radioactive material into the surrounding environment.

4 In 1962, President John F. Kennedy awarded Frances Kelsey the President's Award for Distinguished Federal Civilian Service.

5 V. S. Blazer, L. R. Iwanowicz, D. D. Iwanowicz, D. R. Smith, et al, 'Intersex (Testicular Oocytes) in Smallmouth Bass from the Potomac River and Selected Nearby Drainages', *Journal of Aquatic Animal Health*, Vol. 19, No. 4, pp. 242–53.

6 *Corruption Perceptions Index 2008* (Transparency International). The scale used is 0 (highly corrupt) to 10 (highly clean). At the bottom: Somalia (1.0), Myanmar (1.3) and Iraq (1.3). At the top: Denmark, New Zealand and Sweden all on 9.3.

7 Democratic Republic of the Congo scores 1.7 in the Transparency International *Corruption Perceptions Index 2008*.

8 Russia scores 2.1 in the Transparency International *Corruption Perceptions Index 2008*.

9 Commission of the European Communities Green Paper on better ship dismantling, Brussels, 22 May 2007. COM(2007) 269.

10 'Deadly toxic waste dumping in Côte d'Ivoire clearly a crime', UN News Centre, 29 Sep. 2006, source: http://www.un.org.

11 W. McDonough and M. Braungart, *Cradle-to-Cradle: Remaking the Way We Make Things* (North Point Press, 2002).

12 Directive 2006/12/EC of the European Parliament and of the Council of 5 Apr. 2006 on waste; amended by Directive 2008/98/EC of 19 Nov. 2008.

13 Paul J. Crutzen and Eugene F. Stoermer, 'The Anthropocene', *Global Change Newsletter*, 1 May 2000.

20 SUPPORT REAL CHANGE

1 The United Nations Conference on Environment and Development (often referred to as the Earth Summit), Rio de Janeiro, 3–14 Jun. 1992.

2 The WTO has no specific agreement dealing with the environment. At the end of the Uruguay Round in 1994, trade ministers from participating countries decided to begin a comprehensive work programme on trade and environment in the WTO. They created the Trade and Environment Committee: 'If the committee does identify problems, its solutions must continue to uphold the principles of the WTO trading system'. Source: *Understanding the WTO: Cross-Cutting and New Issues: The Environment: a Specific Concern*, www.wto.org.

3 *Life Cycle Management: A Business Guide to Sustainability* (United Nations Environment Programme, 2007).

4 P. J. McManners, *Adapt and Thrive: The Sustainable Revolution* (Susta Press, 2008).

5 The resident population of the UK in mid-2007 was 60,975,000. Source: www.statistics.gov.uk.

21 LIVING SUSTAINABLY

1 'Ski Dubai' claims to be the largest indoor snow park in the world.

2 Holiday Club Saariselkä, Finland is a tropical spa located inside the Arctic Circle.

3 Many countries in Europe already have community models based on dense developments with high-quality shared facilities, for example, Finland.

4 Phytoremediators are plants that collect heavy metals and radioactive waste from polluted water and contaminated soils.

5 Simon Counsell, Director of the Rainforest Foundation, speaking at the 'Razing the Rainforests: a 21st-Century Challenge' conference at the Royal Geographical Society with IBG, 22 Oct. 2008.

22 FIGHT FOR THE FUTURE

1 The term 'Washington Consensus' was coined in 1989 by John Williamson to describe a set of ten specific economic policy prescriptions that he considered to constitute a 'standard' economic reform package:

- fiscal policy discipline;
- redirection of public spending from subsidies;
- tax reform – broadening the tax base and adopting moderate marginal tax rates;
- interest rates that are market determined and positive (but moderate) in real terms;
- competitive exchange rates;
- trade liberalization
- liberalization of inward foreign direct investment;
- privatization of state enterprises;
- deregulation; and
- legal security for property rights.

2 Terrence E. Fluharty, *Implementing Economic Reforms in Mexico: The Washington Consensus as a Roadmap for Developing Countries* (Texas State University, Dept. of Political Science, 2006).

3 Joseph E. Stiglitz, *Globalization and Its Discontents* (Norton & Company, 2002).

4 The agreements signed at Bretton Woods, New Hampshire, United States in July 1944 laid the basis of the current world economic system, including establishing the IMF and the World Bank.

5 Global Footprint Network, *Ecological Footprint and Biocapacity* (2008 edn), spreadsheet accessed from www.footprintnetwork.org.

23 MY GENERATION: VILLAINS OR HEROES?

1 Powerful estate cars 2008: Audi RS6 (572 bhp), Mercedes AMG (514 bhp) and BMW M5 (507 bhp).

2 'Mission Control: Fido, Guido and Retro', *Time*, 1 Aug. 1969. Source: www.time.com/time/magazine.

Index

Aborigines (Australia) 20
Adapt and Thrive (McManners) 205
Adlakha, Arjun 79
Africa 29, 120, 189, 193, 227–8
ageing populations 82
agrarian society 171
agriculture 4, 35, 73, 164, 168–9, 215, 219, 220
  capacity 39
  genetic engineering 15–16
  green 221
  human health, and 165
  intensive 89
  land 87, 90, 91, 92
    biofuels, and 169
  revolution 102–3
  sustainable 170, 171, 180, 221
  United States 103–4, 226
  urban 136–7
aid agencies 216, 217
air-conditioning 43
air-freight 120, 123
airline industry 123, 207, 208
algae 115
Alps 43
Amazon rainforests 29, 61, 86, 89
ammonia 103
anarchy 3, 51
animal rights 74
animals
  defective genes 16
  feed 174
  population 74
Antarctic 37–8
Anthropocene period 200–1
antibiotics, used in cattle feed 173

Apollo project 232–3
Archimedes 37
archives 3–4, 203
Arctic Ocean 27, 41
Argentina 140
Article 24 (ICAO) 121–2
artificial fertility control 77
asbestos 190, 191, 193
atmosphere 163
  CFCs 98
  CO_2 37, 60, 63, 86, 106, 123, 184, 186
  nitrogen 103
  protection of 163
  water 187
Australia 10, 20, 115
automation 153, 154–6, 221
avian flu, *see* bird flu
aviation 119–20, 128
  21st century 123, 124–8
  civil 121–2
  economics of 121
  environment, and 126–8
  fuel taxes 121–2, 124, 127, 208
    direct 125
  regulatory environment 123
  see also flying

Baltic Sea 181–2
Bangladesh 9–10, 34, 50, 113
  ship dismantling 193, 194
banking system 203
bankruptcy 158
bar-codes 155, 180
BAS (British Antarctic Survey) 38, 191

Index

beef 11
  as commodity 174
  healthy 174
  market 173
  United States 103
behaviours
  change in 63–4
  community 160
  human 19, 61
    resources, shortage/lack of 156
Bernard Matthews Farms Ltd 177–80
bicycles 133, 140, 144
bio cycle 198
biodegradable material 198, 219
biodegradable plastics, *see* plastics, biodegradable
biodiesel 92, 103
biodiversity 60, 168, 203
bioenergy 103
biofuels 29, 88, 91–2, 95, 164, 166, 221
  agriculture 169
  CO_2, and 99
  crops, and 35
    corn 167
  EU 130, 167
  farming 103
  liquid 115
  transport 91, 130
biowaste 97
bird flu 178–80
birth control 77, 81
  underdeveloped world 80
birth rates 79, 82
Biswas-Diener, Robert 93
Blair, Tony, former Prime Minister, UK 24
Blazer, Vicki S. 189
Branca, Francesco 172
Braungart, Michael 199
Brazil 12, 29, 104, 140, 141
Bretton Woods 225, 226
broadband Internet/communications 120, 137
Brown, Gordon, Prime Minister, UK 111
BSE (Bovine Spongiform Encephalopathy) 174

buildings 105, 215
  energy neutral 102
  renewable energy 115
Bush, George W, former US President 114, 122
Bustamante, Martín R. 89

calcium carbonate 185
Cameroon 141
Canada 42
  oil reserves 47, 109
  petroleum exports 47–8
cancer 113
capital flows 162
capital investment 155
capitalism
  community, and 161–2
  foundations 161
  global 161, 164
  United States 161–2, 164
carbon
  credits 42, 106, 125
  cycle 98
  economy, taxing 110–11
  low technology 108
  reductions 122
carbon dioxide emissions 100, 204
  carbon trading, and 106
carbon emissions 29, 37, 42–3
  fossil 107
  politics, and 47
  reduction 130
  regulations 32
  restriction on 51
carbon footprints, agriculture 170
carbon markets 42
  cap 106, 108
  credits 91
  global 107, 108, 109
carbon permits 106
carbon trading 47, 106–9, 125–6, 203
carbonic acid 184
car-centric urban design 130, 131–2
car-free cities 141, 145–6
cars
  cities, and 129, 131–2, 138–9
  developing world 133–4

elimination of   136
fuel tanks   157
green   70, 143
land use   138
manufacture   135
ownership   138–9, 144, 231–2, 235
reliance on   181
taxes   64, 143, 144
Carslaw, Nicola   166
catastrophe   59, 66, 113
cattle feed   173–4
CFCs (chlorofluorocarbons)   98, 99, 108, 191, 199
Chamberlain, Neville   1, 4
Chandler, David   25
Charbit, S.   38
chemicals   14, 61, 176, 187, 188, 191–2
  biodegradable   195
  CFC family   99, 191
  drugs   189
  fish   189
  industrial processes   189–90
  land   184
  ozone-depleting   98
  production processes   192
  substitutes for   191
Chicago Convention   121–2
children   215–16
  costs of raising   81, 82
  see also human breeding
China   10, 25, 28, 46, 158, 227–9
  airlines   120
  cars   129–30
  ecological capacity   13
  human breeding   49, 79
    number of children   77
  manufacturing   209
  power stations, coal-fired   139
cities
  car-free   142
  cars   129, 131–2, 138–9
  design   140, 218
  developed world   129
  pedestrian zones   131
  sustainable   132, 135

civilization   51, 55
  collapse   83, 234
  continuation of   201, 203
  future   69
  interconnection of   60
CJD (Creutzfeldt-Jakob disease)   174
climate change   14, 33, 34, 41–2, 51, 55, 88, 89, 95, 100, 111, 113, 120, 123, 130, 136, 139, 145, 208, 220, 236
  carbon trading, and   125, 203–4
  consequences of   36, 59, 60
  CO_2, and   184
  Earth, and   65–6
  fossil fuels, and   187
  politics, and   42–3
  symptoms   43
cloned sheep   15
coal   48, 99, 100, 108, 112
  heating   102
  UK   101
coastal cities   50
Colchester, Alan   174
Colchester, Nancy   174
Coloma, Luis A.   89
commitment   150
  world level   160
consumption
  China   227
  conspicuous   219
coral reefs   184–5, 201
CO_2 (carbon dioxide)   37, 48, 60, 61, 63, 86, 89, 99, 106, 123, 184, 186, 219
  aviation   122
  reduction in   106–8
  see also atmosphere, CO_2
commodities   27, 73, 94, 158
  food   172
communications   120, 162
community   159–61, 162, 163, 205–6
  agriculture   164
  behaviours   160
  decision making   151–2
  design   4, 19, 66
  destructive forces   152–3
  economics   162

ideal   136
life   141
outcomes   153
power of (physical)   147–50, 164
resources, shortage of   156–8
sustainable   206
values   159, 161, 162, 163
world level   161
see also society
community land trust   90
commuting   120, 123, 137, 143
competitive advantage   31
congestion charges   138
conservation trusts   90
conspicuous consumption   153
consumption
  developing countries   27–8
  global   10
  high   28, 215
  increase in   80
  low   215
  population   73–4
  rates   76
  reduction in world   10, 13, 74, 75
  rise in   55
contamination, of food   172–3
continental shelf   41
convenience stores   181
corn   92, 103, 166–7, 170
corruption   192, 217
  Russia   193
Costa Rica   89
Côte d'Ivoire   194
Cousteau, Jacques   186, 187
cradle-to-cradle production   94
Crawford, Joel   142
Creutzfeldt-Jakob disease, *see* CJD
crops   15, 219–20
  biofuels, and   35, 103
  fluctuations   170
  irrigation   35
  land   130
  no-till   103
  reduced yields   60
  rotation   103
Crutzen, Paul J.   200
culling   74–5, 76, 81

Darfur (Somalia)   21, 157
Darwin, Charles   76
date marking   176–7
Dawson, Jonathan   132
decision making
  community   151
  world level   163
defective genes   16
deforestation   88
DEFRA (Department for Environment, Food and Rural Affairs)   179
Democratic Republic of Congo   193
Denmark   42
deregulation   204–5, 224
deserts   39
  liquid biofuel   115
designer babies   16, 17
developed economies   28
developed nations   30, 51
developed world
  automation   155
  cars   137, 144
  cities   129, 137
developing world   27
  cars   129, 133–4
  city design   140
  green agriculture   221
  population growth   79, 82
Diener, Ed   93
diets   167
  healthy   172
  minimum   169–70
Ding, Y.   38
dirty processes   32
disease genes   16
distance-to-market tax   180
division of labour   161
DNA   16
  human, genetic engineering of   17
drinking water   184
droughts   21, 43
drugs   189

Earth   9, 13, 59, 62, 129, 215, 232, 233–5
  climate change   65–6
  damage to   64, 229

Index

exploitation of 4–5, 10–11, 17, 27–8
fossil fuels 109
ice 38
protection 20–1
sustainability 10, 71
warming period 65
Earth Summit (1992) 204
ecological capacity
　China 13
　Earth 21
　India 13
　United States 13
ecological footprints 10
　Australia 10
　Bangladesh 9–10
　China 10, 227
　Europe 10, 12
　Nordic countries 12
　reduction in 11
　UK 12
　USA 9
economic growth 225
economic policy 226
economics 153, 159, 172, 231
　benefits 92, 93–4
　capitalism 161
　community 162
　development 93
　food supplies 168
　renewable power 97
　success 2, 224
economies
　sustainable 200
　United States 25, 226
ecosystems 4, 9, 21, 23, 165, 168–9, 220, 224, 231
　changes 59
　collapse 68
　conservation of 48
　failure of 10
　global 51
　land 88–9
　population expansion 85
　share of 12
ecovillages 132
education 3, 4
elderly, care for 80

electricity 98
Elliott, Jane 77
emerging economies 31
employees 153–4, 206
employment 153–4, 220
　head count 155
　job security 206
end-of-life disposal 198, 219
energy 3
　alternative sources 33
　choices 4
　consumption/demand 43, 48, 97, 98
　prices 100, 209
　security 112
　shortages 112
　technologies 106
　world 130
energy neutral, buildings 102
environment 162, 221, 235
　benefit 155
　damage/destruction 51, 192–3, 204
　designers 86
　global 187
　impact 92
　improvement 220
　local 32
　policy 205
　protection 20, 50
environmental degradation 32
environmental legislation 31, 70
environmental responsibility 48
ethanol 92, 103, 104
ETS (EU Emissions Trading Scheme) 106
EU 122, 157, 160
　biofuels 130, 167, 170
　identity 161
　waste hierarchy 199
EU Commission 91, 111, 157
EU ETS (European Union Greenhouse Gas Emission Trading Scheme) 122
Europe 10, 21, 43, 55, 161, 164, 189, 193, 227–8
　collapse of 56

forest clearance 90
fossil fuels 106
  gas 47, 112
  markets 120
  oil 112
    prices 114
  society 157
  transport fuel taxes 110
European Union 190
European Union Greenhouse Gas
    Emission Trading Scheme,
    see EU ETS
evolution 14, 76
  theory of 20
exotic holidays 24
exports 158
  subsidized 170

factory
  farming 179
  waste 193
fairtrade 208
Falkland Islands 56
family, right to a 78, 79, 82
farming 29
  efficiency 173
  food dumping 171
  industrialization 168, 171
  machinery 103
farmland 220, 221
FDA (US Food and Drug
    Administration) 189
federalism 160
Ferrigno, Jane G. 38
fertility 76–7
fertilizers 168, 170, 219, 220
financial crisis, 2008 4, 55, 105, 225,
    231
Finland 12, 117
firing ranges 220
fiscal policy 82, 216
fish/ing 181–2
  ban on 182
  chemicals 189
  EU guidelines 182
  heavy metals 185
Fluharty, Terrence E. 225

flying 24, 115, 117–20, 122, 123, 124,
    125–6, 207–8
  see also aviation
Foley, Kevin M. 38
food 20, 157, 171–2
  consumption 11, 165
  crisis 166–71
  crops, and biofuels 92
  dumping 216–17
  health risks 175–6
  localization 180
  prices 91, 92, 166–7, 169, 172, 175
  production 35, 92, 165–6, 168
  requirements 88, 91
  shortages 3, 55, 59
  supplies 91, 130, 165, 216
    imbalance 169
  sustainable 175
  world population 50
foraging 165
forests, see rainforests
fossil carbon 99
fossil fuels 27, 37, 42, 61, 89, 101–4,
    157
  alternatives to 99–100
  ban on 98–100, 114
  burning 89, 105, 108
  climate change 187, 204
  consumption 91, 130, 134
  government
    exploitation 99
    taxing 110
  lower grade sources of 48
  lifestyles, and 94, 95, 97–8
  prices 33–4, 109, 110, 123, 136
  renewable 70
  supplies 3, 46–7
  taxes 32
    UK 110–11
free trade 2, 162, 195, 224

gas 42, 108, 109
  prices 113
  Qatar 47
  reserves 47
  Russia 47, 112
  UK 112

gasoline   91
GDP (Gross Domestic Product)   75, 80, 93–4, 205
genetic code   16
genetic engineering   15
  agriculture   15–16
  human DNA   17
  human embryos   16–17
genocide   21, 74
geo-engineer   86
George, Heather   12
Germany, birth rates   79
Gilman, Diane   132
Gilman, Robert   132
glaciers   39
  Alps   43
Glaeser, Edward L.   142
globalization   25, 42, 120, 121, 149, 162, 169, 200, 216, 224
GHG (greenhouse gas emissions)   39, 42, 65, 86
  reduction in (UK)   110
GM (genetically modified) crops   15, 168
Gottlieb, Joshua D.   142
government finances   110
governments, and sustainability   159–60
green agriculture   221
green aircraft   208
green cars   70, 143
green products   208–9
green revolution   68, 104
green technology   228
Greenland   38
Griggs, M.   38
Gross Domestic Product, *see* GDP
G20   225

habitats, *see* natural habitats
Hardin, Garrett   78
harvests   216
health
  human   165
  public   187
  risks   175–6
H5N1   179

home industry   195
Hong, B. D.   208
hormones   189
Houghton, John T.   38
housing   207
  prices   203
human breeding
  China, number of children   77
  freedom   78–9, 82
  security in old age   80
human consumption   3, 165–6
human embryos   16–17
human genes   19
human health, and agriculture   165
human population
  control   75, 76, 169
  growth   73–5
  interaction   155–6
  size   171
  sustainable limits   75–6
human rights   49, 77, 163
human society   2, 4
human species, survival of   85
human waste   188
Hungary   179
hunting licences   64
hydro energy   97
hydrogen   103

ICAO (International Civil Aviation Organization)   121, 123
ice
  Antarctic   37–8
  Arctic   37
ICJ (International Court of Justice)   160
imaging technology   203
IMF (International Monetary Fund)   162, 224
immigration   82, 215–16
  UK   210–11
impoverishment   165–6
income   20, 93
India   12, 25, 28
  airlines   120
  ecological capacity   13
  population growth   79
  ships   193

individualism 218
Indonesia 221
industrial processes 192, 194
  ecological 194–5
Industrial Revolution 100–1
  coal, and 112
industrialization 28–9, 31, 165, 219
  Earth, survival of 67
  pollution/pollutants 200
infant
  mortality 79, 80, 82
  welfare 81–2
informal settlements 140–4
infrastructure, redesigning 98
International Civil Aviation
    Organization, *see* ICAO
International Court of Justice, *see* ICJ
International Covenant on Economic,
    Social and Cultural Rights 78
International Monetary Fund,
    see IMF
Internet 162
IPCC (Intergovernmmental Panel on
    Climate Change) 39–40, 50,
    203–4
Iran 105
Iraq 192
Irish Sea 185
irrigation 168, 170
Israel 104
IT systems 155
Iwanowicz, D. D. 189
Iwanowicz, Luke R. 189

Japan 12
jobs, *see* employment

Kelsey, Frances 189
Kennedy, John F., former US President
    232
Kyoto Protocol 100, 107, 112, 204

ladybirds 220
laissez-faire capitalism 224
land 87–8
  car infrastructure 138
  national parks 90

  pollution 184
  stabilizing 88–92
landfill 195–6, 197, 210
land trusts 90
lawlessness 152
lead-based additives 190
Leecaster, Molly K. 185
life-cycle design 197–200
  safe 199–200
Life Cycle Initiative: a Business Guide
    to Sustainability (UNEP) 204
lifestyles 20, 23, 27, 31, 35–6, 49
  changes in 11–12, 69–70, 74, 220,
    229
  choices 76, 205
  Europe 228
  flying, and 119–20
  food 169
  fossil fuels 94
  high-consumption 163, 219
  sustainable 64, 67–8, 94, 221–2, 223
  world 163
light bulbs 64
Lobstein, Tim 172
local shops 181
Loh, Jonathan 61
Lovelock, James 55
low-carbon technology 42
loyalty 150
  EU 161
  world level 160

machinery 221
maize, *see* corn
Maldive Islands, and sea levels 50
Malmberg, Ilkka 156
man-made chemicals 61
man-made materials 197, 198
manor houses 218–19
manufacturing 99, 196
  China 209
  localized 200
marine ecosystem 183, 196
markets
  capital 162
  global 158, 169–70
  open 205, 227

Marrakesh Declaration (1994)   204
mass-transit systems   135, 137, 141, 143, 144
material consumption   206
material success   223, 231
McDonough, William   199
McManners, John   56
McManners, Peter J.   34, 67, 127, 129, 139, 205
meat
 consumption   167, 169, 173
 UK   166
  imports   179
mechanization, agriculture   168
mercury   185
metals   185, 193, 198, 219, 220, 251
methane   65, 219
Mexico   225
microclimate   89–90
Middle East   47
 oil   100, 112, 115
minerals   190, 192, 233, 234
mining   99, 219
mobile technology   139
Model T. Ford   129
Monbiot, George   55
money, priority of   154
monoculture   168
'monstrous hybrids'   199
Montreal Protocol on Substances that Deplete the Ozone Layer   98, 191
 Third   100
Moore, Charles J.   185
Moore, Shelly L.   185
mountains   43, 89
Mugabe, Robert, President of Zimbabwe   141
mutations, aquatic life   201
Myanmar   192

nation states   160–2
national accounts   91
national economies   228–9
national parks   41, 51, 89, 117
 land in   90
nationalism   157
Native Americans   20

Newman, Andy   156
nutrients   167
natural gas   103
natural habitats   29, 60, 88–9, 90
 protection   220
natural land   89, 95
 clearance   90
natural resources   91
natural selection   19
natural world   20
nature   76, 87, 89, 203
 cycles   197–8
 working with   215, 217, 219–20
Netherlands   35, 104, 133
New Zealand   226
Nikogosian, Haik   172
nitrogen   103
Noguer, M.   38
Nordic countries   12
North Africa   56
North Pole   37
North Sea   42, 112
nuclear industries   14, 204
nuclear plants   51
nuclear power   104, 112, 113
nuclear reprocessing   185
nuclear waste   112, 185–6
nuclear weapons   51, 112
nutrients, and reproduction   76

Obama, Barack, US President   107, 226, 229
obesity   167, 172
oceans   88, 163, 183, 186–7, 195, 203, 204
 CO_2, and   184
 ice-free   41–2
 poisoning of   14–15, 60, 197
 pollution/pollutants   182, 183–4, 186, 193, 197, 200–1
 radioactive waste   186
 solar-powered machines   86
offshore rigs   41
oil   33–4, 43, 66–7, 108
 consumption   100, 115
 crisis (1970s)   105
 diminishing reserves   41–2
 end of   43, 45

Middle East 100
  prices 45–6, 47, 88, 113–14, 203
    crises 104, 105–6
    UK 113
    United States 113–14
  production 94–5
    United States 101
  shortages 42, 55
  UK 112
oil fields 45–6, 99
  Australia 115
oil-palm plantations 221
oil sands 47, 108
  Canada 109
  production 48
oil shale 48, 108, 109
old age, security in 82
OPEC 45, 100, 104–5
open markets 2
overpopulation 55
ownership 161
  alternative forms of 90
ozone hole/layer 98, 99, 191, 199

packaging 176, 180
Paillard, D. 38
Pakistan 142, 193
panic buying 157
peace 56
  world 160
Pearce, Fred 141
pedestrian zones, cities 131
Peru 120
pesticides 175
photosynthesis 115
planets 233–4, *see also* Earth
planning regulations 181
plants 219
plastics 188–9, 199
  biodegradable 180
  long-life 185, 200
  waste 200
polar bears 43
policies 205
  agriculture 171
  car-free cities 141
  car ownership 136, 137–9

city design 140
  designs 32–3
  food, on 167–8
  sustainable 51, 95
  vehicle infrastructure 134
politics 27, 229
  carbon emissions, and 47
  climate change, and 42–3, 66
  measures 31
  sustainable lifestyles 64, 71
pollution/pollutants 131, 134–5, 170
  industrial 200
  levies on 195
  mutations 201
  oceans 182, 183–4, 186, 193, 196, 200, 201
Pope, Vicky 38
population 9
  consumption, and/or 73–4
  control 83
  expansion, and ecosystems 85
  feeding 50
  growth 4, 49, 71, 78, 81–2, 217, 236
    developing world 79, 82
  reduction, China 227
  resources 216
    imbalance 13, 21
  world 73
poultry, UK 177–8
Pounds, J. Alan 89
poverty 28, 91, 92, 169–70
  UN definition 93
power generation 29
power stations 98
  coal-fired 139
  renewable energy 139–40
predators 49, 220
preservatives 176
privatization 224
production processes 192
products, long-term usage 209
property 161
  personal 131–2
  taxes 181
PV (solar photovoltaic) 209

Qatar, gas reserves 47

Index   263

radiation   14, 57, 60, 61, 112
  background   113, 204
  dirty bomb   112
radioactive terrorism   113
radioactive waste   63
  Irish sea   185
rail networks   120
rainfall   184, 185, 187–8
rainforests   89, 203
  Amazon   29, 61, 86, 89
  protection of   91, 221
Ramstein, G.   38
recession   4
recovery (waste)   199
recycling   94, 196–7
  product life, increase in   198–9
  single stage reuse   199
  waste   199
refuse collection   141
regional communities   160
renewable energy   97, 98, 99
  buildings   115
  power stations   139–40
Renewable Fuel Standard   91
renewable fuels   46, 99
reproduction, nutrients and   76
resources   76
  shortage/lack of   153, 156–8
  sustainable   158
RFID tags   155
rice, shortage   157
Riley, Nancy   77
rivers   39, 43, 184
road networks   131, 132, 134, 231
  underground   144
rubbish, *see* waste
rural-based economy   28–9
Russia   12, 42
  corruption   193
  gas   47, 112

salary   153
salt   172–3
  oceans   187
sanitation   140
Saudi Arabia   46, 47, 100
  oil reserves   109

Schipper, Lee   130
Schneider, Stephen H.   86
Scotland   12, 102
sea defences   35
sea levels   34–5, 38
  Maldive Islands, and   50
  rising   60, 201
self-sufficiency   168
  agriculture   170–1, 180
  community   218
self-worth   150, 161
Sellafield (UK)   185
shanty towns   141–2
ships, end-of-life   193–4
Slatick, Emil   108
Smith, Adam   161
Smith, D. R.   189
society   163
  automation   156
  changes in   66, 67, 236
  collapse of   3, 148–9, 223
  finances   75
  modern   86, 159, 183, 195
  reduction in   75–6
  sustainable   5, 29, 62–3, 69, 159–60, 205, 206, 223–4, 225–6, 232
  variety   163
  see also community
solar energy   97
solar panels   144, 217
solar photovoltaic, *see* PV
solar-powered machines   86
solar radiation   115
solar technology   139
solar water heating   209
Somalia   21, 157, 192
South Africa   140
South America   104, 141
space   218
  private   218–19
space travel   232–4
  moon   233
  planets   233–4
species
  extinction   59, 63, 197
  land-based, decline in   61
standard of living   78

starvation 68, 75, 76, 85, 167, 169–70, 216, 217
states, and society 160
Stern, Nicholas 27, 105
Stiglitz, Joseph 163, 225
Stoermer, Eugene F. 200
subsidiarity 159, 160
suburbanization 68, 69, 129, 131–2
sugar 172–3
supermarkets 166, 173, 175, 176, 178, 180, 181
supply chains 162
  extended 210
  food 170, 177
  meat 166
  supermarket 178
survival instincts 19, 21, 158
survival of the fittest 76
sustainability
  future 235, 238
  society 87, 87, 88, 92–4, 218
    China 227
    United States 226, 228
  thinking 92–3
  world 221–2, 224
Sustainable Revolution 66, 67–71, 203, 205, 207, 209
SUVs (Sports Utility Vehicles) 23–4, 69, 114
Sweden 12, 27, 51, 226
Swithinbank, Charles 38

taxes 235
  cars 143
  cheap fuel, increase in 113
  receipts 124
  transport fuel 138
    UK 110–11, 113
    United States 113–14
team players 158
technical cycle 198, 199
technologies 2, 28, 120
  automation 154, 156
  congestion charges 138
  green 228
  innovation 194
telecommunications 29, 139
teleconferencing 137

terrorism 163
Thalidomide 189
Thomas, Robert Malthus 73
throwaway society 195–7
Tinsley, Stephen 12
tourism 90
toxicity 200
trade
  environmental consequences 225–6
  UK 224
  world 167–8, 187, 204
Trade and Environment Committee (WTO) 204
'Tragedy of the Commons' (Hardin) 78–9
transport/ation 23, 98, 101–2, 105
  energy use 130
  food, costs of 175, 180
  fuel taxes 138
    UK 110–11, 114
  hub 129, 218
    public-transport 206
  network 217
Turkey 193

UK 12, 154, 224–5
  aviation fuel tax exemption 121
  birth rates 79
  coal 101
  fuel prices 33–4
  gas 112
  immigration 210–11
  meat 166
    imports 179
  nuclear reprocessing 185
  oil 112
    prices 104
  population growth 79
  transport fuel taxes 110–11, 113, 114
  Washington Consensus 224–5
  see also transport/ation, fuel taxes
ultraviolet radiation 98
UN 162
  Conference on World Food Security
    Security (2008) 167
  Security Council 160

Universal Declaration of Human Rights 77–8
UNEP (United Nations Environment Programme) 163, 204
　Life Cycle Initiative: a Business Guide to Sustainability (2007) 204
unemployment 152
United Nations Climate Change Conference (2009) 107
United States 9, 32, 163–4, 189, 226–9
　agriculture 103–4, 226
　aviation fuel 122
　biofuels 91, 130, 170
　birth rates 79
　capitalism 161–2, 164
　car-centric cities 141
　car ownership 144
　cars, and 129, 130
　ecological capacity 13
　economies 25, 226
　gasoline prices 113–14
　oil production 101
　ownership of seabed 42
　presidential election campaign 33
　rice, shortage of 157
　taxes, transport fuel 114–14
urban agriculture 136–7
urban communities 129
urban design 129, 136
　bottom up 143
　car-centric 130, 131–2, 133–4, 141, 144, 145
　people-centric 132–3, 145
　top-down 143
urban development 131
urban infrastructure 66
urban land 87
urban living 141
urban planning 98
urban villages 143, 218
US Food and Drug Administration, see FDA

vegetables 175
vegetarians 11
vegetation 89

virgin forests 51
　clearance 168
　protection of 91

wages 206
war 56–7
warming period, Earth 65
Washington Consensus:
　Mexico 225
　UK 224–5
waste 188, 194–5, 219
　international trade in 194
　levies on 195
　recycling 196–7, 199
Waste Framework Directive, see WFD
water 35
　clean 140
　cycles 197
　human needs 187–8
　oceans 39
　treadmill pumps 155
　sea ice, and 37–8
wealth 94, 223
　material 153
　pursuit of 153–4
Wei-Shiuen, Ng 130
Weisberg, Stephen B. 185
West 28, 31, 32, 38
　car ownership, and 144–5
　China, and 228
West Antarctic Ice Sheet 38
Western aid 217
Western Europe 215–6
WFD (Waste Framework Directive) 199
WGMS (World Glacier Monitoring Service) 39
wildernesses 90, 91
Williams, Richard S. 38
wind energy 97
women, status of 82
World Bank 28
world citizens 23
world community 163
World Health Organization 172
world policy 163
World War II 1–2, 55, 225, 232
　and Europe 56
World Bank 224

World Summit on Sustainable
 Development (2002) 204
WTO (World Trade Organization)
 162, 163, 204
Wu, Yangfeng 167

Yom Kippur War 104
Yugoslavia 160

zero-fossil-fuel society 114
Zimbabwe 141